ЯUSSIAИ
ROULETTE

ALSO BY MICHAEL ISIKOFF AND DAVID CORN

Hubris

ALSO BY MICHAEL ISIKOFF

Uncovering Clinton

ALSO BY DAVID CORN

47 Percent
Showdown
The Lies of George W. Bush
Deep Background
Blond Ghost

RUSSIAN ROULETTE

THE INSIDE STORY OF PUTIN'S WAR ON AMERICA AND THE ELECTION OF DONALD TRUMP

MICHAEL ISIKOFF AND DAVID CORN

TWELVE

NEW YORK   BOSTON

Twelve
Hachette Book Group
1290 Avenue of the Americas, New York, NY 10104
twelvebooks.com
twitter.com/twelvebooks

First Edition: March 2018

Twelve is an imprint of Grand Central Publishing. The Twelve name and logo
are trademarks of Hachette Book Group, Inc.

The publisher is not responsible for websites (or their content) that are not
owned by the publisher.

The Hachette Speakers Bureau provides a wide range of authors for speaking events. To find out more, go to www.hachettespeakersbureau.com or call
(866) 376-6591.

Library of Congress Cataloging-in-Publication Data has been applied for.

ISBNs: 978-1-5387-2875-8 (hardcover), 978-1-5387-2874-1 (ebook),
978-1-5387-1473-7 (international)

Printed in the United States of America

LSC-C

10   9   8   7   6   5   4

For Mary Ann and Zach
—M.I.

For Amarins, Maaike, and Welmoed
—D.C.

CONTENTS

Contents

INTRODUCTION

"It's a shakedown."

D onald Trump was suspicious from the start.

It was the afternoon of January 6, 2017, and for two hours, the president-elect had sat in a conference room at Trump Tower and listened to the leaders of the U.S. intelligence community brief him on an extraordinary document: a report their agencies had produced concluding that the Russian government had mounted a massive covert influence campaign aimed at disrupting the country's political system and electing him president of the United States. Trump had controlled his anger during this meeting—at times raising questions, expressing doubts, and clinging to the idea that it might all be a lie, part of some Deep State plot to taint his defeat of Hillary Clinton the previous November and undermine his authority as president.

When the spy chiefs—Director of National Intelligence James Clapper, CIA director John Brennan, and National Security Agency director Adm. Michael Rogers—left the room, one of them stayed behind. FBI director James Comey then handed Trump something else. It was a two-page synopsis of reports prepared by a former British spy alleging that Trump and his campaign had actively collaborated with Moscow. The memos claimed Russian intelligence had collected compromising material on Trump that could be used to blackmail him, including a tape of him engaging in sordid behavior with prostitutes in a Moscow hotel room. The FBI was not giving him this information because it believed the reports, Comey explained to Trump. In fact, the Bureau hadn't confirmed any of the lurid details—and Comey told him that he was not personally under investigation. But the material was circulating within the media and might become public. The intelligence community, Comey said, merely wanted to provide him a heads-up.

When Comey left, Trump was incensed. "It's bullshit," he told his aides. None of this was true. The discussion turned to why Comey had gone through this exercise. Suddenly, it all made sense to Trump. He knew exactly what this was.

"It's a shakedown," Trump exclaimed. They were blackmailing him. Comey—no doubt, with the approval of the others—was trying to send him a message. They had something on him.

Trump had seen this sort of thing before. Certainly, his old mentor Roy Cohn—the notorious fixer for mobsters and crooked pols—knew how this worked. So too did Comey's most famous predecessor, J. Edgar Hoover, who had quietly let it be known to politicians and celebrities that he possessed information that could destroy their careers in a New York minute.

Now, as Trump saw it, Comey and the rest were trying to do this to him. But he was not about to let them.

Trump's anger that day helped set the tone for one of the most tumultuous presidencies in American history. His first year in office would be filled with fits of rage at his political enemies, bizarre early-morning tweet storms, and repeated denunciations of the purveyors of "fake news" who challenged his honesty, his competency, and even his mental stability. Much of this turmoil related to the relentless investigations of Russia's attack on the 2016 election—a subject that infuriated Trump more than anything else. Russia had become a rallying cry for his tormentors—the original sin of his presidency, a scandal that raised questions about both his legitimacy and the nation's vulnerability to covert information warfare. Yet Trump defiantly refused to acknowledge Russia's extensive assault as a real and significant event. In his mind, any inquiry into the matter was nothing but an effort to destroy him.

The Russia scandal, though, dated back decades. For years, Trump had pursued business deals in Russia, continuing to do so even through the first months of his presidential campaign—and this colored how he would engage with the autocratic, repressive, and dangerous Russian leader, Vladimir Putin. The Trump-Russia tale was rooted in the larger post–Cold War geopolitical clash between the United States and Russia, a conflict that Moscow in 2016 shifted into the cyber shadows to gain a strategic advantage.

With Trump unable or unwilling to come to terms with Putin's war on American democracy, it fell to government investigators and reporters to piece together the complete story—an endeavor that could take years to complete. This book is a first step toward that. No matter how Trump regarded the scandal, one thing was for certain: To prevent a future attack, the American public and its leaders had to know and face what had occurred. A thorough accounting was a national necessity.

CHAPTER 1

"Mr. Putin would like to meet Mr. Trump."

It was late in the afternoon of November 9, 2013, in Moscow, and Donald Trump was getting anxious.

This was his second day in the Russian capital, and the brash businessman and reality-TV star was running through a whirlwind schedule to promote that evening's extravaganza at Moscow's Crocus City Hall: the Miss Universe pageant, in which women from eighty-six countries would be judged before a worldwide television audience estimated at one billion.

Trump had purchased the pageant seventeen years earlier, partnering with NBC. It was one of his most prized properties, bringing in millions of dollars a year in revenue and, perhaps as important, burnishing his image as an iconic international playboy celebrity. While in the Russian capital, Trump was also scouting for new and grand business opportunities, having spent decades trying—but failing—to develop high-end projects in Moscow. Miss Universe staffers considered it an open secret that Trump's true agenda in Moscow was not the show but his desire to do business there.

Yet to those around him that afternoon, Trump seemed gripped by one question: Where was Vladimir Putin?

From the moment five months earlier when Trump announced Miss Universe would be staged that year in Moscow, he had seemed obsessed with the idea of meeting the Russian president. "Do you think Putin will be going to The Miss Universe Pageant in November in Moscow—if so, will he become my new best friend?" Trump had tweeted in June.

Once in Moscow, Trump received a private message from the Kremlin, delivered by Aras Agalarov, an oligarch close to Putin and Trump's partner in hosting the Miss Universe event there: "Mr. Putin would like to meet Mr. Trump." That excited Trump. The American developer thought there was a strong chance the Russian leader would attend the pageant. But as his time in Russia wore on, Trump heard nothing else. He became uneasy.

"Is Putin coming?" he kept asking.

With no word from the Kremlin, it was starting to look grim. Then Agalarov conveyed a new message. Dmitry Peskov, Putin's right-hand man and press spokesman, would be calling any moment. Trump was relieved, especially after it was explained to him that few people were closer to Putin than Peskov. If anybody could facilitate a rendezvous with Putin, it was Peskov. "If you get a call from Peskov, it's like you're getting a call from Putin," Rob Goldstone, a British-born publicist who had helped bring the beauty contest to Moscow, told him. But time was running out. The show would be starting soon, and following the broadcast Trump would be departing the city.

Finally, Agalarov's cell phone rang. It was Peskov, and Agalarov handed the phone to an eager Trump.

Trump's trip to Moscow for the Miss Universe contest was a pivotal moment. He had for years longed to develop a glittering Trump Tower in Moscow. With this visit, he would come near—so near— to striking that deal. He would be close to branding the Moscow skyline with his world-famous name and enhancing his own status as a sort of global oligarch.

During his time in Russia, Trump would demonstrate his affinity for the nation's authoritarian leader with flattering and fawning tweets and remarks that were part of a long stretch of comments suggesting an admiration for Putin. Trump's curious statements about Putin—before, during, and after this Moscow jaunt—would later confound U.S. intelligence officials, members of Congress, and Americans of various political inclinations, even Republican Party loyalists.

What could possibly explain Trump's unwavering sympathy for the Russian strongman? His refusal to acknowledge Putin's repressive tactics, his whitewashing of Putin's abuses in Ukraine and Syria, his dismissal of the murders of Putin's critics, his blind eye to Putin's cyberattacks and disinformation campaigns aimed at subverting Western democracies?

Trump's brief trip to Moscow held clues to this mystery. His two days there would later become much discussed because of allegations that he engaged in weird sexual antics while in Russia—claims that were not confirmed. But this visit was significant because it revealed what motivated Trump the most: the opportunity to build more monuments to himself and to make more money. Trump realized that he could attain none of his dreams in Moscow without forging a bond with the former KGB lieutenant colonel who was the president of Russia.

This trek to Russia was the birth of a bromance—or something darker—that would soon upend American politics and then scandalize Trump's presidency. And it began in the most improbable way—as the brainstorm of a hustling music publicist trying to juice the career of a second-tier pop singer.

Trump's Miss Universe landed in Moscow because of an odd couple: Rob Goldstone and Emin Agalarov.

Goldstone was a heavyset, gregarious bon vivant who liked to post photos on Facebook poking fun at himself for being unkempt and overweight. He once wrote a piece for the *New York Times* headlined, "The Tricks and Trials of Traveling While Fat." He had been an Australian tabloid reporter and a publicist for Michael Jackson's

1987 *Bad* tour. Now he co–managed a PR firm, and his top priority was serving the needs of an Azerbaijani pop singer of moderate talent named Emin Agalarov.

Emin—he went by his first name—was young, handsome, and rich. He yearned to be an international star. His father, Aras Agalarov, was a billionaire developer who had made it big in Russia, building commercial and residential complexes, and who also owned properties in the United States. After spending his early years in Russia, Emin grew up in Tenafly, New Jersey, obsessed with Elvis Presley. He imitated the King of Rock and Roll in dress, style, and voice. He later studied business at Marymount Manhattan College and subsequently pursued a double career, working in his father's company and trying to make it as a singer. He married Leyla Aliyeva, the daughter of the president of Azerbaijan, whose regime faced repeated allegations of corruption. After moving to Baku, the country's capital, Emin soon earned a nickname: "the Elvis of Azerbaijan."

Emin cultivated the image of a rakish pop star, chronicling a hedonistic lifestyle on Instagram by posting shots from beaches, nightclubs, and various hot spots. He brandished hats and T-shirts with randy sayings, such as, "If You Had a Bad Day Let's Get Naked." But his music career was stalled. For help, he had turned to Goldstone.

In early 2013, Goldstone was looking to get Emin more media exposure, especially in the United States. A friend offered a suggestion: Perhaps Emin could perform at a Miss Universe pageant. The event had a reputation for showcasing emerging talent. The 2008 contest had featured up-and-comer Lady Gaga. (Trump would later brag—with his usual hyperbole—that this appearance was Lady Gaga's big break.) About the same time, Goldstone and Emin needed an attractive woman for a music video for Emin's latest song—and they wanted the most beautiful woman they could find. It seemed obvious to them that they should reach out to Miss Universe.

This led to meetings with Paula Shugart, the president of the Miss Universe Organization, who reported directly to Trump. She agreed to make the reigning Miss Universe, Olivia Culpo, available for the music video. (Within the Miss Universe outfit, Culpo, who had previously been Miss USA, was widely considered a Trump favorite.) And over the course of several conversations with Shugart, Goldstone and Emin discussed where the next Miss Universe contest would be held. At one point, Emin proposed to Shugart that Miss Universe consider mounting its 2013 pageant in Azerbaijan. That didn't fly with Shugart.

At a subsequent meeting, Emin revised the pitch. "Why don't we have it in Moscow?" he suggested. Shugart was interested but hesitant. The pageant had looked at Moscow previously. It had not identified a suitable venue there, and it was fearful of running into too much red tape. "What if you had a partner who owns the biggest venue in Moscow?" Emin replied. "Between myself and my father, we can cut through the red tape."

The venue Emin was referring to was Crocus City Hall, a grand seven-thousand-seat theater complex built by his father. Moreover, the influential Aras Agalarov could help smooth the way—and bypass the notorious bureaucratic morass that was a regular feature of doing business in Russia.

A native Azerbaijani, Aras Agalarov was known as "Putin's Builder." He had accumulated a billion-dollar-plus real estate fortune in part by catering, like Trump, to the super-wealthy. One of his projects was a Moscow housing community for oligarchs that boasted an artificial beach and waterfall. Agalarov had been tapped by Putin to build the massive infrastructure—conference halls, roadways, and housing—for the 2012 Asian-Pacific Economic Cooperation summit in Vladivostok. He had completed the project in record time. That venture and others—the construction of soccer stadiums for the World Cup in Russia and the building of a superhighway around Moscow—had earned Agalarov Putin's gratitude. Later in 2013, Putin would pin a medal on Agalarov's lapel: "Order of Honor of the Russian Federation."

When Shugart first mentioned to Trump the idea of partnering with a Russian billionaire tight with Putin to bring the Miss Universe contest to Moscow, the celebrity developer was intrigued.

At last, here was an inside track to break into the Russian market. And Agalarov agreed to kick in a good chunk of the estimated $20 million pageant budget. Trump was all for it. A Putin-connected oligarch would be underwriting his endeavor.

But the deal had to include something for Emin. Trump's Miss Universe company guaranteed that Emin would perform two musical numbers during the show. He would be showcased before a global television audience. He and Goldstone believed this could help him achieve his dream: cracking the American pop market.

Even before that, there would be a payoff for Emin. In May, Culpo showed up in Los Angeles for the one-day shoot. Emin was filmed strolling through a deserted nighttime town looking for his love—to the tune of his song "Amor"—and a sultry woman played by Culpo walked in and out of the beam of the flashlight he carried. A few weeks later, the video was done. Emin held a release party at a Moscow nightclub owned by his family. It was a lavish affair. Russian celebrities dropped by. Shugart and Culpo flew in to join the celebration.

In June 2013, Trump arrived in Las Vegas to preside over the Miss USA contest, which was owned by the Miss Universe company. Goldstone, Aras Agalarov, and Emin were in town for the event. Emin posted a photo of himself outside Trump's hotel off the Vegas strip wearing a Trump T-shirt and boasting a hat exclaiming "You're Fired"—the tagline from Trump's hit television show, *The Apprentice*. Trump had yet to meet the Agalarovs. But when they finally got together in the lobby of his hotel, he pointed at Aras Agalarov and exclaimed, "Look who came to me! This is the richest man in Russia!" (Agalarov was not the richest man in Russia.)

On the evening of June 15, the two Russians and their British publicist were planning a big dinner at CUT, a restaurant located at the Palazzo hotel and casino. Much to their surprise, they received a call from Keith Schiller, Trump's longtime security chief and confidant, informing them that his boss wanted to join their party. Sure, they said, please come.

At the dinner for about twenty people in a private room, Emin sat between Trump and Goldstone. Aras Agalarov was across from Trump. Michael Cohen, Trump's personal attorney who acted as the businessman's consigliore, was on the other side of Goldstone.

Also at the table was an unusual associate for Trump: Ike Kaveladze, the U.S.-based vice president of Crocus International, an Agalarov company. In 2000, a Government Accountability Office report identified a business run by Kaveladze as responsible for opening more than two thousand bank accounts at two U.S. banks on behalf of Russian-based brokers. The accounts were used to move more than $1.4 billion from individuals in Russia and Eastern Europe around the globe in an operation the report suggested was "for the purpose of laundering money." His main client at the time was Crocus International. (Kaveladze claimed the GAO probe was "another Russian witch-hunt in the United States.")

Trump was charming and solicitous of his new partners. He asked Aras what kind of jet he owned. A Gulfstream 550, Aras answered. But the Russian billionaire quickly noted that he had a Gulfstream 650 on order. "If that was me," Trump replied, "I would have said I was one of only one hundred people in the world who have a Gulfstream 650 on order." It was a small Trumpian lesson in self-promotion. And Trump, proud of himself, turned to Goldstone to emphasize his point: "There is nobody in the world who is a better self-promoter than Donald Trump."

After the dinner, part of the group headed to an after-party at a raunchy nightclub in the Palazzo mall called The Act.

Shortly after midnight, the entourage arrived at the club. The group included Trump, Emin, Goldstone, Culpo, and Nana Meriwether, the outgoing Miss USA. Trump and Culpo were photographed in the lobby by a local paparazzi. The club's management had heard that Trump might be there that night and had arranged to have plenty of Diet Coke on hand for the teetotaling Trump. (The owners had also discussed whether they should prepare a special performance for the developer, perhaps a dominatrix who would tie him up on stage or a little person transvestite Trump impersonator—and nixed the idea.)

The group was ushered to the owner's box, where Emin had an unusual encounter. Alex Soros, the son of George Soros, the billionaire philanthropist who funded opposition to Putin, was there as Meriwether's date. Emin started chatting with Soros and invited him to see him in Moscow. "You should know," Soros replied, "I'm no fan of Mr. Putin." And, he added, he was a big admirer of Mikhail Khodorkovsky—the oligarch turned Putin critic then serving time in a Siberian prison. Emin laughed it off.

The Act was no ordinary nightclub. Since March, it had been the target of undercover surveillance by the Nevada Gaming Control Board and investigators for the club's landlord—the Palazzo, which was owned by GOP megadonor Sheldon Adelson—after complaints about its obscene performances. The club featured seminude women performing simulated sex acts of bestiality and grotesque sadomasochism—skits that a few months later would prompt a Nevada state judge to issue an injunction barring any more of its "lewd" and "offensive" performances. Among the club's regular acts cited by the judge was one called "Hot for Teacher," in which naked college girls simulate urinating on a professor. In another act, two women disrobe and then "one female stands over the other female and simulates urinating while the other female catches the urine in two wine classes." (The Act shut down after the judge's ruling. There is no public record of which skits were performed the night Trump was present.)

As The Act's scantily clad dancers gyrated in front of them late that night, Emin, Goldstone, Culpo, and the rest toasted Trump's birthday. (He had turned sixty-seven the day before.) Trump remained focused on Emin and their future partnership. "When it comes to doing business in Russia, it's very hard to find people in there you can trust," he told the young pop singer, according to Goldstone. "We're going to have a great relationship."

The next night, toward the end of the Miss USA broadcast, Trump hit the stage to announce that the Miss Universe pageant would be held the coming November in Russia. In front of the audience, the Agalarovs and Trump signed the contract for the event.

Trump declared, "This will be one of the biggest and most beautiful Miss Universe events ever." On the red carpet earlier that evening, Trump had hailed Emin and Aras Agalarov: "These are the most powerful people in all of Russia, the richest men in Russia."

Two days later Trump expressed his desire on Twitter to become Putin's "new best friend." Emin quickly responded with his own tweet: "Mr. @realDonaldTrump anyone you meet becomes your best friend—so I'm sure Mr. Putin will not be an exception in Moscow."

The Moscow event held great potential for Trump to score in Russia. Now he was partnering with a Russian billionaire connected to other oligarchs and favored by Putin. (Trump already had a controversial venture under way in Baku, where he was developing a hotel with the son of the transportation minister of the corrupt regime. This project would soon founder.) "For Trump, this Miss Universe event was all about expanding the Trump Organization brand and getting his names on buildings," a Miss Universe associate recalled.

And anyone who wanted to do big deals in Russia—especially an American—could only do so if Putin was keen on it. "We all knew that the event was approved by Putin," a Miss Universe official later said. "You can't pull off something like this in Russia unless Putin says it's okay." Trump would only be making money in Russia because Putin was permitting him to do so.

Immediately, the contest was slammed by controversy. A few days before the announcement in Las Vegas, the Russian Duma had passed a law that made it illegal to expose children to information about homosexuality. The new antigay measure was the latest move by Putin to appeal to the conservative Orthodox Church and ultranationalist forces. It came amid a disturbing rise in antigay violence throughout Russia. In the southern city of Volgograd a few weeks earlier, a gay man's naked body was found in a courtyard, his skull smashed, his genitals scarred by beer bottles. The atmosphere was "ugly and brutal," a U.S. diplomat who then served in Moscow later said. "There would be these hooligans who would go after gay people in bars and beat them up. There was a pretty vicious campaign against the LGBT community."

Human rights and gay rights advocates in Russia and around the world denounced the new law. Vodka boycotts were launched. There was a push to relocate the Winter Olympics, scheduled to be held the following year in Sochi, Russia. In the United States, the Human Rights Campaign called on Trump and the Miss Universe Organization to move the event out of Russia, noting that under the new law a contestant could be prosecuted if she were to voice support for gay rights.

The uproar over the Russian antigay act confronted Trump with a dilemma—how to distance himself from the law without jeopardizing his big Russia play. The Miss Universe Organization issued a statement asserting that it "believes in equality for all individuals." That didn't stop the protests. Bravo talk show host Andy Cohen and entertainment reporter Giuliana Rancic, who had previously cohosted the pageant, quit the show. Miss Universe officials scrambled and found replacements: Thomas Roberts, an openly gay MSNBC anchor, and former Spice Girl Mel B.

Roberts explained his decision in an op-ed on MSNBC.com: "Boycotting and vilifying from the outside is too easy. Rather, I choose to offer my support of the LGBT community in Russia by going to Moscow and hosting this event as a journalist, an anchor, and a man who happens to be gay. Let people see I am no different than anyone else."

This was a godsend for Trump. He granted Roberts an interview on MSNBC. "I think you're going to do fantastically," he told Roberts, "and I love the fact that you feel the same about the whole situation as me." Inevitably, the conversation turned toward Putin and whether he would appear at the pageant. "I know for a fact that he wants very much to come," Trump said, "but we'll have to see. We haven't heard yet, but we have invited him."

Though U.S. relations with Moscow were at this point deteriorating, Trump was touting Putin as a wily and strong leader. In September, Putin published an op-ed in the *New York Times* that opposed a possible U.S. military strike against the government of Bashar al-Assad in Syria (in retaliation for its use of chemical weapons) and that denounced President Barack Obama for referring to American exceptionalism. The next day, Trump on Fox News commended Putin's move. "It really makes him look like a great leader," he said.

The following month, Trump appeared on David Letterman's late-night show. The host asked if Trump had ever done any deals with the Russians. "I've done a lot of business with the Russians," Trump replied, adding, "They're smart and they're tough." Letterman inquired if Trump had ever met Putin. "He's a tough guy," Trump said. "I met him once." In fact, there was no record he ever had.

Trump landed in Moscow on November 8, having flown there with casino owner Phil Ruffin on Ruffin's private jet. (Ruffin, a longtime Trump friend, was married to a former Miss Ukraine who had competed in the 2004 Miss Universe contest.) Trump headed to the Ritz-Carlton where he was booked into the presidential suite that Obama had stayed in when he was in Moscow four years earlier.

There was a brief meeting with Miss Universe executives and the Agalarovs. Schiller would later tell congressional investigators that a Russian approached Trump's party with an offer: He wanted to send five women to Trump's hotel room that night. Was this traditional Russian courtesy—or an overture by Russian intelligence to collect *kompromat* (compromising material) on the prominent visitor? Schiller said he didn't take the offer seriously and told the Russian, "We don't do that type of stuff."

Trump was soon whisked to a gala lunch at one of the two Moscow branches of Nobu, the famous sushi restaurant. (Nobu Matsuhisa, its founder, was one of the celebrity judges for the Miss Universe telecast. Agalarov was one of the co-owners of the restaurant; another co-investor was actor Robert De Niro.) An assortment of Russian businessmen was there, including Herman Gref, the chief executive of Sberbank, a Russian state-owned bank and one of the cosponsors of the Miss Universe pageant.

Trump was treated with much reverence. He gave a brief welcoming talk. "Ask me a question," he told the crowd. The first query was about the European debt crisis and the impact that the financial woes of Greece would have on it. "Interesting," Trump replied. "Have any of you ever seen *The Apprentice*?" Trump spoke at length about his hit television show, repeatedly noting what a tremendous success it was. He said not a word about Greece or debt. When he was done with his remarks, he thanked them all for coming and received a standing ovation. (Later, Aras Agalarov, reminiscing about this lunch, would note, "If [Trump] does not know the subject, he will talk about a subject he knows.")

Gref, a close Putin adviser, was pleased with his face time with Trump. "There was a good feeling from the meeting," he later said. "He's a sensible person . . . [with] a good attitude toward Russia."

Trump next went to the theater in Crocus City Hall. It was the day before the show. This was Trump's chance to review the contestants and exercise an option he always retained under the rules of his pageants: to overrule the selection of judges and pick the contestants he wanted among the finalists. In short, no woman was a finalist until Trump said so.

At each pageant, Miss Universe staffers would set up a special room for Trump backstage. It had to conform to his precise requirements. He needed his favorite snacks: Nutter Butters and white Tic Tacs. And Diet Coke. There could be no distracting pictures on the wall. The room had to be immaculate. He required unscented soap and hand towels—rolled, not folded.

In this room would be videos of the finalists who had been selected days earlier in a preliminary competition and the other contestants, particularly footage of the women in gowns and swimsuits. Here, a day or two before the final telecast, Trump would review the judges' decisions.

Frequently, Trump would toss out finalists and replace them with others he preferred. "If there were too many of women of color, he would make changes," a Miss Universe staffer later noted. Another Miss Universe staffer recalled, "He often thought a woman was too ethnic or too dark-skinned. He had a particular type of woman he thought was a winner. Others were too ethnic. He liked a type. There was Olivia Culpo, Dayanara Torres [the 1993 winner], and, no surprise, East European women." On occasion, according to this staffer, Trump would reject a woman "who had snubbed his advances."

Once in a while, Shugart would politely challenge Trump's choices. Sometimes she would win the argument, sometimes not. "If he didn't like a woman because she looked too ethnic, you could sometimes persuade him by telling him she was a princess and married to a football player," a staffer later explained.

That night, Aras Agalarov hosted a party at Crocus City Hall to celebrate his fifty-eighth birthday. Various VIPs were invited. Trump by now was exhausted. He spent much of the time sitting with Shugart and Schiller. At one point, Goldstone approached him with a request from Emin. The pop star was filming a new music video. Could Trump the next day shoot a scene that would be based on *The Apprentice*? Trump agreed, but it had to be early— between 7:45 and 8:10 in the morning. Sure, Goldstone said. Twenty-five minutes of Trump would have to do.

About 1:30 A.M., Trump left the party and headed to the Ritz-Carlton hotel a few blocks from the Kremlin. This would be his only night in Moscow. According to Schiller, on the way to the hotel, he told Trump about the earlier offer of women, and he and Trump laughed about it. In Schiller's account, after Trump was in his room, he stood guard outside for a while and then left.

The morning of November 9, Trump showed up for Emin's shoot. He was needed for the final scene. The video would open with a boardroom meeting with Emin and others reviewing Miss Universe contestants. Emin would doze off and dream of being with the various contestants. Enter Trump for the climax—Emin wakes up with Trump shouting at him: "What's wrong with you, Emin? Emin, let's get with it. You're always late. You're just another pretty face. I'm really tired of you. You're fired!" Trump's bit would only last fifteen seconds. Yet soon Emin would release a video that he could promote as featuring the world-famous Trump.

The rest of the day was as hectic as the first: a press conference with three hundred Russian reporters and more interviews, including one with Roberts in which Trump was pressed again about Putin.

Do you have a relationship with Putin and any sway with the Russian leader? Roberts asked him. Trump was unequivocal: "I do have a relationship." He paused. "I can tell you that he's very interested in what we're doing here today. He's probably very interested in what you and I are saying today. And I'm sure he's going to be seeing it in some form."

Trump could barely contain his praise for Russia's president: "Look, he's done a very brilliant job in terms of what he represents and who he's representing. If you look at what he's done with Syria, if you look at so many of the different things, he has really eaten our president's lunch. Let's not kid ourselves. He's done an amazing job. . . . He's put himself at the forefront of the world as a leader in a short period of time."

But Trump's comments about a "relationship" with Putin were, at this point, wishful thinking. The word had spread through the Miss Universe staff that Trump fiercely craved Putin's attendance at the pageant. In preparation for Putin's possible appearance, Thomas Roberts and Mel B were taught several words in Russian to welcome the Russian president: "hello," "thank you," and so on. With her cockney accent, Mel B had trouble pronouncing the Russian words. She was told she had to get this right because Putin might come.

By late afternoon, Trump's anxiety was palpable. There had been no word. He kept asking if anybody had heard from Putin. Then Agalarov's phone rang. "Mr. Peskov would like to speak to Mr. Trump," Agalarov said.

Trump and Peskov spoke for a few minutes. Afterward, Trump recounted the conversation to Goldstone. Peskov, he said, was apologetic. Putin very much wanted to meet Trump. But there was a problem nobody had anticipated: a Moscow traffic jam. King Willem-Alexander and Queen Maxima of the Netherlands were in town, and Putin was obligated to meet them at the Kremlin. But the royal couple had gotten stuck in traffic and was late, making it impossible for the Russian president to find time for Trump. Nor would he be able to attend the Miss Universe pageant that evening.

Putin wanted to make amends, though. Peskov conveyed an invitation for Trump to attend the upcoming Olympics, where perhaps he and Putin could then meet. He also told Trump that Putin would be sending a high-level emissary to the evening's event—Vladimir Kozhin, a senior Putin aide. And, Peskov told Trump, Putin had a gift for him.

It was a crushing disappointment for Trump. But he quickly thought of how to spin it, suggesting to an associate that after the telecast they could spread the word that Putin had dropped by. "No one will know for sure if he came or not," he said.

One reason Trump's hoped-for meeting with the Russian president never materialized was his attention to another project. Trump was originally scheduled to spend two nights in Moscow—which would have yielded a wider window for a get-together with Putin. But Trump had decided to attend the celebration of evangelist Billy Graham's ninety-fifth birthday on November 7 in North Carolina. In Russia, Trump told Goldstone that it had been necessary for him to show up at the Graham event: "There is something I'm planning down the road, and it's really important."

Goldstone knew exactly what Trump was talking about: a run for the White House. Franklin Graham, the evangelist's son, was an influential figure among religious conservatives. When Trump two years earlier was championing birtherism—the baseless conspiracy theory that Barack Obama had been born in Kenya and was ineligible to be president—Graham joined the birther bandwagon, raising questions about the president's birth certificate. Appearing at this event and currying favor with Franklin Graham was a mandatory stop for Trump, if he were serious about seeking the Republican presidential nomination.

Before the Miss Universe broadcast, there was the obligatory red-carpet event. Camera crews from around the world recorded the strutting celebrities. A triumphant-looking Trump posed with Aras and Emin Agalarov for the paparazzi. Trump dodged a question about whether Emin had been booked to perform based on merit.

"Russia has just been an amazing place," Trump exclaimed. "You see what's happening here. It's incredible." Behind him was a banner featuring the logos of the Trump Organization, Miss Universe, Sberbank, Mercedes, and NBC. The NBC peacock was in black and white, without its usual rainbow of colors. Officials at Agalarov's company had ordered Miss Universe staffers to eschew the rainbow, fearing it would be seen as a gay pride message.

Thomas Roberts walked the red carpet with his husband. He wore a bright pink tuxedo jacket—something he would never do back home in New York. He was sending his own message. In interviews, he explicitly denounced Putin's antigay laws.

Other celebs and local notables strolled past the entertainment reporters. The group included Kozhin and a curious guest: Alimzhan Tokhtakhounov, aka "the Little Taiwanese," one of Russia's most prominent suspected mobsters and a fugitive from U.S. justice. Tokhtakhounov had an odd link to Trump's signature property: Seven months earlier he had been indicted in the United States for protecting a high-stakes illegal gambling operation run out of Trump Tower. Additional Trump guests included Chuck LaBella, an NBC executive who worked on Trump's *Celebrity Apprentice*, and Bob Van Ronkel, an American expatriate who ran a business specializing in bringing Hollywood celebrities to Russian events. (Van Ronkel once had tried to produce an American television show extolling the KGB and its heroic exploits.)

The show went off well. Trump sat in the front row next to Agalarov. Emin performed two of his Euro-pop numbers. Aerosmith's Steven Tyler, one of the judges, pumped out his classic hit "Dream On." For the finale, Culpo crowned Miss Venezuela the new Miss Universe. There was no mention during the broadcast of the controversy over the antigay law.

After the event, there was a rowdy after-party with lots of vodka and loud music. A twenty-six-year-old aspiring actress, Edita Shaumyan, made her way into the VIP section, entering the roped-off area the same time as a famous Russian rap singer named Timati. Shaumyan caught Trump's eye. He approached her, gestured to Timati, and asked, "Wait, is this your boyfriend? You're not free?" She said no. "You're beautiful," Trump told her. "Wow, your eyes, your eyes." According to Shaumyan, "He said, 'Let's go to America. Come with me to America.' And I said, 'No, no, no. I'm an Armenian. We're very strict. You need to meet my mother first.'" When other women approached trying to get photographs with Trump, he took hold of Shaumyan's arm and said, "Don't go. Stay. Stay." Shaumyan took selfies with him. (She later produced five photos and a video of her with Trump that night.) But nothing further happened. Trump later had somebody give Shaumyan his business card with his phone number on it. She never called.

From the party Trump headed to the airport. He was going straight home on another Ruffin jet. The next day, he called Roberts. He told him he was pleased with the show and that it had been a smash, with great ratings. That was not accurate—at least not in the United States. The telecast drew 3.8 million viewers, much less than the 6.1 million who had watched it the previous year.

In the following days, various media outlets in Russia and the United States reported that Trump had used his visit to Moscow to launch a major project in the Russian capital. "US 'Miss Universe' Billionaire Plans Russian Trump Tower," declared the headline on RT, the Russian government-owned TV channel and website. The *Moscow Times* proclaimed, "Donald Trump Planning Skyscraper in Moscow." Trump's partners in the Trump SoHo project he had developed in New York City—Alex Sapir and Rotem Rosen—had come to Moscow for the event and met with Agalarov and Trump to discuss the possibilities.

It seemed things were moving fast. The state-owned Sberbank announced it had struck a "strategic cooperation agreement" with the Crocus Group to finance about 70 percent of a project that would include a tower bearing the Trump name. If the deal went ahead, Trump would officially be doing business in Moscow with the Russian government.

"The Russian market is attracted to me," Trump told *Real Estate Weekly*. "I have a great relationship with many Russians." He added, with his customary exaggeration, "almost all of the oligarchs" had been at the Miss Universe event.

Back in the United States, Trump tweeted out the good news: "I just got back from Russia-learned lots & lots. Moscow is a very interesting and amazing place!" The next day he tweeted at Aras Agalarov, "I had a great weekend with you and your family. You have done a FANTASTIC job. TRUMP TOWER-MOSCOW is next. EMIN was WOW!"

The project moved further along than publicly known. A letter of intent to build the new Trump Tower was signed by the Trump Organization and Agalarov's company. Donald Trump Jr. was placed in charge of the project. A few months later, Ivanka Trump flew to Russia and scouted sites with Emin for the new venture. "We thought that building a Trump Tower next to an Agalarov tower—having the two big names—could be a really cool project to execute," Emin later said.

Trump was finally on his way in Russia. And shortly after the Miss Universe event, Agalarov's daughter showed up at the Miss Universe office in New York City bearing a gift for Trump from Putin. It was a black lacquered box. Inside was a sealed letter from the Russian autocrat. What the letter said has never been revealed.

CHAPTER 2

"We did not recognize the degree it would tick Putin off."

In November 2006, Alexander Litvinenko was writhing in agony in a London hospital room. A forty-three-year-old former officer of the FSB, Russia's domestic intelligence service, Litvinenko was an outspoken political dissident living in exile in England. For weeks, he had been vomiting uncontrollably, suffering excruciating cramps, and losing body strength—the result of a mysterious poison that invaded his body after he had met for tea with two former Russian intelligence agents in a hotel bar off Grosvenor Square. Aware that he had a short time to live, Litvinenko signed a statement that pointed the finger at the man he believed had ordered his murder: Vladimir Putin.

"You have shown yourself to be as barbaric and ruthless as your most hostile critics have claimed," Litvinenko proclaimed in the statement. He added, "You may succeed in silencing one man but the howl of protest from around the world will reverberate, Mr. Putin, in your ears for the rest of your life. May God forgive you for what you have done, not only to me, but to beloved Russia."

Litvinenko died from heart failure two days later. And when his powerful *j'accuse* was read aloud at a press conference, it presented the British government with a political and diplomatic dilemma. Was it possible that Litvinenko, who had become a British citizen, was right—that the president of Russia had ordered his assassination? Would Putin go so far as to commit murder on British soil? If so, how should the government respond?

Scotland Yard opened a criminal investigation into Litvinenko's death. But that would take time and would be focused on finding legal culpability. The government of Prime Minister Gordon Brown had a more immediate need—an intelligence inquiry that would assess Russian government complicity and what the Litvinenko case revealed about Putin's regime. Tasked with this assignment, MI6, the British spy service, turned to its top Russia specialist to lead the investigation. His name was Christopher David Steele.

A Cambridge graduate with a photographic memory, Steele knew the turf well. Between 1990 and 1993, he had served in Moscow as a spy under diplomatic cover. It was a tumultuous period when the Soviet Union collapsed, a new Russia Federation was born, and the Communist Party staged a coup to regain control— but was beaten back by a defiant Boris Yeltsin, who climbed on a tank and stood the plotters down. Steele watched the confrontation unfold on the streets of Moscow and sent detailed reports to London.

After Moscow, Steele served in Paris and then returned to London to become MI6's chief Russia analyst. In this post, Steele briefed the prime minister, the foreign ministers, and other British government officials on what they needed to know about developments within the Kremlin.

As he dug into the Litvinenko case, Steele looked for patterns. He soon found one. A few weeks before Litvinenko was poisoned, Anna Politkovskaya, one of Russia's most prominent journalists, was shot to death outside her Moscow apartment. Politkovskaya had been a fearless Putin critic and a relentless chronicler of Russia's human rights abuses in the war-torn Russian Republic of Chechnya. And she had been a friend and collaborator of Litvinenko, often visiting him in London. Two murders within weeks, both victims were friends and outspoken foes of Putin. Surely, Steele believed, this was more than a coincidence.

A turning point in the case came when a British doctor figured out the poison slipped into Litvinenko's tea was polonium-210—a highly radioactive substance almost exclusively under the control of Russia's nuclear agency. Someone high up must have approved providing this substance to the two Russian assassins who flew from Moscow to London to meet Litvinenko. (The two Russian operatives had left behind a trail of radioactive contaminants—in hotel rooms, bathrooms, and on a British Airways aircraft.)

Soon Steele was in the Cabinet Office briefing room in Whitehall reporting to Brown and his senior ministers on what he had found. This was likely a state-sponsored assassination, he told them, and the orders probably came from Putin through Nikolai Patrushev, then the director of the FSB, the successor to the KGB. Steele put the odds at 80 to 90 percent.*

The implications were enormous. An assassination in the heart of London, with radioactive poison contaminating multiple sites— this seemed a menacing turn by Putin, the authoritarian, nationalistic, wily, and pugilistic leader, who had been Russia's president since 2000. "If al Qaeda had done something like this, people would have been up in arms," Steele later told colleagues. "There was polonium all over London. [Brown and his ministers] were genuinely shocked. Here was a member of the United Nations Security Council that had just committed an act of nuclear terrorism."

The question was, what to do about it? Should the British government retaliate against Putin and make clear he couldn't get away with it? These were not questions Whitehall was eager to deal with. The Brown government expelled a few Russian diplomats, but no sanctions were imposed, and business with Moscow went on as usual.

Among those also reluctant to grapple with troubling questions

---

* A 2016 British inquiry reached the same conclusion, finding Putin "probably approved" the Litvinenko murder.

raised by Litvinenko's murder was MI6's partner across the Atlantic: the CIA. When Steele's U.S. intelligence colleagues were apprised of his conclusions in the Litvinenko case, they were not excited or overly concerned. "It's your problem, not ours," they said.

A decade after Litvinenko's assassination, the U.S. government would face a similar situation: how to handle an attack from Putin. And Steele would again be in the middle of the fray.

In early 2009, Michael McFaul, an American expert on Russia, was in Moscow, and he visited his old friend Garry Kasparov, the one-time world chess champion. Kasparov, a man with bushy eyebrows and an intense bearing, had become a well-known Russian opposition leader and passionate foe of Putin. But now McFaul and Kasparov had a fundamental disagreement over a simple yet basic question: Could the United States do business with a Russian government that was still controlled by Putin?

McFaul had spent years in Russia studying the rise of the Russian state after the fall of the Soviet Union. And he had been much more than an objective, just-the-facts academic chronicling history. In the early 1990s, when the Soviet Union was in a chaotic free fall, McFaul, a graduate student in his mid-twenties, was a passionate comrade of the young pro-democracy and free-market activists pushing for change, advising them on strategies and hooking them up with government agencies and foundations in the West that could support their efforts. Some Russians suspected McFaul was a CIA spy conniving to undermine the Soviet system—and what would come afterward—to Washington's benefit. They were wrong. But that was often the Soviet way of looking at things.

Now, over a dozen years later, McFaul was indeed working for the U.S. government. Barack Obama, a freshman senator, had just been elected the first African American president of the United States. McFaul, who had advised Obama during his campaign, was the new president's point man on Russia, working in the White House and managing the Moscow brief for the National Security Council.

Obama had declared his intent to "reset" U.S.-Russia relations after a stormy period during the George W. Bush years. No one in Obama's circle was under any illusion this would be easy. Putin and Russia had been increasingly hostile to American and Western interests—and aggressive. In August 2008, Russia invaded Georgia in support of pro-Russia separatists. But as the new Obama team saw it, there was reason to believe a page could be turned.

Putin, after serving two terms, had stepped down the previous March, succeeded as president by his protégé, Dmitry Medvedev. Putin still lurked in the background as prime minister and the power behind the throne. But Medvedev had a softer image. He was in his early forties and a fan of heavy metal bands. He came from an academic background; he was a lawyer who had lectured at a St. Petersburg law school. He looked like someone Obama might be able to do business with—especially on areas of common interest, including countering terrorism and controlling nuclear weapons.

McFaul and another NSC aide, Celeste Wallander, laid out the strategy for the reset in a memo for the new White House national security staff. It outlined "first steps toward a new US-Russia relationship" and called for focusing on two to three "high priority issues...that can generate goodwill and produce early successes." The memo pointedly recognized the deterioration of political and human rights in Russia, but noted such issues as arms control and nuclear nonproliferation were too important "to be held hostage to an increasingly authoritarian internal situation." McFaul and Wallander were promoting what they considered to be a cautious experiment.

That was the plan. But in Kasparov's apartment, over dinner served by the dissident's mother, McFaul was having a tough time selling this idea to the former grandmaster and two other opposition leaders: Boris Nemtsov and Vladimir Ryzhkov. Of course, Putin was corrupt and untrustworthy, McFaul acknowledged. But Putin would only go so far, he argued. And Obama thought he could "make deals" by working with Medvedev, who seemed more willing to cooperate with the West. If they offered Russia concessions during this process, it would help Medvedev, who would then have more room to "open up" Russia. And, if all went well, Putin would gradually fade from the picture.

Nemtsov and Ryzhkov were willing to hear out McFaul. But they were skeptical. Ryzhkov was afraid the reset could come at the expense of human rights, fair elections, and corruption. They each told McFaul that the real power was in the hands of Putin. McFaul's pitch reminded them of when George W. Bush tried to engage Putin eight years earlier. At a joint press conference with Putin in 2001, Bush declared, "I looked the man in the eye. I found him to be very straightforward and trustworthy. . . . I was able to get a sense of his soul." Then came the Russian president's crackdown on political foes, extensive human rights abuses in Chechnya, and the military intervention in Georgia.

Kasparov was certain Obama's reset would end badly. Don't you realize who Putin is? he told McFaul. Don't you know he cares nothing about what the West thinks? Medvedev, he insisted, was a nobody. He would never go against Putin's wishes. "You're going to waste three to four years," Kasparov told him.

The two men sparred through the dinner. McFaul believed he was hardly naïve about Putin. He had met Putin in 1991, when Putin was a minor official in St. Petersburg, and McFaul had been one of the first Russian scholars in the United States to spot Putin as a serious and potentially troublesome force when he became a senior government official in the late 1990s. He contended the reset was a reasonable course that could yield important results in the short run.

For Kasparov, that was bunk, and the only way to deal with Putin was to hit him hard. The reset was a move that Putin would exploit to preserve his power at home and triumph over the West. The new U.S. president and his aides, Kasparov thought, didn't understand the canny and ruthless Putin. They didn't get his dark soul.

The Obama administration remained committed to the reset. But the warnings of Kasparov and the dissidents presaged fierce policy debates that would play out behind the scenes within the U.S. government in the years to come.

* * *

One of the key officials in charge of implementing Obama's Russia reset was Hillary Clinton, the new secretary of state. But things got off to inauspicious start. In March 2009, Clinton first met her Russian counterpart, Foreign Minister Sergey Lavrov, in Geneva, Switzerland, and, before television cameras at the Intercontinental Hotel, she handed him a green gift-wrapped present. Inside was a button with the word PEREGRUZKA and under it the English word RESET. The gag gift was a stunt, dreamed up by Philippe Reines, her longtime media adviser, a political operative with no diplomatic experience. Whatever the PR merits of this silly move, the execution was botched. The Americans who prepared the gift had muffed the translation.

"You got it wrong," Lavrov said. "It should be *perezagruzka*. This means 'overcharged.'"

Clinton laughed loudly and replied, "We won't let you do that to us. I promise."

Clinton's relations with Lavrov, though outwardly cordial, were fraught with tension and distrust. The wily and savvy diplomat, who fancied expensive Italian suits and fine cigars, was a Putin loyalist. Always tanned, he was rigid, sarcastic, and struck a condescending manner, especially with women. After one of her meetings with Lavrov, Clinton asked a State Department official, "What is the *deal* with Lavrov?" She thought he was a jerk.

The official told her Lavrov was a difficult person—and probably more so when he was compelled to deal with women as equals. Clinton laughed and asked if Lavrov could deliver the goods. The diplomat replied that Lavrov certainly held the trust of Medvedev and, more important, Putin.

"That's all I need to know," Clinton said. She would do what she could. She had always been considered more hawkish within Democratic policy circles. But she was committed to the reset.

In various meetings and communications, Clinton and Lavrov hammered out the details of this new engagement. They set up a session between Obama and Medvedev in London in April, where the leaders announced the two countries would begin talks for a new nuclear arms treaty. In July, Obama visited Moscow, and he and Medvedev signed an agreement that would allow U.S. military planes to fly through Russian air space to deliver supplies to U.S. troops fighting in Afghanistan—a top priority for the Pentagon. Months later, in September, Obama and Medvedev met again at the annual U.N. General Assembly meeting in New York, and Medvedev signaled Russia would be amenable in joining the United States and other Western nations in pressuring Iran to limit its nuclear program.

But there were puzzling moments in Clinton's dealings with Lavrov. During their meetings, the Russian minister kept asking Clinton to intervene on behalf of a billionaire Russian oligarch, Oleg Deripaska, who had been periodically blocked from entering the United States because U.S. officials suspected he was tied to organized crime in Russia. Lavrov wanted Clinton to help Deripaska obtain a visa.

Deripaska was known as one of Putin's favorite oligarchs. He had made billions of dollars in the aluminum business in the 1990s. Just why Lavrov was pressing the issue was unclear. But Lavrov and others "raised it on many, many occasions," recalled a U.S. official who worked in the U.S. embassy in Moscow. "It was amazing the way they pushed this from many different angles."

Clinton never acted on Lavrov's requests. And it wouldn't be until years later that the public would learn that one of Deripaska's U.S. business partners was a controversial American lobbyist and political consultant named Paul Manafort.

One of the key goals of the reset was to get Moscow to fully join the U.S. effort to prevent Iran from developing nuclear weapons. Medvedev was moving in this direction, but an important question for Obama was whether Putin was aboard.

In March 2010, Clinton, while in Moscow, was handed the assignment of visiting Putin to ascertain if he would back Medvedev on Iran. She realized there could be no Iran deal without Putin. And she knew he was arrogant, mercurial, and difficult to deal with. Later she would note, "When I sat with Putin in meetings, he looked more like one of those guys on the subway who imperiously spread their legs wide, encroaching on everyone else's space, as if to say, 'I take what I want.'" She also saw Putin as an autocrat with little respect for women. Still, she had to figure out how to handle him.

At Putin's dacha, Clinton made the pitch to him: You previously gave Medvedev the green light to work with the rest of us at the U.N. Security Council to increase pressure on Iran and now it is time to see this through.

Putin did not explicitly agree. But he took a much softer approach than he had in public. He led Clinton and her colleagues to conclude that he would not block the U.S.-backed initiative to intensify the sanctions on Tehran.

At one point, Clinton, to lighten the mood, asked Putin about his efforts to save the tigers in Siberia. Putin marched Clinton and her team of aides out of the room and down the stairs—they passed a room where several senior Russian officials had long been waiting for Putin—and toward a room with a gigantic map of Russia covering one wall. There he enthusiastically told her about an upcoming conference he would be convening in November in St. Petersburg devoted to preserving tigers. He explained that he had seen a show on television reporting that the snow leopard had become endangered in Russia. He told Clinton he was embarrassed to say that he had watched this program on the Discovery Channel. "It took the United States to tell us this," Putin said.

He asked Clinton if she would attend the tiger summit. She diplomatically replied that she would consider it.

Putin also informed Clinton that he had planned a trip to tag polar bears. He asked if her husband would like to join him on this expedition. (Bill Clinton had undergone heart surgery a few weeks earlier.) Clinton said she would convey the invitation to her husband and if he couldn't go, maybe she would. Putin raised an eyebrow. She knew what that meant: Putin didn't go polar bear tagging with sixty-two-year-old women.

When the Putin meeting was done, the two held a press conference, and Putin launched into a long list of complaints about the United States. Clinton ignored the lecture and hailed the U.S.-Russia nuclear arms reduction treaty nearing completion.

Afterward, she got into her car to ride to the airport. She and her aides were in good spirits. They believed she had managed Putin well and perhaps scored an important policy win. One aide piped up: "There's no way Bill can go polar bear tagging, so the secretary will have to go to the tiger summit." They all laughed. The nuclear arms treaty talks were close to done, and now it looked as if Russia was going to be helpful on the Iran front. For the moment, they thought they had Putin on their side. Maybe the reset could work.

Obama's cultivation of Medvedev seemed to be paying off. In April 2010, the two leaders met in Prague, and during a celebratory ceremony in the majestic hall of Prague Castle, they signed the New START treaty, which would compel each nation to reduce its arsenal of strategic nuclear weapons. The cuts would not be great, but the accord would revive an inspection process that ended several months earlier and that would be crucial for the greater reductions that each country pledged to pursue. "We're having a real conversation," McFaul enthusiastically told reporters. Weeks later, the Russians would vote with the Americans in the Security Council for a new round of sanctions for Iran.

But a different conversation was being held about Russia among U.S. law enforcement and intelligence officials that spring. It was about a Russian espionage operation seeking to penetrate the U.S. government.

This was a sensational tale straight out of a Cold War spy novel. For years, the FBI had been monitoring a network of ten Russian sleeper agents—"illegals," in spy parlance—who had been dispatched to meld into American communities. The Russian spies had arrived nearly a decade earlier, using forged documents and stolen identities, with instructions to blend into American society: they should become good neighbors, raise families, and send their children to local schools. Their mission, according to a message intercepted by the FBI, was "to search and develop ties in policy-making circles in the U.S." One of the spies became a tax adviser to Alan Patricof, a powerhouse Democratic fundraiser close to Bill and Hillary Clinton—a connection that some at the FBI found alarming.

The Bureau had been tipped off to the network years earlier by a high-ranking Russian intelligence official who had defected. But by June 2010, officials at FBI headquarters had become nervous. They had intercepted communications sent to Moscow and feared one of the spies was about to flee—and the rest could quickly follow. Now seemed to be the time to move in and nab them.

At a meeting in the White House Situation Room, FBI director Robert Mueller informed Obama's aides the Bureau intended to roll up the Russians. But deputy national security adviser Tom Donilon raised an objection. Medvedev had just arrived in Washington for more talks with Obama. To bust a Russian spy ring could blow up the reset, he argued.

The discussion got intense—until Leon Panetta, the CIA director, weighed in. He said that Donilon needed to think long and hard about a potential *Washington Post* headline that would read, "The U.S. failed to arrest a group of Russian spies." At that point, Panetta later noted, "I saw the lights go off in his head." Soon after the meeting, according to Panetta, Donilon okayed the arrest, but he asked the FBI to wait until Medvedev was out of American airspace.

The Bureau apprehended the spies on June 27 and the story grabbed international headlines. Much of the attention focused on one of the agents, a voluptuous twenty-eight-year-old redhead named Anna Chapman. A spy swap was quickly arranged, and the ten illegals were sent back to Russia. They were greeted as heroes by Putin, who welcomed them at a celebration, where he and the spies sang the theme song from *The Shield and the Sword,* a popular Russian miniseries from the 1960s about a Soviet double agent in Nazi Germany. Chapman posed for the Russian version of *Maxim* and was named by the magazine as one of Russia's "100 sexiest women." (This operation later inspired the television show *The Americans.*)

What intelligence, if any, the Russians had obtained from this spy network was never clear. ("We never discussed anything but paying the bills," Patricof, the Democratic fundraiser, told the *Washington Post*.) But for veteran U.S. counterintelligence officers, the case was an eye-opener. Never mind the end of the Cold War and Obama's reset. The determination of Russia's spy service to infiltrate American political and government circles had not waned. And the level of investment the Russians had made in this decade-long operation demonstrated how committed they were to the effort. Inside Russia House—as the CIA's Russian operations division was known—senior officers, many of them still hard-bitten Cold Warriors, saw it as a sign that Russia remained a committed adversary and the reset was doomed. "They never stopped fucking with us," John Sipher, the deputy director of Russia House, later noted. "But that was not something they wanted to hear about downtown."

The day after the Russian spies were arrested, Bill Clinton arrived in Moscow to deliver the keynote speech at a conference sponsored by Renaissance Capital, a Russian investment banking firm with links to the Kremlin. Clinton was paid a whopping $500,000* for his ninety-minute appearance, which drew an audience of top Russian government officials. Though his wife was secretary of state, the former president had not curbed his lucrative overseas speech-making, even when the gigs were underwritten by groups that might have interests before the State Department.

In the case of Renaissance Capital, the firm at that time was promoting a stock offering of a company called Uranium One— a mining firm that controlled about 20 percent of uranium production capacity within the United States. And Russia's nuclear agency, Rosatom, was in the process of purchasing a controlling interest in Uranium One, pending approval of a U.S. government

---

* This was four times more than the $125,000 Clinton earned the last time he spoke in Moscow in 2005 at an event sponsored by a British firm.

foreign investment review board on which Hillary Clinton sat with eight other senior U.S. officials.

There was no evidence that Hillary Clinton ever involved herself in the Uranium One review; a Clinton subordinate would later say he represented the State Department in deliberations over the deal. But her husband's trip to Moscow was an example of a persistent criticism raised about this power couple: They were too often blind to possible conflicts of interest. Around the time of the Uranium One deal, the company chairman's family foundation donated about $2.35 million to Clinton Foundation programs.

While in Moscow, Bill Clinton met with Putin, who gave him a stern lecture about the FBI's arrest of the illegals—and hinted it could upset Washington's efforts to improve relations. "You have come to Moscow at the very right time," Putin told the former president. "Your police have let themselves go, putting people in jail. I really expect that the positive achievements that have been made in relations between our states of late will not be harmed by the latest events."

In November, Medvedev attended a NATO summit in Lisbon. Though Putin had often demonized NATO, Medvedev signed a joint statement proclaiming that Russia and NATO had "embarked on a new stage of cooperation toward a true strategic partnership." The Russian president stated, "We recognized that the cold spell and period of grievances is over." Obama went further, declaring, "We see Russia as a partner, not an adversary."

Was that how Putin saw it? Putin had once called the collapse of the Soviet Union the "greatest geopolitical catastrophe of the century." He was a Russian nationalist to his core. He wanted to extend Russian power, restoring its spheres of influence. He was an autocrat in the long tradition of Russian strongmen and had little interest in joining the club of Western liberal democracies—or winning its approval. Becoming a strategic partner of the United States and NATO was not his goal. He was not looking to accommodate. He aimed to restore Russian greatness in what he appeared to believe was a zero-sum game of global power. And true to his KGB training, he viewed the United States and its military actions with perpetual suspicion. How long would he—could he—abide Medvedev playing nice with Obama?

In a 2007 speech, Putin had accused the United States of trying to impose a "unipolar" world on Russia and other nations. President George Bush's invasion of Iraq was Exhibit A. He would soon have Exhibit B: the U.S. intervention in Libya.

When the Arab Spring erupted in late 2010, with demonstrators assailing corrupt autocratic rulers and calling for democracy, Putin saw danger. Authoritarian governments were beginning to topple. A frenzy of regime change was under way, with the Obama administration mainly cheering on the pro-democracy protests.

By February 2011, the protests had hit Libya and soon turned into armed rebellion against the country's dictator, Muammar Qaddafi. At the U.N., Washington pushed for a resolution that would allow the United States and other nations to attack Qaddafi's troops to protect Libyan rebels and civilians. U.S. Ambassador Susan Rice lobbied the Russians hard to support the measure—or at least to not veto it. Medvedev did abstain, the measure passed, and Obama administration officials considered this a great diplomatic coup—another dividend of the reset. Soon American, British, French, and Canadian forces were launching cruise missile attacks and air sorties against Qaddafi's troops.

Putin was furious—at the United States, for once again intervening in the Arab world, and at Medvedev, for not standing up to what he viewed as Washington's arrogance. He declared that the U.N. resolution "resembles medieval calls for crusades." And he ticked off a list of past U.S. actions he deemed criminal: "During the Clinton era they bombed Belgrade, Bush sent forces into Afghanistan, then under an invented, false pretext they sent forces into Iraq, liquidated the entire Iraqi leadership—even children in Saddam Hussein's family died. Now it is Libya's turn, under the pretext of protecting the peaceful population." He seemed to be thinking, if the United States could go this far in overthrowing governments around the world, could Russia be next?

Obama's foreign policy team was caught off guard. "We did not recognize the degree it would tick Putin off," recalled Jake Sullivan, then the director of policy and planning at the State Department.

Medvedev had one more year in his term, and it had been an open question whether Putin would allow him another term as president or would return to claim the position for himself. Putin's harsh response to the Libyan action signaled the end of Medvedev's days as president.

Hillary Clinton now believed the Obama administration needed to start preparing for Putin's return to full power. She had skipped the tiger conservation summit held the previous November to which Putin had invited her. But afterward she did talk to a U.S. government official who had attended the conference—not to discuss tigers but to spend time with Putin's entourage.

This U.S. official had picked up some intriguing intelligence and reported it to Clinton: Putin was making personnel changes. Russians who had recently worked on Medvedev's presidential staff were switching to Putin's staff. This suggested Putin was indeed planning to boot Medvedev and run in the 2012 presidential elections.

Clinton sent a memo to the White House: It was time to begin thinking about Putin's restoration and what that might mean for U.S. policy. Her memo peeved other administration officials, including people in her own State Department, who saw her as being too quick to yield to a default hawkishness. Many administration officials still hoped they could squeeze more out of reengagement.

In September 2011, Putin made it official. At a joint appearance with Medvedev, Putin announced he would be running for president—and Medvedev would step aside and take his job as prime minister. For U.S. officials, who had pinned so much on working with Medvedev, it was a crushing disappointment.

The move also was a jolt to the Russian body politic. The worst fears of Kasparov, Nemtsov, and other opposition leaders about Putin were now confirmed—and in a way that showed contempt for any semblance of a democratic process. "People didn't like being treated like a doormat in which the Kremlin wiped their feet on," Vladimir Kara-Murza, a charismatic young Russian opposition figure, later observed. "It's not okay when two guys come out and say, ok, we sat down, we talked among ourselves, and we decided, 'He's going to be president and I'm going to be prime minister.' People decided: We are not cattle."

"We are not cattle"—it would soon become a rallying cry for Russia's opposition.

After the announcement, the U.S. embassy began picking up signs of popular opposition to Putin. At one point, Putin went to a boxing match and entered the ring. He was booed by the audience. "You could feel there was disquiet about another six years of Putin," John Beyrle, then the U.S. ambassador in Russia, recalled.

It seemed a clash was coming.

CHAPTER 3

"Are we here because Clinton texted us?"

Russia was heading toward a political crisis—and Putin would blame it on Hillary Clinton.

In early December 2011, Russia held nationwide parliamentary elections. Election monitors reported blatant cheating, including the brazen stuffing of ballot boxes. A video of an elections chairman apparently marking off a stack of ballots went viral. Within days, protesters took to the streets in central Moscow, shouting, "Russia without Putin!" and "Putin is a thief!" Several hundred were arrested. Russian election monitoring groups, as well as anti-Putin websites and radio stations, reported being the victims of online attacks. Worse for Putin, his United Russia Party collected about half of the vote, a major drop in its support that would mean a significant loss of seats in the Duma. (The runner-up Communist Party had 19 percent.)

The day after the election, Clinton was attending an international conference on Afghanistan in Bonn. With Lavrov looking on, she all but questioned the legitimacy of the Russian election. The United States had "serious concerns about the conduct of the elections," she said. "We are also concerned by reports that independent Russian election observers...were harassed, had cyberattacks on their websites, totally contrary to what should be the protected rights of people to observe elections and participate in them and disseminate information." She noted that she was "proud" of Russians who had tried to ensure a fair election and that "Russian voters deserve a full investigation of all credible reports of electoral fraud and manipulation." The next day, Clinton repeated the criticism. "The Russian people, like people everywhere, deserve the right to have their voices heard and their votes counted," she said. "And that means they deserve fair, free, transparent elections and leaders who are accountable to them."

How remarkable were these comments? McFaul had cleared Clinton's statement, deciding that the secretary of state—not a lower-level official or press spokesperson—should speak for the United States on this matter. "I wanted to get the Russians' attention," he later recalled. But for some U.S. officials, Clinton's affirmation of American support for fair democratic elections was not so momentous—just routine talking points. "We say that all the time," Wallander later observed. "It was really standard State Department stuff."

That was not how Putin saw it. The protests rattled him. U.S. officials who watched video and studied photographs at the time thought he appeared shaken by the outpouring of unrest. In Putin's paranoid worldview, there were no coincidences. When things went badly for him and Russia, he saw the hidden hand of the Americans trying to impose their "unipolar" world. He looked around for somebody to blame for the demonstrations—and pointed his finger at the American secretary of state.

During his official presidential campaign announcement that week, Putin, speaking to a group of grim-faced political allies assembled around a conference table, declared that Clinton had "set the tone for certain actors inside the country; she gave the signal." He was blaming her for instigating the protesters challenging him. He claimed the anti-Putin demonstrations sweeping through his country were the result of hundreds of millions of dollars in "foreign money." He added, "We are all grown-ups here. We all understand the organizers are acting according to a well-known scenario and in their own mercenary political interests."

Afterward, tens of thousands took to the streets in Moscow, St. Petersburg, and dozens of other cities demanding honest elections and denouncing Putin. Protesters mocked Putin's claim that Clinton was engineering the demonstrations. At one protest, a speaker asked the crowd, "Are we here because Clinton texted us?"

Putin, proud and vain, hated to be challenged and ridiculed. And Clinton, as he saw it, was behind all this. For him, this grudge would smolder for years—with consequences no one in the U.S. government could foresee.

In March 2012, to nobody's surprise, Putin was elected as Russia's president for the third time. About now, Clinton sent a classified memo to the White House that laid out the case for a new policy approach to Russia. As he returned to power, Putin was cracking down harshly on dissent and stirring up nationalist fever. She warned that Putin intended to re-Sovietize Russia and, she wrote, "was deeply resentful of the U.S. and suspicious of our actions." Her memo offered no prescriptions. She was recommending that the White House rethink its reset.

The White House team, including Tom Donilon, now national security adviser, was reluctant to give up on what they considered a signature foreign policy initiative for the president. Obama's top national security aides still thought they could find ways to engage with Putin, at least on a handful of specific fronts, including further nuclear arms reductions—a personal priority of the president. And other issues were on the top of the foreign policy agenda— including trying to find an end to the bloody civil war in Syria triggered by protests against Bashar al-Assad, the country's brutal dictator staunchly backed by Putin.

In September, at an Asia-Pacific Economic Cooperation gathering in Vladivostok, Clinton met with Lavrov and pressed him on collaborating with the United States to resolve the Syrian conflict. But there was no give from the Russian.

At this session, Lavrov told Clinton that Putin was about to kick the U.S. Agency for International Development out of Russia. Since the end of the Cold War, USAID had supported Russian groups that protect human rights, defend the environment, and promote fair elections—spending about $50 million annually in recent years. The eviction of USAID was aimed at bolstering Putin's claim that the United States had been mucking about in Russia's politics to weaken him.

Clinton was incensed and walked out of the meeting, leaving her notes behind and telling Lavrov he could read them if he cared to. Clinton saw this decision as another sign of Putin's growing repression and increasing paranoia.

At the APEC dinner, Clinton did have a memorable exchange with Putin. She was seated next to the Russian president, and she mentioned she had recently visited a memorial in St. Petersburg for the victims of the Nazi siege of that city during World War II. Putin responded with a harrowing story. During the war, he told Clinton, his father, a soldier, came home from the front lines for a short break. Near the apartment he shared with his wife, he saw bodies stacked on the street. Men were loading them on to a truck. In the pile, he spotted a leg with a shoe he recognized. It was his wife's shoe. He demanded her body. The men first refused but then relented. He picked up the body and realized his wife was not dead. He carried her to their apartment. She recuperated. Eight years later, she gave birth to Vladimir Putin.

Afterward, Clinton shared this account with McFaul, who was now the U.S. ambassador in Moscow. He had never heard it. Neither of them knew if this was true. Was Putin, well known for playing head games with foreign leaders, trying to impress—or intimidate—Clinton with his tale of steely determination? Whatever Putin's intent, it was one hell of an origin story.

Clinton and a few others in the administration kept angling for a revision of the Russia policy. But there was another concern at the White House at this point. It was an election year. "We don't want to have a rethink of our policy, when the president is running for reelection," McFaul later said. And the president and his team wanted to cite the reset as a foreign policy success. They certainly did not prefer the knotty dilemma of dealing with Putin becoming a campaign issue.

Russia had sparked a minor election controversy when Obama in March was caught on a hot mic at a summit in Seoul telling Medvedev, who was in his last days as president, "After my election, I have more flexibility." Obama was primarily referring to talks over whether the United States would install missile defense systems in Europe—an issue that rankled Moscow. But it looked as if the president might be trying to cut a private deal with the Russians—and keep his plans concealed from voters. Republicans pounced. "But for the accident of an open microphone, the president's intentions would have been known by Mr. Putin but not by the American people," exclaimed Republican Senator Roger Wicker of Mississippi.

Mitt Romney, the presumptive GOP presidential nominee, blasted Obama's reset and declared that Russia was "without question our number one geopolitical foe." Obama's aides saw an opening to ridicule Romney for being stuck in the past. "I'm pretty sure the Cold War ended when some of the folks in this room were still in elementary school," Jay Carney, the White House press secretary and a former Moscow correspondent, cracked to reporters. The issue came to a head during the third and final presidential debate between the two candidates. Obama took the offensive: "When you were asked, what's the biggest geopolitical threat facing America, you said Russia. Not al Qaeda. You said Russia. And the 1980s are now calling to ask for their foreign policy back, because the Cold War's been over for 20 years."

Romney was thrown on the defensive; he insisted he had "clear eyes on this." Most pundits saw Obama as winning the exchange. But it hardly mattered. This was an election that was being fought out on other grounds—Obama's management of the economy, health care, Romney's business career. The question of Putin and Russia was barely on the radar screen of most voters.

Obama won decisively. But years later, some Obama administration officials would look back on the campaign's ridicule of Romney over his Russia stance and wince. "We should have realized the reset was over earlier," a senior Obama national security official later said. Leon Panetta, who served as Obama's CIA director and then his secretary of defense, would agree, contending that the White House had been wrong to "pooh-pooh" Romney's remarks. "It was not a smart move to downplay the threat from Russia," he noted.

In the weeks after the election, the U.S. Congress took a step that intensified the mounting tensions between Washington and Moscow by passing a bipartisan measure known as the Magnitsky Act.

The story of Sergei Magnitsky was a tragedy. He was a thirty-seven-year-old Russian tax lawyer who had died a painful death in a Moscow prison cell in 2009. He had been hired by Bill Browder, an American-born financier who headed Hermitage Capital Management, a London-based hedge fund. Browder's company was one of the biggest investors in Russia—until it ran afoul of Putin's regime. In 2007, Browder's offices were raided by Russian police, its books seized, and its operations shut down.

The financier, who by that point was banned from Russia, asked Magnitsky to determine the reasons for the raid. During his inquiry, Magnitsky discovered that Russian police and tax officials had used documents pilfered from Hermitage Capital to mount a tax fraud that netted them $230 million. This seemed a blatant example of the corruption rife among senior Russian officials.

After Magnitsky filed a criminal complaint accusing Russian officials of fraud, he was arrested and charged with tax evasion. While in custody, he grew painfully ill, suffering from gallstones and pancreatitis. He made repeated requests for medical assistance that were denied. Hunched over in agonizing pain, he documented his mistreatment in 450 handwritten complaints. After his death, an independent investigation found his body was badly bruised, the result of multiple beatings by prison guards.

In the years since, Russian dissidents and human rights groups had promoted the Magnitsky case as a symbol of Russian governmental abuse—a topic the dissidents believed was receiving too little attention from the Obama administration. And Browder initiated a campaign—for him, it was more like a crusade—to pass a law in the United States that would impose stiff sanctions on Russian officials suspected of involvement in the death of his tax adviser. Russia's leading dissidents—including Kasparov, Nemtsov, and Kara-Murza—supported the measure, viewing it as a powerful warning to Putin and his oligarch friends that the Kremlin's crackdown on the opposition would have consequences and make Russia an international pariah.

The campaign for the Magnitsky Act put the White House in a difficult spot. Obama wanted to promote human rights causes—so long as they did not interfere with other foreign policy objectives. Administration officials had quietly opposed the bill; they saw it as congressional meddling in executive branch prerogatives and a complication for already strained U.S.-Russian relations. According to Kara-Murza, at a 2011 reception at the Russian embassy in Washington, McFaul, then still the NSC's top Russia official, berated him for lobbying on behalf of the measure. McFaul, he later recalled, buttonholed him and said, "How dare you Russians tell our Congress what to do? It's not up to you to tell us to pass this law. We have to decide this ourselves." Years later, Kara-Murza said, McFaul confessed over coffee, "You were right on the Magnitsky law. And we were wrong." (McFaul subsequently said he had only a vague memory of the Russian embassy encounter. As for the conversation over coffee, he did not dispute Kara-Murza's account: "I'm sure I said something like that.")

In the end, Obama signed the Magnitsky Act into law. Predictably, the Russian government struck back. The Duma passed a law cutting off U.S. adoptions of Russian children. (Between 1999 and 2012, Americans had adopted close to fifty thousand Russian children.) And the Foreign Ministry released a list barring eighteen current and former U.S. officials from Russia.

As Clinton prepared to step down as secretary of state in January 2013, she sent an exit memo to Obama essentially declaring the reset dead. She portrayed Putin as a looming threat to world order—most alarmingly in his backing of Assad's brutal dictatorship in Syria.

Don't appear too eager to work with Putin, she counseled Obama. Don't flatter him with high-level attention. Don't accept his invitation to a summit in Moscow. Putin understood and valued strength more than cooperation. "Not everyone at the White House agreed with my relatively harsh analysis," she later noted. When an aide asked Donilon if he had seen Clinton's memo on Russia, Donilon snapped, "I've seen it"—and cut off further discussion.

The new chill was evident in a disturbing development: a spike in the harassment of U.S. embassy officials serving in Russia. This was an old Soviet tactic: physically and psychologically intimidating Americans serving in Russia. During the Cold War, the Soviets had beamed radioactive microwaves at the U.S. embassy in Moscow, and thugs had assaulted U.S. officials on the street.

Now embassy officials were followed wherever they went. They had their apartments broken into. One came home to find his dog poisoned. Another found his bird dead. Yet another discovered human feces in the middle of the floor. "They were roughing up people, slashing their tires, breaking into their houses, turning off the heat, breaking up meetings of embassy officials with contacts, everything just short of physical violence," recalled one U.S. official who served in Moscow during this period. One day when Chad Norberg, a human rights officer in the St. Petersburg consulate, was at a mall with his seven-year-old son, a Russian security officer tailing them grabbed the boy and violently shook him. Norberg punched the assailant. It was all a setup. A video of the incident ended up on Russian television, a supposed case of an American diplomat attacking an innocent man. Norberg left Russia for another posting.

No one experienced the harassment more intensely than McFaul, who had arrived in Moscow as ambassador in early 2012. Once in the Russian capital, he received death threats. His children were followed on their way to school and soccer practice, infuriating the new ambassador. McFaul one winter afternoon went to visit the home of a human rights activist, Lev Ponomaryov. When he arrived, he was greeted by an unruly mob, including two reporters with TV cameras from NTV, a pro-Kremlin outlet, blocking his way and shouting questions about why he was there. "They got under his skin," a diplomat who witnessed the encounter recalled. "He lost his temper." McFaul lashed back, accusing the reporters of conducting illegal surveillance, reading his emails, and listening in on his phone calls. "How did you know I was going to be here?" he exclaimed. He protested that his diplomatic rights had been violated and asserted that Russia had turned into *"dikaya strana"*—a wild, uncivilized country.

The provocation served its purpose. McFaul's outburst was shown on Russian TV that night. Not long after, McFaul was attending a reception at the Kremlin, and a Russian friend took him aside and cautioned him to "lay low" because "you are really on thin ice." "What do you mean?" McFaul asked. Putin, he was told, considered him a "rabble-rouser" and he should be "very careful." Another time, at a party, McFaul was ominously warned by a Russian friend that Putin viewed him as a CIA spy who had been dispatched to instigate a revolution against him.

As the incidents mounted, McFaul asked the White House for a vigorous response and didn't receive it. Part of the problem was that it looked personal for McFaul. But the failure of the Obama administration to react more forcefully to the harassment led to frustrations among embassy officials. "The White House wouldn't do anything," one senior official later said. "The Russians had good reason to believe they could do whatever they wanted and not get any pushback."

In early 2013, McFaul—who had initiated the reset as an experiment and then hailed its accomplishments—sent a classified cable to the new secretary of state, John Kerry, the former senator, that essentially endorsed Clinton's stark assessment: Putin was steering Russia in a bad direction and the reset was over. "It was rather ironic," McFaul later observed. "I was the author of the reset. At first, some people thought I was too soft on the Russians. Then I was too hard on the Russians. But my thinking was, if Russia changes, we have to change."

In February 2013, Gen. Valery Gerasimov, the chief of staff of Russia's armed forces, published an article in an obscure Russian military journal advocating that Russia adapt its military strategies to the modern world. The piece initially received little attention within the U.S. national security establishment. But after Radio Liberty published a translation, U.S. officials took notice. Here was a Russian military leader proposing a new doctrine that could shape how Russia would engage—and do battle—with the United States.

In the article, Gerasimov explored how social media had fueled the Arab Spring. He noted in the internet-dominated world there were new means for waging war: "political, economic, informational." And these measures could involve "the protest potential of the population." In other words, information warfare could be used to weaponize political divisions within another nation. Gerasimov was crafting a doctrine of "hybrid warfare"—a new form of conflict in which "frontal engagements" by army battalions and fighter aircraft would become a "thing of the past," replaced by hackers and skilled propagandists trained to exploit existing rifts within the ranks of the adversary.

"The very 'rules of war' have changed," Gerasimov wrote. "The role of nonmilitary means of achieving political and strategic goals has grown, and, in many cases, they have exceeded the force of weapons in their effectiveness.... Long-distance, contactless actions against the enemy are becoming the main means of achieving combat and operational goals." Gerasimov did not spell out what "contactless actions" would replace ground troops. But it was not hard to figure out what he was talking about.

The Russian intelligence services had become increasingly aggressive and sophisticated in their cyber hacks, penetrating government, business, and media networks all over the world. Russian hackers showed their might in 2007 when they blitzed Estonia. After the Estonian government removed a statue of a Soviet soldier, a massive cyberattack shut down the country's banking system, the sanitation system, and the websites of government agencies and news organizations. The country was paralyzed for days. And in 2008, Russian cyber warriors broke into the computers of the

U.S. Central Command—which oversaw U.S. military actions throughout the Middle East—with an ingenious trick. Their operatives seeded bazaars in Kabul, where U.S. soldiers shopped, with thumb drives for sale that were embedded with malware. All it took was one soldier with one infected thumb drive, plugged into a laptop hooked up to the U.S. Central Command network, for the Russians to secretly obtain U.S. military battle plans.

Russia's cyberattacks were only one page in the Gerasimov playbook. Another was a revival of the old Soviet tactic of dirty tricks. And the Kremlin would soon deploy one against a high-level target: a senior U.S. diplomat.

In November, Viktor Yanukovych, the corrupt and Putin-friendly president of Ukraine, suddenly abandoned an agreement for closer trade ties with the European Union. The accord had been widely seen as an indicator Ukraine was moving out of Russia's orbit and aligning itself with the West. Putin, naturally, was opposed, and he successfully leaned on Yanukovych and his party to kill the deal.

In the weeks following Yanukovych's pivot back to Putin, angry protesters gathered in Kiev, decrying Yanukovych's reversal and his corruption. In early December, eight hundred thousand attended one rally, and protesters occupied Kiev's city hall and the Maidan, the central square of the city. One day, Victoria Nuland, the assistant secretary of state for European and Eurasian affairs known for her tough stance on Russia, visited the Maidan and handed out sandwiches.

As political unrest ensued, Putin threw Yanukovych a lifeline: He agreed to buy $15 billion of Ukraine's debt and to cut gas prices by a third. But that was not enough. The protests continued, growing violent and spreading to other parts of the country. The Maidan became a war zone. Clashes between protesters and riot police turned deadly.

Throughout the crisis, the Kremlin accused Washington of orchestrating the chaos and arming opposition rebels to undermine a Putin ally on Russia's border. Obama administration officials, fearing Ukraine could descend into bloody civil war, were talking intensively with Ukrainian, European, and Russian officials, attempting to hammer out a deal that would end the violence and restore stability. Obama spoke to Putin several times. He insisted that Washington was not fomenting another revolution. Obama pointed out that if they could reach an agreement here, Washington and Moscow could put their relationship on a better track and explore the possibility of massive nuclear weapons reductions.

On January 27, 2014, Nuland was home in Washington and received a call from Geoffrey Pyatt, the U.S. ambassador to Ukraine. As part of the ongoing negotiations, Nuland and Pyatt were working with the Ukrainian opposition to create a coalition government that would include Yanukovych and opposition leaders. On this call, the two Americans candidly discussed the merits of various opposition leaders who could join the coalition. They also expressed frustration that the European Union was not doing more to help end the crisis.

"Fuck the EU," Nuland told the ambassador.

Ten days later, an audio file of their entire conversation was posted on YouTube. There was little question who was responsible. The clip was first promoted on Twitter by a Russian official and then widely publicized by Russian media. Russians cited it as gotcha evidence that the United States was meddling and trying to rig the political outcome in Ukraine.

"I realized immediately what's going on," Nuland later observed. "He [Putin] is trying to discredit me or get me fired."

Nuland apologized and weathered the storm. She received a supportive phone call from Obama. The administration criticized Moscow for exploiting the audio, and the episode soon was subsumed by more dramatic developments in the Ukraine crisis. Yet the dumping on the internet of an intercepted diplomatic phone call suggested the Russians were prepared to act boldly in the arena of information warfare and to take aggressive and provocative steps

abruptly fled Kiev on February 22, and the opposition took over. Obama officials believed they had acted to avert violence and maintain stability in Ukraine. Putin saw it another way: The United States had mounted a coup to overthrow his ally and impose an anti-Putin government on Russia's border. Now the question was how he would respond.

When he returned to Moscow the morning after the Olympics finale, according to reports picked up by the U.S. embassy, Putin was furious at his intelligence agencies and determined to reassert Russian dominance and choke off what he saw as another U.S.-inspired revolution. "This is my backyard," Putin told British Prime Minister David Cameron in a phone call to discuss the crisis. "The West has repeatedly humiliated me, over Libya, over Syria, etc., for the last ten years."

The U.S. intelligence community feared Putin might be preparing to move into Crimea, a peninsula in southeastern Ukraine that was home to many ethnic Russians. There were reports of Russian military exercises that could be used as a cover for invasion. But State Department officials and some White House officials were reluctant to believe that Putin would go that far. Ukraine was an independent country of 45 million people—it had been since the Soviet Union's breakup in 1991. Crimea was part of its sovereign territory. The prevailing thinking in Washington was that Putin was most likely trying to ensure he would have maximum influence with the new Ukrainian government.

In the days following the end of the Olympics, a veteran U.S. official assigned to the Moscow embassy, looking for intelligence on Putin's plans, reached out to a secret source—a senior Russian government official who had access to the Russian president's inner circle.

The source had become a gold mine of information for the U.S. government, passing along juicy tidbits about the debates and rival factions maneuvering for power inside the Kremlin. Much of his information was gossipy stuff—who was up, who was down, who had Putin's ear and who didn't. But now with so much on the line, his U.S. contact needed to know: What was Putin's game plan?

Were the reports of a possible military move into Crimea real or a ploy?

The source laughed and said with great emotion, "Annexation will happen. It is 110 percent." The decision, he disclosed, had already been made by Putin and his advisers. And it would not stop there. Putin's regime was crafting plans to expand its influence throughout Ukraine by deploying troops and seizing other territory in eastern Ukraine. War was inevitable.

The secret source's information proved on target. A week later, Russian forces took over Crimea and grabbed the Black Sea port of Sevastopol. Soon enough, Putin announced Crimea's formal annexation into the Russian Federation—the first seizure of land from another nation in Europe since the end of World War II. And in the coming weeks and months, the fighting would spread to other parts of Ukraine, with pro-Russia militants backed and assisted by Putin occupying government buildings and combatting local and government forces in eastern Ukraine.

In response to Putin's actions in Ukraine, the United States and the European Union quickly began slapping severe economic sanctions on Russia. At a fund-raiser, Clinton, now preparing for her not-yet-announced presidential run, compared Putin's moves in Ukraine to "what Hitler did back in the 30s."

Putin was unfazed. On March 18, the Russian leader delivered a fierce and emotionally charged speech in the Grand Kremlin Palace, justifying his action. He declared that Crimea represented "our shared history and pride." He invoked the spirit of Prince Vladimir the Great, who in the year 988 had been baptized in Khersones, the ancient name for Crimea, giving birth to a Christian Russia. "After a long, hard and exhaustive journey at sea, Crimea and Sevastopol are returning to their home harbor, to the native shores, to the home port, to Russia!" Putin proclaimed. He was met with thunderous applause.

The secret source, who had tipped off the United States to Putin's plans, was not in a formal sense a spy. He was not being paid. He was not being run by a U.S. intelligence agency with a handler giving him secret instructions, arranging clandestine dead drops or furtive overseas liaisons. But this Russian official had become one of the U.S. government's most significant sources for information on what was occurring inside Putin's court.

The source was aware of the dangers he faced by talking to the U.S. official who was in touch with him. At times, he would turn up the television and the radio in his office to full volume, the better to thwart FSB eavesdroppers. He would scribble notes and pass them back and forth to his American visitor. And as the conflict in Ukraine continued, with reports of "little green men"—heavily armed but out-of-uniform Russian troops—fighting on the ground against the Ukrainian Army, his information became increasingly invaluable and troubling.

The Kremlin was divided, he told the U.S. official. There were relative moderates, led by Lavrov and Peskov, who urged caution, warning that Western sanctions in response to the Ukraine intervention would isolate Russia and endanger its economy. But they were being outgunned by a clique of hardliners. This group included Yury Kovalchuk, a billionaire owner of Rossiya bank, who was a friend of the president from St. Petersburg and known as "Putin's banker," and the *siloviki*, the leaders of the security forces. Alexander Bortnikov, the FSB chief, Nikolai Patrushev, now a senior security official, and their comrades wanted Moscow to defy sanctions and seize even more territory in the Russian-speaking provinces of Ukraine.

More alarming, the source claimed that Putin was increasingly being influenced by a telegenic, ultranationalist Orthodox Russian monk, Father Tikhon Shevkunov, whose principal message was that Putin had a divine mission to save Russia from its demise and to defend Christian values against the liberal, secular West. This monk had become a regular at Putin's side, even accompanying him on foreign trips. There had been rumors swirling around the Kremlin that the xenophobic Father Tikhon had become Putin's confessor and, having ushered him into Orthodox faith, was his *dukhovnik*, or godfather. The Russian official depicted the monk as a modern-day Rasputin. Whenever it seemed the moderates were making headway in the battle over Russian foreign policy, Kovalchuk—the banker—would bring in the monk to buck Putin up.

There was more disturbing intelligence from this Russian official: Putin and his inner circle had nothing but utter contempt for Obama and his administration—much of it cast in racist terms. Putin and his top advisers routinely denigrated Obama and his national security team as "weak" and "indecisive"—and then, contradictorily, blamed him for meddling in Russia's internal affairs. In Putin's presence, Obama would be called a "monkey," and it was not uncommon for the American president to be referred to as the N-word.

The small number of U.S. officials privy to the reports from this source wondered if Putin and his crew truly viewed Obama in such crude terms. But the source's credibility was bolstered by a recent episode. Months earlier, Irina Rodnina, a Russian figure skater, posted a racist tweet showing a doctored photo of Obama and First Lady Michelle Obama looking like monkeys and admiring a banana. The U.S. embassy lodged a protest, and Rodnina claimed on Twitter that her account had been hacked. When the Sochi Olympics opened, Putin selected Rodnina, a member of his United Russia Party in the Duma, as one of two Russian athletes to light the Olympic torch. This seemed like a not-too-veiled message.

The Russian source delivered what was perhaps his most stunning and consequential revelation later that spring, as the Ukrainian crisis continued. He told his American contact that the Kremlin was planning a wide-ranging, multifaceted campaign to attack Western institutions and undermine Western democracies. The clandestine operation was to include cyberattacks, information warfare, propaganda, and social media campaigns. Here was the Gerasimov doctrine at work.

"You have no idea how extensive these networks are in Europe—Germany, Italy, France, and the U.K.—and in the U.S.," the Russian informant told the U.S. official. "Russia has penetrated media organizations, lobbying firms, political parties, governments, and militaries in all these places."

The Russian informant offered few details—not the names of any agents or the particulars of who was to be attacked and when. But he noted that Russia regularly used its own state-controlled media organizations, including RT (formerly known as Russia Today), and Russian nongovernment organizations to plant agents that worked directly for Russian security agencies. There were fierce rivalries among these agencies, the official explained. But they had made progress in co-opting institutions and senior officials in Eastern Europe.

The source also reported there was a burgeoning relationship between Russian agents and France's right-wing National Front led by Marine Le Pen. (In December of that year, it would be revealed that the National Front had received a $9.8 million loan from a Russian bank with close ties to the Kremlin.) An alliance between Putin, who had been indoctrinated by the communist KGB, and an extreme conservative, xenophobic political party whose longtime leader, Jean-Marie Le Pen, had once dismissed the Nazi gas chambers as a mere "detail," seemed odd. But, the source explained, this fit Putin's larger strategic vision: "to destroy NATO, destroy the European Union, and seriously harm the United States."

"It was so startling," the U.S. official in contact with the Russian source later said. Russia's use of disinformation and propaganda was no surprise. Moscow's reliance on such tactics stretched back decades into the Soviet era. What was disturbing in this case, the U.S. official recalled, was "the size and the magnitude and the seriousness and their intent. It was a glimpse into the building up of a capacity for mounting influence operations against us—with the intention to do us harm."

Why was this Russian sharing all this information with an official of the U.S. government? As a boy, the source had been in a communist youth league. He later joined the Communist Party. But, he told his American contact, he eventually became disillusioned with Kremlin propaganda. He listened stealthily late at night to Radio Free Europe and the Voice of America to get what he considered to be more accurate information about world events. He was heartened by President Ronald Reagan's anti-Soviet rhetoric. That was what he expected from the U.S. government—to stand firm against aggressors and human rights violators. And that, he said sadly, was not what he was seeing from the Obama administration. Washington was imposing tough sanctions on Russia. But as far as this Russian official viewed it, such measures were not sufficient for confronting what Putin was up to.

The U.S. official wrote accounts of his conversations with this informant's disclosure in multiple emails sent to senior U.S. officials at the embassy and the National Security Council. He briefed the CIA's station chief at the embassy. And he dispatched classified "NODIS" (No Distribution) cables to the upper echelon of the State Department and the U.S. intelligence community. He ended up filing more than a dozen reports sharing this intelligence. He recalled receiving a response from a senior State Department official calling his memos "excellent reporting, very useful." But the feedback the U.S. official received was mostly about what the secret source had to say about Ukraine. That was the crisis of the moment. The secret source's warnings about Russia's information warfare plans in the United States and Europe garnered little attention. "Anybody who had any doubt about Putin's intentions," the U.S. official later said, "just wasn't reading what we reported."

The sanctions imposed by the United States and the European Union did place the West and Moscow on a more combative footing. They also affected Donald Trump.

In early 2014, as the Ukrainian crisis raged, Trump, Ivanka, and Donald Jr. had been enthusiastically pursuing their deal with the Agalarovs to develop a Trump Tower in Moscow. Yet Trump, still enamored with Putin after the Miss Universe contest, couldn't seem to work out a coherent response to Putin's aggression in Ukraine.

On Twitter, he aimed his barbs at Obama rather than the bellicose Russian president. He taunted Obama, suggesting he was not strong enough to take on Putin. "Because of President Obama's failed leadership," Trump tweeted, "we have put Vladimir Putin

& Russia back on the world stage!—No reason for this." Yet in an interview, Trump backed the sanctions Obama had pressed for.

Still, Trump continued to express admiration for Putin. Asked about Putin's invasion of Ukraine, Trump extolled Putin's leadership qualities: "Well, he's done an amazing job to taking the mantle. And he's taken it away from the president. And you look at what he's doing. And so smart. When you see the riots in a country because they're the Russians, okay, 'We'll go and take it over.' And he really goes step by step by step, and you have to give him a lot of credit."

Trump appeared to be venerating Putin for assaulting Ukraine and violating international norms. And Trump praised Putin for having been so hospitable to him during the Miss Universe event: "We just left Moscow. He could not have been nicer. He was so nice and so everything." Trump would not criticize the man whose permission he would need to build a Trump Tower in Moscow.

But the Obama and EU sanctions were making it tougher for the Trump-Agalarov deal to proceed. Russia's economy was still struggling in the wake of the recent global financial crisis, and the price of oil, a major source of revenue for Russia, was plummeting. In 2014, economic growth in Russia would almost come to a standstill.

The Ukraine sanctions would be another kick in Russia's faltering economy. And one round imposed by the EU targeted the source of financing for the Trump-Agalarov project: Sberbank. In July, the EU imposed sanctions on all Russian banks in which the Russian government held a majority interest—that included Sberbank. Its access to capital was now hindered.

In this environment, the plans for the Trump Tower in Moscow crumbled. According to the Trump Organization, Ivanka Trump, after touring potential sites in Moscow with Emin, killed the deal for business reasons. But Rob Goldstone—the manager and publicist who had helped Trump gain his best foothold in Russia—suspected the demise of Trump's Moscow project with the Agalarovs influenced Trump's view of sanctions: "They had interrupted a business deal that Trump was keenly interested in."

That deal was dead. But Trump's involvement with Russia and Putin was not done. He still had a close bond with an influential oligarch, Aras Agalarov, wired into the Kremlin. And he stayed in touch with his Miss Universe pals, Emin Agalarov and Goldstone. A year after Putin's invasion in Ukraine, Trump had Emin and Goldstone as guests to his office in Trump Tower. As Goldstone recalled it, they found Trump listening to the blaring sounds of a "hideous" rap video about Trump. The lyrics were ridiculing Trump, and Goldstone asked, "Have you listened to the words?" Trump replied, "Who cares about the words? It has 90 million hits on YouTube." While they chatted, Trump was encouraging to Emin: "Maybe next time, you'll be performing at the White House."

Months after the secret source began providing information to the United States about Putin's ambitious information warfare campaign against the West, a woman in St. Petersburg took the first steps that would lead to the disclosure of a big part of the Kremlin's operation.

Lyudmila Savchuk, in her early thirties, was employed at an unusual company with a secretive mission that she found increasingly sinister. So she reached out to a local investigative journalist. "You don't know me, but I'm working on a troll farm," Savhuck told the reporter, Andrei Soshnikov. "I hate this place. I want to destroy this place."

Over the next several weeks, Savchuk met with Soshnikov in a St. Petersburg coffee shop, slipping him documents and an undercover video about life inside the Internet Research Agency. Located in a nondescript but heavily guarded office building, with no name on the glass front doors, the Internet Research Agency had little to do with research. Instead, it employed hundreds of Russians who created fake internet identities and planted stories on social media platforms—Facebook, VKontakte (a Russian version of Facebook), Twitter, and Instagram.

These professional trolls worked in twelve-hour shifts and were measured by how many posts they filed and how many comments, likes, and shares their items received. Their fake identities were created with considerable care; the trolls would scour Facebook pages in Poland, for example, and steal the photos of Slavic-looking men and women for their phony social media personas. There were lots of attractive women—with images lifted from the pages of models and actors. The messages they were to disseminate were spelled out by management: promote Vladimir Putin, ridicule Russian opposition leaders, deride the European Union, insult Barack Obama (sometimes with racist imagery), and smear Ukraine's new president, Petro Poroshenko.

Savchuk worked in a branch of the Internet Research Agency known as Special Projects. Her mission was to concoct creative and engaging personas to entice readers on social media. One of the creations she helped develop was "Cantadora," a fortune-teller who offered readers advice on ghosts, recipes, personal relationships, and feng shui. Interspersed in Cantadora's folksy postings were prophecies on political figures—she foresaw great things for Putin—and comments on world events affecting Russia.

For Savchuk, the final straw came after opposition leader Boris Nemtsov was gunned down and murdered crossing a bridge one block from the Kremlin in February 2015. The suspicion was widespread among Russian dissidents and in the West that Putin was behind the assassination. "It was the moment I realized," she later said, "that they could kill anyone, they could kill all of us."

But Savchuk and her colleagues were ordered to promote an alternative message: Nemtsov's murder was the work of Ukrainian oligarchs aligned with the despised Poroshenko. There was no evidence Nemtsov's murder was tied to Ukrainian agents. "I don't want to do their dirty work," Savchuk told Soshnikov.

Soon after, Soshnikov revealed the existence of the Internet Research Agency in the Russian newspaper *Moi Raion*, and made a big splash. The IRA launched a mole hunt and discovered surveillance footage of Savchuk having secretly filmed the video she leaked to Soshnikov—and fired her. After the article was published, an antigovernment Russian hacking group, Anonymous International, cracked into the Internet Research Agency's computers and discovered that payments to the trolls were being made through a holding company owned by Yevgeny Prigozhin, a Russian oligarch and restaurateur close to the Russian president and known as "Putin's chef."

That was not the end of the story. An enterprising American journalist named Adrian Chen followed up. He discovered that the previous year—on September 11, 2014—several Twitter accounts had tweeted out messages about an explosion at a chemical plant in St. Mary Parish, Louisiana. Soon hundreds of tweets about this disaster were being sent to media outlets and politicians around the country. They contained images of explosions, flames, and smoke spewing forth from the chemical plant. There were screen shots of a CNN website page reporting on the disaster. A Wikipedia page about it popped up. Prominent political figures started receiving messages about the explosion. One Twitter account directed a tweet at GOP strategist Karl Rove: "Karl, Is this really ISIS who is responsible for #ColumbianChemicals? Tell @Obama that we should bomb Iraq!"

None of this was real. There had been no chemical explosion in Louisiana that day. The CNN and Wikipedia pages were fake. The entire operation, Chen wrote in the *New York Times* in June 2015, "was a highly coordinated disinformation campaign, involving dozens of fake accounts that posted hundreds of tweets for hours, targeting a list of figures precisely chosen to generate maximum attention." Chen had discovered that the fraudulent tweets had been posted via a web tool registered five years earlier in St. Petersburg—from an email address used by the executive director of the Internet Research Agency.

This whole operation—seemingly designed to convince Americans another 9/11 was at hand—harkened back to an old Soviet hallmark known as "active measures." Throughout the Cold War, Soviet intelligence agencies had sought to sow dissension in the West and stir up anti-American sentiment through false narratives, phony documents, and concocted news stories.

"Our active measures knew no bounds," Oleg Kalugin, a former senior KGB official, wrote in his memoirs. He described how he and his colleagues typed up hundreds of anonymous hate letters, purportedly from American white supremacists, and sent them to African diplomats at the United Nations to portray the United States as an irredeemably racist country. The active measures operations were relentless. The CIA was behind the John Kennedy assassination. The CIA orchestrated the killing of Martin Luther King Jr. The CIA engineered the 1978 mass murder and suicide of more than nine hundred people at a religious cult in Jonestown, Guyana. The AIDS virus was manufactured by American biological warfare specialists. The KGB had tried to push all these stories, planting them with overseas journalists and watching them spread across the globe. In the 1970s, in an attempt to influence an American election, Russian intelligence fabricated an FBI memo and other documents to make it seem as if Democratic Senator Henry "Scoop" Jackson, a fierce critic of Soviet human rights abuses, was a closeted homosexual and a member of a gay sex club.

The Internet Research Agency combined this old tactic with new technologies and did so on a new battlefield: social media. The exposés about the IRA did nothing to hinder or halt its operations. And Putin's trolls were preparing for the most expansive active measures campaign of all.

In the fall of 2014, weeks after the Louisiana chemical plant hoax, Michael Daniel, the director of White House cyber policy, received a call from Richard Ledgett, the deputy director of the NSA. "We think we have a problem," Ledgett said. "We're seeing signs the Russians have gotten access to the White House."

For years, U.S. officials had been grappling with Russian cyber intrusions. As far back as 1996, Russian hackers penetrated Defense Department networks and stole documents that if piled up would be three times the height of the Washington Monument. In the 2000s, the Chinese were perceived as the biggest cyber threat to the United States—they were stealing data from government databases and American companies practically at will, prompting concerns about a massive theft of U.S. intellectual property. But the Chinese were noisy about it. They left readily identifiable fingerprints. Ledgett, though, had long since become convinced that the Russians were the more sophisticated and stealthy adversary. When it came to cyber intrusions, "the Chinese would break into your house, smash the windows and steal your cutlery," he later explained. "The Russians would pick your lock, reset the alarm, and steal the last five checks in your checkbook so you wouldn't even know they were there."

This latest Russian assault began as a spearphishing operation aimed at State Department computers. A department employee somewhere opened a spoof email and clicked on an attachment embedded with malware. From there, the malware spread to computers throughout the State Department and U.S. embassies. The department had to shut down its nonclassified global network, leaving foreign service officers unable to access their emails. Then the malware jumped to the unclassified network of the White House.

Administration officials sought to play down the intrusions, insisting no classified systems had been breached. (The State Department told reporters its computer networks had been shut down for routine maintenance.) But the penetration was highly disruptive and worrisome. Once into the networks, the Russian attackers had obtained system administrator privileges and begun writing new code to exfiltrate data. They targeted State Department and National Security Council officials dealing with Russia policy, the war in Syria, and the Ukraine crisis, including a previous target of Moscow: Victoria Nuland. They stole a tremendous amount of documents. Obama's private schedule was accessed, downloaded, and beamed back to Moscow.

Holed up in an NSA war room dubbed the "Battleship," Ledgett and his colleagues worked around the clock to expel the intruders. But it proved far more difficult than before. When NSA cyber defenders cut the links between the Russians' command and control server and the malware in the networks, the invaders kept coming back, inserting more malware and retrieving more data. "It was hand-to-hand combat," Ledgett later observed. "It was like a fencing match—with thrust and counterthrust." In past cyberattacks, the hackers usually fled once discovered. This was different.

"You don't know me, but I'm working on a troll farm."

At the White House, Daniel, too, was struck by the Russians' new aggressiveness—and their noisiness. "It was almost like they double-dared us," he recalled. "They became even more brazen. They didn't care that we could see them. The Russians had made a strategic decision, and they were sending us a signal."

As soon as he had learned of the breach, Daniel alerted White House chief of staff Denis McDonough. For the next few weeks, Daniel, McDonough, and Lisa Monaco, Obama's homeland security adviser, met repeatedly to formulate a response. Most of the discussion centered on cyber defense. The White House team concluded there was no way to preserve the existing White House computer network. The cyber experts working on the case could never guarantee that the Russians were completely expelled. The only solution was to burn it down.

That meant turning the system off and replacing it—a project that cost several million dollars. White House staffers lost access to their shared drive folders and the memos and notes they had stored. The full story of this cyber battle would be kept secret.

Daniel believed the matter was serious enough to require a policy response targeting Russia. There was little doubt what had provoked the new aggressiveness: the Ukraine-related sanctions.

This cyber brawl certainly showed that the White House needed to shore up its defenses. But should the administration take a swing at Moscow? The idea was raised within the National Security Council and directly with Obama. But there were crucial areas where the president still was seeking Moscow's cooperation in his final two years in office—countering terrorism, resolving the horrific Syria conflict, and restraining Iran's nuclear program. Those were the bigger prizes. And there were other mitigating factors: The Russian operation had targeted unclassified systems, and the hackers had not done anything publicly with the material they stole.

"This was an intelligence operation," Obama told his top aides, according to Ledgett. "It's just like we would do to them."

The White House made a decision. It would not strike back.

CHAPTER 5

"This is the new version of Watergate."

One day in September 2015, FBI agent Adrian Hawkins placed a call to the Democratic National Committee headquarters in Washington, D.C., and asked to speak to the person in charge of technology.

He was routed to the DNC help desk, which transferred the call to Yared Tamene, a young IT specialist with The MIS Department, a consulting firm hired by the DNC. After identifying himself, Hawkins told Tamene that he had reason to believe that at least one computer on the DNC's network was compromised. He asked if the DNC was aware of this and what it was doing.

Tamene had nothing to do with cybersecurity and knew little about the subject. He was a mid-level network administrator; his basic IT duties for the DNC were to set up computer accounts for employees and be on call to deal with any problems.

When he got the call, Tamene was wary. Was this a joke or, worse, a dirty trick? He asked Hawkins if he could prove he was an FBI agent, and, as Tamene later wrote in a memo, "he did not provide me with an adequate response.... At this point, I had no way of differentiating the call I received from a prank call."

* * *

Hawkins, though, was real. He was a well-regarded agent in the FBI's cyber squad. And he was following a legitimate lead in a case that would come to affect a presidential election.

Earlier in the year, U.S. cyber warriors intercepted a target list of about thirty U.S. government agencies, think tanks, and several political organizations designated for cyberattacks by a group of hackers known as APT 29. APT stood for Advanced Persistent Threat—technojargon for a sophisticated set of actors who penetrate networks, insert viruses, and extract data over prolonged periods of time.

APT 29 was among the more determined of the known APTs. It was suspected of being associated with Russian intelligence, most likely the SVR, the country's foreign intelligence arm, and being behind the penetrations of the unclassified networks of the White House and the State Department in late 2014. More recently, it had infiltrated a network of the U.S. Joint Chiefs of Staff.

It was not unprecedented for a foreign espionage service to target the computers of U.S. political parties. The FBI's cyber watchers certainly knew that a flood of cyber assaults was occurring daily. Computer networks at major businesses, institutions, and government agencies were constantly at risk of penetration. In 2008, the FBI discovered that Chinese government hackers had infiltrated the campaigns of Barack Obama and John McCain, prompting the White House to alert both that their internal data had been compromised. In June 2015, the Chinese mounted a massive hack of the Office of Personnel Management and swiped personal information on an estimated 21 million people. The previous November, hackers who would be identified with the North Korean government raided the network of Sony Pictures. (Of course, the United States mounted its own offensive cyber operations. In 2010, Obama directed the National Security Agency to launch a cyberattack on Iran's nuclear program that destroyed about one thousand centrifuges used for uranium enrichment—a move that set back Iran's nuclear program and, as White House officials saw it, forestalled a military strike by Israel.)

The APT 29 target list was fresh evidence the Russian cyber threat was ongoing—and widening. It was another key clue that Moscow was planning the sort of information warfare campaign that the secret Russian source had told his American contact about a year before. To some in the FBI cyber division, it seemed ominous—especially when matched with other intelligence about what the Russians were up to. "We could see they were preparing their guys for something," said one FBI cyber agent who reviewed the intelligence reports. "It's like they were getting up in the morning and strapping on their body armor. They were activating infrastructure all over the world."

Hawkins, a diligent agent who had a habit of documenting every phone call and meeting, was assigned the job of alerting some of the targets. One of those on his list was the Democratic National Committee.

Hawkins's initial contact with the DNC, though, was the first in a series of botched communications and misunderstandings between the Bureau and the party that would result in bitter feelings, angry accusations, and, most important, a missed opportunity to thwart a Russian attack on an election. In time, a host of questions would arise. How hard did the FBI try to alert the DNC that its computer network was under attack by a foreign government? Why didn't the Bureau raise the issue with senior party officials? And why didn't the IT staffers—Tamene and his colleagues—take the FBI's warnings more seriously and report them to the DNC's top officials?

In that first phone call, Tamene, who thought Hawkins was being overly secretive and not forthcoming, made sure not to provide the agent any specific information about the DNC network. Hawkins instructed Tamene to look for the malware called "the Dukes" (which was actually the name of a group of hackers). He asked that Tamene not discuss the possible cyberattack or this conversation using DNC phones or email. Tamene agreed, but he still wondered if this whole thing was fake. Hawkins said nothing about Russia or any other foreign actor.

Tamene was unimpressed by the vague warning. He did do a quick internet search for information on the Dukes—which had recently been linked by a cybersecurity firm, Symantec, to high-profile cyberattacks originating in Russia. He also conducted what he later called a cursory review of the log files of the DNC's system, searching for any signs of a Dukes attack on the network. He found nothing. He told Andrew Brown, the technology director at the DNC, about the phone call from Hawkins and reported he did not see any evidence of a cyber penetration.

Case closed, it seemed.

In October, Hawkins called Tamene again several times and left voice mails. Tamene ignored them. "I did not return his calls as I had nothing to report," he later wrote in his memo detailing his contacts with the FBI.

Hawkins did not give up. In November, he called once more. This time, Tamene took the call and informed the FBI agent he had found nothing on the DNC's network to corroborate Hawkins's claims.

Hawkins then provided new information: At least one computer on the DNC's network was infected and it was "calling home" to Russia—that is, beaconing to an IP address in that country. This, Hawkins indicated, could be evidence that the DNC had experienced a "state-sponsored attack." He asked Tamene to look for any signs of the IP address in the DNC's firewall logs.

This conversation got Tamene's attention. He promised to look for the IP address and alerted Brown about the call. Tamene wondered if his searches were missing signs of the intrusion. He conducted tests and uncovered no issues that would prevent detecting evidence of a cyber break-in.

In January 2016—while the divisive presidential primary contest pitting Hillary Clinton against Bernie Sanders was fully preoccupying the DNC—Hawkins called Tamene yet again and asked to meet in person. A few days later, Tamene and two colleagues drove to an FBI office in Ashburn, Virginia, a small city thirty miles outside Washington. Hawkins greeted them, flashed his FBI badge, and handed out his business card, finally convincing Tamene and his colleagues that this was no ruse.

Hawkins provided the ITers a log of internet traffic from an IP address at the DNC to a redacted IP address. The log indicated that the Democrats had been penetrated and one of its computers was indeed "calling home" to the redacted address. Hawkins asked them not to block this unauthorized activity, if they could find it on their network. Take whatever steps might be necessary to mitigate the risk of the penetration, Hawkins said, but please don't show your hand to the hackers. (This was standard practice when trying to identify an adversary within a network.)

Once more, Tamene and a colleague went looking for signs of an infiltration. They searched network logs but could not find the traffic detailed in the document Hawkins had shared with them. They wondered if the hackers had somehow spoofed their system to hide their tracks.

In mid-February, Hawkins emailed Tamene (at Tamene's non-DNC email account) and provided him the specific IP destination address to search for—that is, the "home" the DNC network had been calling. This was the first time the FBI man had shared this crucial piece of information. But even with the IP address, Tamene and the others could not locate any network data confirming the penetration. At the end of the month, Hawkins emailed Tamene to say that his cybersecurity colleagues were still detecting activity indicating the DNC's network was compromised. Tamene replied that he and his associates were actively monitoring the network and had nothing new to report.

It was now five months since the FBI had first approached the DNC. The case at hand involved malware linked to Russia. Yet, remarkably, no one was treating this potential break-in as urgent. A cyber fire was raging within the DNC network, and no alarm was ringing.

On Saturday, March 19, 2016, at 4:34 A.M., John Podesta, the Hillary Clinton campaign chairman, received what looked like an email from Google about his personal Gmail account.

"Hi John Someone just used your password to try to sign in to your Google Account," read the email from "the Gmail Team." It noted that the attempted intrusion had come from an IP address in Ukraine. The email went on: "Google stopped this sign-in attempt. You should change your password immediately." The Gmail Team helpfully included a link to a site where Podesta could make the recommended password change.

That morning, Podesta forwarded the email to his chief of staff, Sara Latham, who then sent it along to Charles Delavan, a young IT staffer at the Clinton campaign. At 9:54 AM that morning, Delavan replied, "This is a legitimate email. John needs to change his password immediately, and ensure that two-factor authentication is turned on his account... It is absolutely imperative that this is done ASAP."

Delavan later asserted to colleagues that he had committed a typo. He had meant to write that "this is *not* a legitimate email." Not everybody on the Clinton campaign would believe him. But Delavan had an argument in his favor. In his response to Latham, he had included the genuine link Podesta needed to use to change his password.

Yet for some reason Podesta clicked on the link in the phony email and used a bogus site to create a new password. The Russians now had the keys to his emails and access to the most private messages of Clinton World going back years.

The phishing email sent to Podesta was part of a massive assault launched by another APT. This one was called APT 28, and it was tied to the GRU, Russia's military intelligence. Cybersecurity experts would later determine it had launched nineteen thousand separate attacks between March 2015 and May 2016.

These Russian hackers had targeted more than four thousand people in 116 countries, including close to six hundred in the United States, including many current and past military and diplomatic officials. On their hit list were Secretary of State John Kerry, former Secretary of State Colin Powell, Michael McFaul, now out of government service, the pope's representative in Kiev, and the anti-Putin Russian punk band Pussy Riot. More than 130 Democratic targets—including Jennifer Palmieri, the Clinton campaign's communications director, and Huma Abedin, Clinton's longtime aide and confidante—were sent phishing emails. APT 28 set its sights on the Clinton Foundation and the Center for American Progress, a progressive policy shop close to Hillary Clinton that Podesta had started.

This cyber assault resulted in the Russian hackers infiltrating about four hundred accounts. But one mattered the most. With a click, they had snared the top official in the Clinton campaign. And no one in the campaign had a clue.

On a March day, Robby Mook, Hillary Clinton's thirty-six-year-old, data-driven campaign manager, was in his eleventh-floor office at the campaign's national headquarters in Brooklyn, and he was freaking out.

The FBI was at the door. Mook got the word that agents from the New York field office had shown up—unannounced—and wanted to talk to someone in charge. What could this be about? Palmieri saw the FBI agents entering the campaign offices, and she began to fear the worst.

There was reason for concern: The FBI was probing Clinton's use of a private email server for official business when she was secretary of state in an investigation that had the potential to destroy her campaign.

For over a year, Clinton's email server controversy had been prominently in the news—and a drag on her presidential bid. It started with a *New York Times* report revealing that Clinton had used a personal email account—set up on a server in the basement of her Chappaqua, New York, home—for her government work at Foggy Bottom, in apparent violation of government rules, including a requirement that official correspondence be archived and preserved. State Department officials had been clueless about the secretary's arrangement. When they received congressional and Freedom of Information Act requests for Clinton's emails on assorted subjects, they dutifully searched the department's computer system and responded they could find no such documents— unaware that the material actually resided on a private server in suburban New York. Days after the story hit, Clinton disclosed that she had returned thirty thousand work-related emails to the State Department, but she had destroyed another thirty-two thousand that her lawyers had determined were "personal."

Clinton had handed her foes new ammunition to portray her as a secretive conniver, a politician with no regard for transparency who believed she could sidestep the rules. Her more conspiratorial-minded antagonists asserted she had relied on private email to cover up personal malfeasance, perhaps including her response to the tragic attack in 2012 at the U.S. facilities in Benghazi, Libya, in which four Americans were killed. There was no real evidence of this, and Clinton insisted she had used the private email solely as a matter of "convenience." Still, the inspectors general of the State Department and the Office of the Director of National Intelligence launched inquiries. After finding evidence that some classified emails had moved through the private server—contrary to Clinton's initial assertions—the inspectors general alerted the Justice Department to what they described as a "potential compromise of classified information." By the summer, Clinton and her use of the private email server were under criminal investigation by the FBI.

Now, months later, Clinton was pulling ahead of Sanders in the Democratic primary contest—having barely defeated him in the Iowa caucuses and been walloped by him in the New Hampshire contest. But Clinton and her advisers were constantly nervous that an unforeseen event—some new discovery by the FBI in the email case—could blow up her campaign. The FBI investigation hung over the campaign like the sword of Damocles. So when the FBI showed up at Clinton headquarters, Mook and the others had cause to fret. As the agents entered the offices, Mook was told they had come to discuss the campaign's email server. His first thought was that the FBI was going to grab this server as part of the Clinton email investigation.

Mook was spooked by the Bureau. The FBI, as he saw it, had been screwing Clinton with the email probe. Clinton aides questioned why it was taking so long for the Bureau to wrap it up. Some suspected the FBI was purposefully stretching it out to hurt Clinton. And now why hadn't the agents called first to schedule a meeting?

Mook's suspicions were so strong that he worried that agents at the Bureau might even plot to trap him or other Clinton aides. He didn't want to be part of any conversation with the FBI in which sensitive or classified information might be discussed. Every day, Mook was mentally juggling reams of information and data, and he was afraid that after a conversation with the FBI that included classified material he might inadvertently mention a piece of secret information during a media interview. Then he, too, could become the target of an FBI investigation.

This was the reality within Clinton world: The Clinton team was so paranoid about the FBI that Clinton's campaign manager did not want to be in the same room with its agents.

Mook instructed the campaign's lawyer, Marc Elias, a Washington, D.C.-based partner at the tony Perkins Coie law firm, and members of the campaign's IT and cybersecurity teams, including Shane Hable, the campaign's chief information officer, to deal with the agents.

In the meeting, the FBI agents informed Elias, Hable, and the others that it had learned the campaign was the target of a sophisticated spearphishing attack designed to compromise its computer systems. They did not name the culprit.

The campaign had long been aware of attempts to penetrate its network. The Clinton IT team had seen that the campaign was constantly under vicious cyber fire. Mook himself had received phishing emails. The campaign's techies had not been able to nail down where these attacks were coming from. But they concluded the assault was not the work of a college kid or lone hacker; it was probably state-sponsored. "We were always under the assumption that the Russians and Chinese were trying to hack us," Palmieri later said.

The campaign was on a heightened state of cyber alert and taking precautions. It expunged emails after thirty days—precisely so hackers, in the case of a breach, could not make off with a treasure trove of messages that could be used to sabotage Clinton's presidential effort. The campaign practically harassed staffers about employing good password habits and using two-step authorization.

(Podesta apparently did not get the memo.) As far as the IT folks could tell, the Clinton campaign had not been compromised.

The Clinton officials in the room asked if the agents could say who was targeting the campaign and if the FBI could share the data showing these attacks. The agents replied that they could not provide any definitive answers. The Clinton officials wondered why the FBI had bothered to go through the trouble of visiting the office, if the agents had nothing useful to offer beyond this obvious warning. It seemed a waste of time—or something else.

"I was paranoid," Mook later recalled. "I thought it was a ruse."

Perhaps the most important aspect of the meeting was what was not said. For months, FBI agents in Washington suspected that the Democratic National Committee had been penetrated by the APT 29 hackers linked to Russia. These hackers now possibly possessed political intelligence about the Clinton campaign and the 2016 presidential election. But the FBI agents in this meeting mentioned nothing about that. Agents are rigorously trained to say as little as possible about cases they are working on. It just wasn't their job to tell the Clinton campaign aides what was happening to their colleagues at the DNC.

On the afternoon of April 19, 2016, Michael Sussmann got a cryptic email from one of his colleagues at the Perkins Coie law firm about a potential problem at the DNC: "Any chance you would be free to join a call with me and the DNC at some point between 2 and 4 P.M. tomorrow? Apparently some IT guy at the DNC has been talking to the FBI for a while about their suspicions that the DNC system has been compromised to send SPAM and the FBI is now asking for the DNC to share files regarding account logon information."

Sussmann, a soft-spoken former Justice Department computer crimes prosecutor, was one of the premier cyber lawyers in Washington. His practice included representing big corporations that had been hacked. Because his firm's partner, Elias, represented the DNC (along with the Clinton campaign and virtually all the related Democratic party committees and super PACs), Sussmann did double duty as the Democratic Party's chief outside cyber adviser. And he was puzzled by the email. "Some IT guy" had been talking to the FBI for a while, and nobody had told him?

In recent weeks, FBI agent Hawkins, after not communicating with the DNC for over a month, had once again been in contact with Tamene to say the FBI was still spotting activity indicating a Russian compromise within its network. Sussmann contacted the Bureau and was told that cyber thieves may have used stolen credentials to log on to DNC accounts and swipe files from email accounts. The Bureau needed the DNC's logs so it could determine precisely which accounts had been penetrated.

By this point, Lindsey Reynolds, the DNC chief operating officer, had been looped in. But, as Mook had been, she was not eager to cooperate with the FBI. Reynolds was concerned that sensitive DNC material might leak out and that if information were handed over to the Bureau, it could later be obtained under the Freedom of Information Act.

Sussmann sought to reassure her—and set her straight. In an email to Reynolds, he wrote, "This is part of a national security investigation so any information they have goes into a classified file and is not subject to FOIA. Most important . . . they really are helping you."

Sussmann was now convinced the hack was a highly sophisticated operation and serious. No stranger to the lingo of the cyber world, he summed it up in an email after one of his briefings from the Bureau:

> FBI believes the adversary had (or has?) access to the DNC's internal network. It probably then used a keystroke logger or "mimiketz" malware, which rips from memory cleartext passwords. After the adversary gets credentials, it will stage the exfiltration on the victim (DNC) network and send the data to the cloud. And if the adversary gets bumped off the network, they just use the stolen credentials, because there is no 2-factor barrier.

But the DNC techies still had not found the breach or identified the attacker.

Three days later, on April 29, the DNC resolved what had been the major cyber controversy of the 2016 presidential campaign. And it had nothing to do with Russian hackers.

The previous December, Sanders staffers had exploited a computer glitch to gain access to confidential Clinton campaign voter information contained within a DNC database. The DNC subsequently blocked the Sanders campaign from the database—an action that impeded the Sanders campaign's voter contact efforts at the start of the Democratic primaries and caucuses. As the Sanders camp saw it, it was more proof the DNC was trying to rig the Democratic race in Clinton's favor. His campaign sued the Democratic Party.

The DNC turned to an outside cybersecurity firm called CrowdStrike to mount an independent investigation. The firm, with sleek offices in an office building in northern Virginia, was part of a new generation of cybersecurity firms that specialized in computer forensics and identifying foreign actors attacking American networks. Among its principals was Shawn Henry, a tough-talking former chief of the FBI's cyber division. In 2008, he had been the FBI official who had alerted the Obama and McCain campaigns that they had been infiltrated by Chinese cyber spies. Another CrowdStrike principal was Dmitri Alperovitch, a cocky, Russian-born technology expert, who had played a key role in fingering Chinese military hackers who had penetrated U.S. and European networks. In 2014, Alperovitch and CrowdStrike had quickly identified the North Korean government as the source of the hack that slammed Sony Pictures.

The Sanders episode was a small matter. CrowdStrike soon found evidence that four Sanders staffers had gained unauthorized access and rummaged through Clinton voter files. But the breach had not gone beyond that. The DNC, hoping to avoid an inter-party rift, agreed to let the Sanders camp once again have access to the database, and the Sanders campaign dropped the lawsuit.

As the settlement of this minor cyber kerfuffle was being wheeled out and covered by the political press, a far more dramatic development was transpiring at DNC headquarters.

That day, Reynolds was pulling into the driveway of her home when she got an alarming phone call from Tamene. The contractor he worked for had finally discovered the intrusion.

"Lindsey, I need to tell you, there was suspicious activity in the system," he said. "In the middle of the night." Reynolds quickly figured out what was going on. "Was that Moscow time?" she asked. Yes, Tamene told her. He explained that the hackers had logged on to the DNC network using Tamene's own stolen credentials—while Tamene himself was fast asleep.

For the first time, the enormity of the situation dawned on Reynolds. She had spent years at the DNC. At one point, she worked in a basement office that was adjacent to a historic monument: a file cabinet from the old DNC headquarters at the Watergate that had been burgled by secret operatives of Richard Nixon's campaign. That crime resulted in the biggest political scandal in American history. It occurred to Reynolds: "This is the new version of Watergate. This is the way they do it now. You don't need crowbars anymore."

Reynolds immediately called Amy Dacey, the DNC's chief executive officer. Until now, Dacey had known nothing of the possible Russian penetration. The next day, she informed the DNC's chair, Representative Debbie Wasserman Schultz. And Sussmann retained CrowdStrike with a new task: to investigate the breach and kick the Kremlin's modern-day burglars out of the DNC.

One of CrowdStrike's first moves was to advise the DNC officials to do nothing. Don't shut down the system. Don't stop using it. The reason: Any dramatic action or change in routine could alert the hackers they had been spotted, and then the intruders might take steps to make it impossible to ferret them out of the system. But this move—possibly unavoidable—would come back to haunt the DNC.

CrowdStrike and the lawyers warned the small circle of DNC

officials in the know to keep their mouths shut. And this meant not telling anyone in the Clinton campaign. The few DNC officials and IT staffers aware of the intrusion were to create personal email addresses for any communicating about the hack. CrowdStrike did not want the hackers to pick up any whiff the DNC was on to them.

CrowdStrike immediately got to work trying to determine the basics and, with the aid of a sophisticated security system it had developed called Falcon, quickly identified the perps: two separate bands of Russian cyber spies that had been engaged in extensive political and economic espionage for years. Each of these groups was highly sophisticated and familiar to CrowdStrike. Each used superb tradecraft and advanced methods associated with government-level capabilities that allowed them to bypass firewalls and escape detection.

"We realized that these actors were very well known to us," Alperovitch later told a reporter. There were several significant tells, including a misspelled URL, the use of a certain IP address, and Russian time-stamps. A small piece of computer code was another clue. "We could attribute them to the Russian govern-ment," Alperovitch said.

One of these bands of hackers had been dubbed Cozy Bear by cybersecurity experts. They were the same suspects known as APT 29, the Russian hacking group whose target list had been intercepted by U.S. intelligence a year earlier. This outfit had been linked to the previous attacks on the White House and State Department networks.

The other group was APT 28—the hackers associated with Rus-sian military intelligence—which had been given the name Fancy Bear. This gang had been active since the mid-2000s, sneaking into the systems of aerospace, energy, media, and government targets, with a distinct focus on defense ministries and military organiza-tions. It had developed a variety of implants—software placed in a system that allowed hackers access—which had been tweaked and improved over the years and went by various names, including X-Agent, X-Tunnel, and Foozer. Its software was designed to cover up or erase telltale signs of penetration. Fancy Bear specialized in registering domain names that closely resembled the domain names of the websites of their targets. A user would inadvertently come to their fake site, sign in, and—presto!—Fancy Bear had a password it could use to gain access to the target. A year earlier, it had been publicly linked to the hacking of the German Bundestag and France's TV5Monde.

CrowdStrike concluded Cozy Bear had been inside the DNC network since at least July 2015. Fancy Bear had only recently snuck into the DNC computers in April 2016 by exploiting a connection from the Democratic Congressional Campaign Committee, the Democratic group that raised money and supported House candidates. And, it seemed, the Russians might have gained entry to the DNC system by snooping into the LastPass accounts holding the passwords of employees of The MIS Department, the consulting firm overseeing the DNC network.

Surprisingly, the security firm uncovered no evidence that the two Russian groups had collaborated. It appeared that the DNC had been hit twice by separate teams of Russian cyber bandits. And the Russian hackers, CrowdStrike could tell, had been exfiltrating—that is, stealing—a host of DNC material, including emails and databases. Among the pilfered material was the DNC's entire opposition research file on Donald Trump.

It was a complete compromise. There was no telling what the Russians had. Or what they would do with it.

CHAPTER 6

"Felix Sater, boy, I have to even think about it."

By early December 2015, Donald Trump was the leader in the Republican presidential race. Polls had him ahead of his rivals by up to twenty points. Six months earlier, he had entered the contest as a long shot and was widely considered a novelty candidate. After all, he had gone through numerous business and personal scandals. He had been accused of associating with organized crime figures, screwing over workers and contractors, and making degrading comments about women (such as when he called Rosie O'Donnell a "slob" with a "fat ugly face"). As a candidate, he had hurled slurs and violated norms and conventions. Members of his own party recoiled at what they considered to be his offensive remarks, such as his campaign announcement speech when he referred to Mexicans as "rapists." They decried his lack of policy knowledge and denounced his insult-driven politics. They were firmly convinced his erratic behavior, arrogance, narcissism, temperament, and poor judgment would prevent him from getting the nomination.

Yet Trump knew how to put on a good show. He drew large numbers of fans to rallies where he angrily decried the political establishment, flogged the media, mocked his rivals, touted his success, and promised that Trump—he tended to refer to himself in the third person—would do great things for America. He was crushing it, shrewdly exploiting deep-seated resentments, especially among rural white voters. He was defying expectations, turning the GOP inside out, providing cable-news catnip, and cruising toward the first primaries and caucuses.

In his short stint as a candidate, Trump had set records with fact-checkers. It seemed no major presidential candidate in modern times had bent or busted the truth as much as Trump did. But there was some brazen dissembling he did in early December that was largely overlooked but necessary for Trump to preserve his chance of becoming president. It was about a onetime felon turned FBI informant named Felix Sater and about Trump's connection to Russia. And nobody at the time—no reporter, none of Trump's opponents—caught its full significance.

With Trump at the head of the pack, the Associated Press was combing over various aspects of his past, and its review included one of many checkered episodes: In the 2000s, Trump had worked with the Russian-born Sater, a New York real estate developer who had served time in prison for assault and who had once been part of a stock swindle involving members of the Mafia and Russian organized crime. Trump had developed with Sater's company the glitzy Trump SoHo hotel and condominium complex in lower Manhattan. After Sater's criminal past was revealed by the *New York Times* in 2007, Trump distanced himself from Sater. But three years later, the tycoon was once again collaborating with Sater in the pursuit of various deals, including a major project in Russia. Trump's relationship with Sater was curious and for years had drawn the interest of journalists who covered Trump.

On December 2, AP reporter Jeff Horwitz managed to get Trump on the phone for a brief interview, and he asked him about Sater.

"Felix Sater, boy, I have to even think about it," Trump replied. "I'm not that familiar with him."

In a subsequent call, Alan Garten, the Trump Organization's

chief lawyer, confirmed for Horwitz that Sater had been an adviser to Trump's company for six months in 2010.

What neither Trump nor Garten said was that Trump was right then in the middle of a business deal with Sater to develop a tower project in Moscow—less than two years after his project with the Agalarovs had crashed.

While running for president and claiming he would put the nation's interest first (and ahead of his own business interests), Trump was once again trying to build a Trump Tower in Moscow. The earlier deal with the Agalarovs had imploded after Obama imposed sanctions over Putin's intervention in Ukraine. But now, a year and a half later, Trump was privately negotiating with another Russian development company—and Sater, a former felon turned FBI informant, was the go-between. The deal would require approval from the Russian government, meaning the fate of Trump's new project was ultimately at the mercy of the Kremlin.

Trump said nothing about this deal publicly. But here was a potentially serious conflict of interest: A candidate was seeking the White House and simultaneously pursuing a business venture that could proceed only if the government of a foreign adversary gave it the green light.

When the AP story appeared a few days later with Trump stating he wouldn't recognize Sater, journalists aware of Trump's previous dealings with Sater chuckled. It was absurd for Trump to claim he had forgotten his old business associate. But they figured Trump was resorting to a ludicrous whopper just to cover up an old connection to a mobbed-up swindler. They didn't realize Trump had reason to hide a prospective Russian real estate deal that if publicly disclosed could blow up as a campaign issue.

A few months earlier, around September 2015, Sater had approached Michael Cohen, Trump's lawyer, with a proposal for the construction of a luxury hotel, office, and residential condominium building in the Russian capital that would be called the Trump World Tower Moscow. Cohen was Trump's fierce defender—in legal proceedings and in the media. A quick-talking Long Island native, he was known as Trump's pit bull. He also was a deal maker within the Trump company, and he had first met Sater when they were high school students.

Sater's proposal called for a tower that would have fifteen floors of hotels rooms, 250 luxury condominiums, and commercial space. A Russian company named I.C. Expert Investment Company—which had no track record for developing such complexes—would construct the building, and Trump would license his name to it. The Russian firm had previously been involved in building a large mid-priced apartment project that had been plagued by delays and problems. Cohen later said he "primarily communicated" with the Russian firm through Sater. And he noted that Sater was overseeing the details: acquiring a site, rounding up financing, and landing the necessary government permits. In late October 2015, Trump signed a letter of intent with I.C. Expert Investment to move forward with the venture.

The arrangement would put $4 million in up-front fees in Trump's pocket and grant him a percentage of the sales. He would have control over the marketing and design of the project and the right to name the hotel's luxury spa after Ivanka, his daughter. (One possibility: "The Spa by Ivanka Trump.") Trump's company would manage the hotel portion of the tower.

This was a serious endeavor. Trump's firm solicited building designs from different architects. Ivanka Trump suggested possible architects for the project. There were discussions regarding potential financing for the proposal. I.C. Expert Investment projects were occasionally underwritten by Russian banks under U.S. economic sanctions, including Sberbank, which had cosponsored the Miss Universe pageant in Moscow. According to Sater, he lined up financial support from VTB Bank, an institution partially owned by the Kremlin and also under U.S. sanctions. So the Trump Organization was cobbling together a deal that could well depend on Russian financing from blacklisted banks linked to Putin's regime. (VTB subsequently denied it was involved in the project.)

In the letter of intent, the chairman of I.C. Expert, Andrey Rozov, stated he owned 100 percent of the firm. According to the

Russian tax registry, I.C. Expert was owned by three off-shore companies, with one of those firms controlled by a Cypriot lawyer deeply involved in Russian finance. It was unclear how this deal had started—a Russian company with a questionable pedigree offering Trump a potentially lucrative project as he was campaigning for president and publicly addressing issues of importance to Moscow. (Cohen later said that Rozov had made an "unsolicited proposal," that he had accepted Rozov's claims about his ownership of I.C. Expert, that no "additional due diligence" was necessary at this stage, and that he never met Rozov.)

Sater, who was prone to embellishment, pitched this venture as much more than a real estate deal. He presented the deal as beneficial to Trump's presidential campaign and the fate of U.S.-Russia relations. In an email to Cohen, he wrote, "Lets make this happen and build a Trump Moscow. And possibly fix relations between the countries by showing everyone that commerce & business are much better and more practical than politics. That should be Putins message as well, and we will help him agree on that message. Help world peace and make a lot of money, I would say thats a great lifetime goal for us to go after."

In a subsequent email to Cohen, Sater noted, "I arranged for Ivanka to sit in Putins private chair at his desk and office in the Kremlin [during a 2006 trip]. I will get Putin on this program and we will get Donald elected. . . . Buddy our boy can become president of the USA and we can engineer it. I will get all of Putins team to buy in on this, I will manage this process."

Sater told Cohen that he was eager to show his Russian contacts videos of Trump making positive comments about Russia and boasted he could arrange for Putin to praise Trump. And he informed Cohen that if Trump were elected, he would like to be named U.S. ambassador to the Bahamas.

While Cohen and Sater pushed ahead with this confidential project, Trump continued his ardent defense of Putin in public. In mid-December 2015, Trump appeared on MSNBC's *Morning Joe* and declared that Putin was a better leader than Obama. When host Joe Scarborough asserted that Putin "kills journalists that don't agree with him," Trump scoffed at him: "He's running his country and at least he's a leader, unlike what we have in this country....I think our country does plenty of killing also." Two days later, Trump again dismissed allegations Putin was linked to the murders of dissidents and journalists in Russia: "In all fairness to Putin, you're saying he killed people. I haven't seen that. I don't know that he has. Have you been able to prove that?" He brushed aside the 2006 assassination of Alexander Litvinenko.

In mid-January 2016, the project was stalling. A site for the tower had not yet been acquired. The necessary permits had not yet been secured. Sater suggested that Cohen, on behalf of Trump, reach out to Putin's office and request help. But Sater had no real in with the Kremlin, and neither did Cohen. Trump's lawyer started calling journalists asking if they had the email address of Dmitry Peskov, Putin's spokesman. One of those who got the call was Maggie Haberman of the *New York Times*, who had been covering Trump for years. She told Cohen she did not have Peskov's email. Cohen ended up sending his plea for help to the general email address he obtained from the Kremlin's website—and never received a response.

Toward the end of the month, according to Cohen, he decided on his own—without Trump's input—to abandon the project for what he called "business reasons."

This proposal was done. But through five of the first eight months of Trump's campaign, the deal had been alive. It could potentially have enriched Trump and his family but also threatened his presidential bid. Trump kept it hush-hush. And he pretended he barely knew Felix Sater.

The story of Trump's odd relationship with Sater was part of the larger tale of Trump's determination to do a deal in Russia. For nearly three decades, Trump had expanded his business empire throughout the world—building and developing office towers, hotels, and golf courses in Panama, India, Turkey, Ireland, Scotland, Dubai, Canada, and the Philippines. But, much to his frustration, Russia was one market he could never crack.

His efforts began with an all-expenses-paid trip sponsored by the Soviet government in 1987, where he toured possible sites for a Trump Tower project in downtown Moscow. In an interview at the time, he explained that the hotel would mainly be for wealthy people visiting Russia "who didn't want to have to come to Moscow and sacrifice their lifestyle." There was one huge sticking point. The tower would have to be a joint venture between Trump and the Soviet government, with the Soviets retaining 51 percent ownership. That was a deal killer for Trump. (Shortly before he took this shot at a Russian project, Trump told Bernard Lown, a doctor who shared the 1985 Nobel Peace Prize with a Soviet physician for promoting nuclear disarmament, that he wanted to be given a special ambassadorship by President Reagan so he could negotiate a nuclear arms deal with the Soviet Union—which he could nail down "within one hour.")

It was several years before Trump made another push in Russia. In late October 1996, the Trump Organization announced that Trump was heading to Moscow to discuss developing a Trump Tower complex. It was five years since the collapse of the Soviet Union, and Russia was experiencing a spree of privatization and chaotic crony capitalism. Trump had spent much of the early 1990s, as his casino empire cratered, going through—and surviving—a string of bankruptcies, and he had shifted his general business strategy from building projects of his own to licensing his name to other construction projects and then managing the finished hotel or residences.

Trump landed in the Russian capital for a three-day visit. "We're looking at building a super-luxury residential tower, which I think Moscow desperately wants and needs," he said.

This time he seemed closer to a deal. Trump had joined forces with Liggett-Ducat Ltd., a Russian cigarette manufacturer that was a subsidiary of the U.S.-based Brooke Group. The Russian firm had already started developing an office center on land in Moscow it held a lease on. And the Brooke company had recruited Trump to develop what would be Europe's first Trump Tower on this site. The schedule called for its completion by 2000. "We have tremendous financial commitments from various groups," Trump said, while in Moscow. "We're ready to go anytime we want to go."

But nothing came of that deal—or a later proposal by a Russian investment firm for Trump to renovate the shabby Hotel Moskva, an ugly gray monolith across from the Kremlin. By 1998, a Trump Organization spokesman told the *Moscow Times* that Trump's Russian plans were "on the back, back, back burner. We haven't thought about Moscow for some time. That's not to say, as far as I know, that he's discarded the idea."

Russia may also have held an appeal for Trump beyond business ventures. In the middle of an on-air spat with Trump in 2001 on Howard Stern's radio show, gossip columnist A. J. Benza took a shot at Trump by saying, "He bangs Russian people." In the mid-1990s, Benza had been a prominent celebrity-chasing journalist at the *New York Daily News*, and he had often written about Trump. Referring to those days, Benza told Stern that Trump "used to call me when I was a columnist and say, 'I was just in Russia. The girls have no morals. You gotta get out there.'"

Trump didn't give up on Russia—and he soon was sharing his dream of a tower in Moscow with Sater.

As Trump had expanded his father's development business into Manhattan real estate and New Jersey casinos in the 1980s and 1990s, he had collaborated with a variety of unsavory players: crooked union officials, Mafia bosses and wise guys, and Roy Cohn, the onetime chief counsel to Senator Joe McCarthy who became a top New York lawyer for mobsters and politicians facing corruption charges. For Trump, due diligence about his business associates and customers was never a high priority. In the early 1980s, Trump began his casino empire in Atlantic City, New Jersey, by leasing property owned by two mob associates. In 1988, Trump bought a racehorse for $500,000 from an associate of Mafia kingpin John Gotti. (Trump later stiffed Gotti's man on the deal when the horse turned up lame.) But Sater might have been one of his most bizarre associates with a criminal record.

Sater was born in 1966 in what is now Russia and grew up in the

Brighton Beach neighborhood of Brooklyn. He became a licensed stockbroker, but his career in finance was interrupted in 1991, when he got into a barroom brawl and stabbed a man in the face with the stem of a margarita glass. Sater ended up serving about a year in prison on a felony conviction. Later, he and others assumed control of a brokerage that scammed customers through pump-and-dump and other stock manipulation schemes and then laundered the proceeds—more than $40 million. The operation included members of the Russian mob and assorted Mafia crime families.

In 1998, the FBI came calling. A subsequent indictment named Sater as an "unindicted co-conspirator." But Sater cut a deal with the feds, in which he pleaded guilty to one count of racketeering and agreed to provide information about his co-conspirators. The prosecutors promised to recommend a reduced sentence for Sater, if he held up his end of the bargain.

Sater did serve up information that helped the FBI in 2000 roll up others involved in that $40 million stock scheme linked to the Russian mob and the Mafia. He was living a double life as an FBI informant and a real estate developer. By early 2002, he was working at Bayrock, a real estate development and investment firm run by Tevfik Arif, a former Soviet official from Kazakhstan. (Bayrock often collaborated with the Sapir Organization, another development firm that was founded by Tamir Sapir, a billionaire from the former Soviet republic of Georgia.) Bayrock's offices were in Trump Tower.

Sater and Bayrock were soon doing deals with Trump. In one sworn deposition, Sater recalled that he would pitch ideas to Trump—"just me and him." In 2003, Bayrock announced it would build a nineteen-story condominium tower and hotel in Phoenix with the Trump Organization. (The project never went through.) Bayrock licensed the Trump name for a hotel and condominium complex in Fort Lauderdale, Florida. (That project flopped and prompted lawsuits claiming fraud.)

Bayrock and Trump also cooked up the Trump SoHo condominium-hotel in New York City, the only Bayrock project into which Trump invested any of his own money. Sater and Trump both appeared at the launch party for this project. (The Trump SoHo deal led to a lawsuit in which purchasers of units claimed they had been defrauded by Trump, his adult children, and others. Trump and his codefendants would settle the case in 2011 without admitting any wrongdoing.)

Throughout this stretch, Sater worked hard on finding Trump a project in Russia. In 2005, Trump handed Bayrock the exclusive rights to develop a Trump venture in Russia. Sater would later testify that he would visit Moscow and upon his return, "I'd come back, pop my head into Mr. Trump's office and tell him, you know, 'Moving forward on the Moscow deal.' And he would say, 'All right.'" At one point Sater and Bayrock even zeroed in on a potential site: a closed pencil factory that had been named for American radicals Nicola Sacco and Bartolomeo Vanzetti. "I showed [Trump] photos, I showed him the site, showed him the view from the site. It's pretty spectacular," Sater testified.

Sater and Bayrock were also a bridge to Russian money for Trump. In a 2007 deposition, Trump said that Bayrock brought Russian investors to his Trump Tower office to discuss deals in Moscow, and he noted that "he was pondering investing there." Trump added, "It's ridiculous that I wouldn't be investing in Russia. Russia is one of the hottest places in the world for investment." Their plans were big, he noted: "This was going to be the Trump International Hotel and Tower in Moscow, Kiev, Istanbul, et cetera, and Warsaw, Poland."

Sater, though, was a dangerous partner for any developer to have. If his previous conviction for racketeering—which remained a secret at this point—became known, investors could claim they had been misled by Bayrock and their partners, including Trump. And in 2007, the manager of the proposed Trump-Bayrock project in Phoenix claimed in a lawsuit that Sater threatened to have a cousin shock his testicles, cut his legs off, and leave him "dead in the trunk of his car" if he disclosed Sater's "suspected improprieties and past criminal conduct." Sater strongly denied this happened; the case was settled.

* * *

In December 2007, the Trump-Sater relationship hit a bump when the *New York Times* reported that the real estate tycoon was doing deals with a man who had conspired "with the Mafia to launder money and defraud investors." With Sater exposed as a felon and crook, anyone engaged in business with him would be in a tough spot. The *Times* also noted that Sater, oddly enough, had become involved "in a plan to buy antiaircraft missiles on the black market for the Central Intelligence Agency."

Trump told the newspaper he knew nothing of Sater's past.

During a deposition in an unrelated lawsuit days after the article was published, Trump was queried about Sater and the *Times*'s bombshell piece. He insisted he had only had "limited" interactions with Sater. "Have you severed your ties with the Bayrock Group as a result of this?" Trump was asked. He answered, "Well, I'm looking into it, because I wasn't happy with the story."

Trump also declared during the deposition, "We will be in Moscow at some point."

Sater left Bayrock, after the *Times* story ran. By then, his Moscow project with Trump had fizzled.

Though Sater had been outed as felon and fraud, Trump did not cut his ties to him. In 2010, Sater joined the Trump Organization as a consultant, seeking out deals. His business cards described him as a "senior advisor to Donald Trump." The arrangement lasted for only six months, according to the Trump Organization. After Sater left Bayrock, the firm became embroiled in lawsuits. A former Bayrock official sued the company, charging that it had engaged in money laundering and cash skimming. Bayrock countered that the official was a disgruntled employee aiming to make a fast buck.

Sater's work for the FBI had been praised by Justice Department officials, and later on Attorney General Loretta Lynch would tell Congress that he had provided "information crucial to national security and the conviction of over 20" mob associates. But in a report he wrote for his lawyers, Sater displayed a penchant for self-aggrandizement, calling himself "one of the all-time great cooperators." He claimed to have foiled assassination plots against President

George W. Bush and Colin Powell and provided credible information about the whereabouts of Osama bin Laden. He wrote he had
"saved thousands, perhaps tens of thousands, of lives," including
those of American servicemen and women in Afghanistan, and
"exposed himself to great danger in the process." Felix Sater, he
declared "is, without exaggeration, a national hero."

But he was not a hero Trump wanted to be publicly associated
with—not once the media had disclosed Sater's unsavory past. In a
2013 deposition—previewing what he would say two years later as
a presidential candidate—Trump insisted, "If he were sitting in the
room right now, I really wouldn't know what he looked like."

Trump's Sater connection had not led Trump to success in Moscow. But Trump and his family business had taken other stabs at
scoring a deal in Russia—and at exploiting the flow of funds pouring out of the country's oligarch-driven economy.

"Donald Trump to Sell His Name"—that was the headline for
a June 2008 article in *Kommersant*, a Russian newspaper. Donald
Trump Jr., then the executive vice president of development and
acquisitions for the Trump Organization, had come to Moscow
to deliver the keynote address at a "Real Estate in Russia" conference. Four hundred people from eighteen countries—would-be
investors and developers, folks looking to cash in on the zooming
Russian economy—had gathered at the Marriott Grand Hotel to
schmooze, network, pick up tips, and get rich. Speaking alongside
Russian officials and executives, Trump's eldest son announced
that the Trump Organization was bullish on Russia and aiming
to build elite hotels and apartments in Moscow, St. Petersburg, and
Sochi, the site of the upcoming 2014 Winter Olympics. His family
was also seeking to license the Trump name to other developers
in Russia. The previous year, Trump had registered his name as a
trademark in Russia.

A few months later, Trump's son spoke to a real estate conference in Manhattan and reported that he had personally been seeking out deals in Russia. He said that he had made half a dozen trips
there in the previous eighteen months. But one big issue, he said,

was, "Can I actually trust the person I am doing the deal with?" He and his father were worried about the rampant corruption in Russia. "As much as we want to take our business over there," he explained, "Russia is just a different world. . . . It is a question of who knows who, whose brother is paying off who, etc." He added, "It really is a scary place." Deals went forward only if the right people wanted them to happen.

But there was good news. Trump told the crowd his firm was riding high on money flowing out of Russia. Trump and his partners were having success selling condos and investment properties to wealthy Russians. In 2006, for instance, Trump's partners in a Panama project headed to Moscow to sell condos to well-heeled Muscovites. And Trump Jr. touted Russia as a key source for profits. "Russians make up a pretty disproportionate cross-section of a lot of our assets . . . certainly with our project in SoHo and anywhere in New York," he explained. "We see a lot of money pouring in from Russia."*

Around this time, another weird and somewhat mysterious character intersected with the Trumps' desire to exploit the Russian market: Sergei Millian, who would later claim to have been a broker marketing some Trump properties to wealthy Russians.

Millian was the president of the Russian-American Chamber of Commerce in the USA (RACC) and the owner of a translation service. RACC had a name more impressive than its record. Millian had started the nonprofit in Atlanta in 2006, and it had survived on shoestring budgets. The group championed closer commercial ties between Russia and the United States. According to RACC's website, Millian and his compatriots facilitated cooperation between American firms and the Russian government and Russian corporate leaders.

---

* In 2017, golf writer James Dodson recounted a 2014 conversation with Eric Trump, Trump's second oldest son, in which this Trump said his father's business did not rely on U.S. banks for financing its various golf resort projects and explained, "We have all the funding we need out of Russia." Eric Trump later denied saying that.

But how much could Millian do, when the budget for his group was only in the five figures? At one point, the organization was based in the apartment in Astoria, Queens, where Millian lived.

An online bio said Millian had graduated from the Minsk State Linguistic University with the equivalent of a master's degree in 2000. He was born in Belarus but secretive about how he had come to the United States. He wouldn't say how he had obtained U.S. citizenship. He once went by the name Siarhei Kukuts.

But Millian had seemingly struck up a relationship with the Trumps. In the April 2009 issue of the Russian-American Chamber of Commerce newsletter, he reported that he was working with Russian investors looking to purchase property in the United States and had signed an agreement with the Trump Organization "to jointly service the Russian clients' commercial, residential and industrial real estate needs."

Millian claimed he had met Trump in 2008 when Trump was promoting the Trump Hollywood development in Florida. He would later tell reporters he had signed a contract to sell apartments in the project to Russian investors—and that his efforts were a big success. "I was very happy so many Russians were able to purchase condominiums in that project," he recalled. He told another reporter that Trump "likes to be able to make lot of money with Russians." Millian estimated that Trump had made "hundreds of millions of dollars . . . as a result of interaction with Russian businessmen."*

One aspect of the Millian story was particularly curious. In 2011, he and the Russian-American Chamber of Commerce would partner with Rossotrudnichestvo, a Russian government organization that promoted Russian culture abroad. The two

---

* A 2017 Reuters review of real estate records found that at least sixty-three individuals with Russian passports or addresses bought at least $98 million worth of property in seven Trump-branded luxury towers in southern Florida. The identity of hundreds of other owners was masked by shell companies and could not be determined. But most of this money did not end up with Trump. He was not the owner of these projects. He had licensed his name and reaped a small percentage in commissions on the initial sales.

groups mounted a ten-day exchange that brought fifty entrepreneurs to Moscow and the Vladimir region. Afterward, Millian praised the Russian group in a letter to Russian President Dimitry Medvedev. But Rossotrudnichestvo would soon be under investigation by the FBI for using junkets to recruit Americans for Russian intelligence. American participants were questioned by FBI agents about any overtures that were made to them during these all-expense paid trips. Shortly after the probe began, Yury Zaytsev, the head of the Washington, D.C., arm of Rossotrudnichestvo and the lead organizer of the trips, quietly returned to Moscow. He dismissed the FBI probe as "no more than an echo of the Cold War."

The Trump Organization would later deny having forged any formal business connection with Millian. But Millian would come to play an oversized role in the Trump-Russia story by apparently making sensational and unverified claims about what had gone on inside a Moscow hotel room.

Throughout the 2000s, Trump continuously worked different angles on Russia. In 2006, Trump became executive producer of a Russian version of *The Apprentice*. The following year, he initiated a marketing blitz to sell Trump Vodka in Russia. Trump even tried to start a mixed martial arts venture that featured Fedor Emelianenko, a Russian heavyweight champ whose fans included Putin. The enterprise went bust.

But Trump did hit the jackpot in one eyebrow-raising deal with a Russian oligarch. In 2004, Trump had bought a Palm Beach estate from a nursing home magnate who had recently lost his fortune. The price tag: $45 million. Trump vowed to renovate the property into "the second greatest house in America." The first was his nearby Mar-a-Lago club. But Trump decided two years later to flip this mansion. His asking price: $125 million.

There were no takers. Then the housing market crashed. Trump discounted the property 20 percent. Still, it sat on the market.

In 2008, a buyer came to Trump's rescue: a Russian oligarch named Dmitry Rybolovlev. He had an intriguing pedigree. He had spent a year in prison in the 1990s on murder charges of which he was later cleared. In 1995, during the Wild West days in Russia, Rybolovlev, at the age of twenty-nine, became chairman of one of Russia's largest fertilizer firms. Earning the nickname "the fertilizer king," Rybolovlev soon was one of Russia's wealthiest men. Forbes estimated he was worth $12.5 billion by 2008.

He paid Trump $95 million for the estate. Trump pocketed a $50 million profit.

All of Trump's wheeling and dealing in Russia had not paid off with a Moscow project. But it was still his dream. Trump had attempted repeatedly to change the Moscow skyline and add his name to it. He and the Agalarovs had come close after Miss Universe in 2013. Then in 2015 Trump got back into business with Sater, trying to wrangle a project in Moscow, while selling himself to voters as an America First superPatriot. Was he trying to leverage his status as the Republican front-runner to finally score a Moscow deal? Did he assume there was no way he would win the presidency and cared more about achieving a decades-old ambition?

This Sater deal had been a highly unusual move for a presidential candidate. But shortly after the project died, Trump began discovering a kind of success he had never before known: He started winning Republican primaries and blowing away his establishment rivals.

CHAPTER 7

"He's been a Russian stooge for fifteen years."

Paul Manafort wanted back in the game. The veteran D.C. lobbyist had once been a big player in Republican Party politics—a
delegate counter for Gerald Ford in 1976 and the manager of GOP
conventions for George H. W. Bush in 1988 and Robert Dole in
1996. Now sixty-six, he had not worked on a campaign in years but
saw his chance. Trump was rolling over his foes in the early 2016
primaries and caucuses. Yet his ragtag campaign operation lacked
political operatives experienced in the mechanics of presidential
nomination contests. Manafort offered his services to the Republican front-runner.

In a memo sent through a mutual friend, private equity mogul
Tom Barrack, Manafort laid out the case for why Trump should
hire him. "I have managed Presidential campaigns around the
world," Manafort wrote. He suggested he was the perfect man for
a candidate who vowed to drain the swamp in the nation's capital. "I have avoided the political establishment in Washington since
2005," Manafort wrote. "I will not bring Washington baggage."

That pitch—combined with his offer to take no salary—
worked. Trump told aides he liked Manafort's appearance, with

his perpetual tan and well-coiffed hair. And Manafort had another asset: Years earlier he had bought an apartment in Trump Tower. In late March, at the urging of Barrack and son-in-law Jared Kushner, Trump brought Manafort on board as a senior strategist in charge of the complicated delegate selection process.

Yet if Trump thought Manafort wouldn't bring along any baggage, he couldn't have been more wrong. Once again, Trump had failed to do the most minimal due diligence. When Victoria Nuland, the assistant secretary of state who oversaw Russia policy, read about Manafort's hiring, she knew instantly what baggage he carried. "Manafort!" she thought. "He's been a Russian stooge for fifteen years."

For well over a decade, Manafort had been raking in millions from his consulting work—often behind the scenes—for Ukrainian and Russian clients. He had established himself as one of Ukraine's premier political fixers and the chief strategist for the country's pro-Russia Party of Regions when it was led by Viktor Yanukovych. He had spent so much time in Ukraine that he viewed the country as his private fiefdom—as Roger Stone Jr., Manafort's old friend and former partner, once discovered in a jarring fashion.

Stone, a longtime Trump adviser and self-proclaimed dirty trickster, was in a Kiev restaurant in 2007 while consulting for a Ukrainian politician named Volodymyr Lytvyn (who was once allegedly caught on tape talking about the need to silence an investigative journalist, whose decapitated corpse was later found in a forest). Suddenly, as he would later tell the story, Stone's dinner was interrupted. "What the fuck are you doing here?" demanded an American. It was Phil Griffin, a fellow GOP operative, then part of a team Manafort had assembled to work for Yanukovych, a Lytvyn rival. Soon after that encounter, Manafort called Stone. He was furious. Manafort screamed at his old friend, "What are you doing in *my* country!"

Years earlier, Manafort and Stone had been partners in one of Washington's most notorious lobbying and consulting firms—Black, Manafort and Stone. It was a trailblazing enterprise that brought Washington influence-peddling to lucrative new heights. Boasting of insider access to senior officials in the Reagan administration, the three wily principals—Stone, Manafort, and Charlie Black—made big bucks as political consultants for Republican candidates running for the House and Senate. Then they collected huge fees lobbying the lawmakers they had helped elect on behalf of corporate clients. Prominent firms lined up to retain their services: Salomon Brothers, Rupert Murdoch's News Corporation, the Tobacco Institute, the National Rifle Association, and the Trump Organization.

What made their company especially controversial was a specialty the taciturn Manafort carved out: representing the interests of some of the world's most corrupt and reprehensible dictators. In exchange for hefty retainers—often seven figures—Black, Manafort and Stone endeavored to burnish the images of these clients, portraying them as respectable partners of Washington in the global war against communism.

Their clientele was an international rogues' gallery: Ferdinand Marcos of the Philippines, Mobutu Sese Seko of Zaire, and Mohamed Siad Barre of Somalia. The unsavory character of the clients concerned some of those who worked for the firm. "Are we sure we want *this* guy as a client?" Riva Levinson, then a twenty-five-year-old lobbyist at the firm, asked Manafort after she was dispatched to meet with the Somalian strongman Siad Barre, who had been recently accused in one human rights report of summary killings, torture, and rape. Manafort seemed annoyed that such a question was being asked. "We all know Barre is a bad guy, Riva," he told her. "We just have to make sure he's *our* bad guy. Have a great trip."

One notorious Manafort client was Jonas Savimbi, an egomaniacal, ex-Maoist, Angolan rebel waging a guerilla war against his country's Marxist government and leading an army accused of recruiting child soldiers and raping and torturing civilians. Manafort dispatched lobbyists to Capitol Hill to meet with congressional aides and persuade them the allegations were overblown and that Savimbi deserved U.S. government support. When top corporate lobbyist Wayne Berman, who had just joined the firm, was invited by Manafort to attend a Washington cocktail reception for Savimbi, he got queasy. He checked out Savimbi with a top State Department official. "The guy makes all his money from drugs, diamonds, and kidnapping," the official told him. Berman was now alarmed about the reputational risk he and his A-list corporate clients, such as Texaco and Salomon Brothers, might face if he was associated with such Manafort clients. "You need to get out of there right away!" his wife said. And he did, quitting the firm and breaking all ties with Manafort.

In the 2000s, after his lobbying firm was sold off, Manafort expanded into another highly profitable endeavor. A new firm he formed with Rick Davis, another GOP consultant, offered a variety of consulting services to foreign politicians and businesspeople. One of its top clients was Oleg Deripaska, the Russian billionaire aluminum king, who, according to a confidential U.S. embassy cable, was "among the 2–3 oligarchs Putin turns to on a regular basis."

In 2005, Manafort successfully pitched Deripaska on a $10 million plan to provide him assorted consulting services. "This model can greatly benefit the Putin Government if employed at the correct levels," Manafort wrote in a memo to the oligarch. He noted that this project could "re-focus, both internally and externally, the policies of the Putin government."

Manafort's alliance with Deripaska would soon prove politically embarrassing. In early 2006, a letter from Deripaska to Manafort and Davis popped up unexpectedly on the fax machine of the Reform Institute, a nonprofit that had been set up by Republican Senator John McCain to promote his policy agenda. Davis, one of McCain's top advisers, was the group's president.

In the letter, Deripaska thanked the two consultants for setting up an "intimate" meeting for him with McCain and two other GOP senators at the ski chalet of a Canadian gold mining executive outside Davos, Switzerland. Some of McCain's aides who read the fax were aghast. The U.S. government, suspecting Deripaska was connected to organized crime, had recently denied him a visa to travel to the United States—a move that was first reported by a *Wall Street Journal* reporter named Glenn Simpson.

McCain at the time was planning to run for president in 2008 as a champion of transparency and democratic values around the world. Yet here was Davis, McCain's top adviser, and Manafort brokering a meeting between the Arizona senator and a Russian billionaire the U.S. government wanted to keep out of the country. The letter eventually leaked and caused a brief headache for McCain, just as his campaign was getting underway. Davis, who by then was McCain's campaign manager, had to end his business relationship with Manafort. Later, the McCain campaign scrapped a plan for Manafort to manage the 2008 Republican National Convention. He was too hot.

In the crush of the 2008 campaign, the Manafort-Deripaska connection faded from public attention. But it was the first public tip-off that Manafort was neck deep in secretive offshore commerce with a Putin-allied Russian oligarch—an arrangement that might be profitable but could also wind up highly compromising.

It was Deripaska who set Manafort on the path to riches and influence in Ukraine. He introduced the American to a Ukrainian steel and coal magnate named Rinat Akhmetov. And Akhmetov gave Manafort an important but tough task: Rehabilitate the image of the Kremlin's closest Ukrainian ally—Yanukovych.

This was not an easy sell. Yanukovych was a sour, heavyset man with a checkered past. As a teenager, he had spent time in prison for robbery and assault. In 2004, Yanukovych and his political party experienced a crushing defeat in a raucous election marked by the mysterious dioxin poisoning of Viktor Yushchenko, the opposition leader who ended up winning the presidency.

Manafort set up an office in Kiev and hired a crew of more than forty pollsters and advisers. Among them was Democratic consultant Tad Devine, who would later become Bernie Sanders's chief strategist during the 2016 presidential campaign. Another top member on Manafort's staff, Konstantin Kilimnik, who was known as "Kostya," had a more mysterious background. A former Russian Army translator, he told associates that he had learned to speak fluent English while serving in the GRU, Russia's military intelligence service. "'Kostya, the guy from the GRU'—that's how we talked about him," a political operative who worked in Moscow later said.*

Manafort and his team deployed state-of-the art, American-style politics and image–making to boost Yanukovych's public persona. He advised Yanukovych to wear Italian suits. He pushed imagery of Yanukovych as a strong leader, using photos of him with Putin. Manafort figured out which hot-button issues to use to enhance Yanukovych's and the Party of Region's popularity, focusing on the rights of Russian-speaking Ukrainians and opposition to Ukraine entering the NATO alliance.

"The Party of Regions is working to change its image from that of a haven for mobsters into that of a legitimate political party," a U.S. embassy official wrote in a cable. "Tapping the deep pockets of [Akhmetov], Regions has hired veteran K Street political help for its 'extreme makeover' effort…[Manafort's firm] is among the political consultants that have been hired to do the nipping and tucking."

Manafort was also pitching Yanukovych in Washington, peddling him as a modernizer who could lead his country away from Russia and into the arms of the West. In December 2006, he escorted Yanukovych to Washington and arranged for the Ukrainian to meet Vice President Dick Cheney, speak to newspaper editorial boards, and deliver a speech at a think tank in which the pro-Russian pol now depicted himself as an aspiring statesman committed to democracy and bringing Ukraine closer to Europe.

Manafort's efforts triggered complaints to the FBI that he was acting as an undeclared foreign lobbyist—in violation of the For-

---

* A 2017 Justice Department court filing noted that an unidentified Manafort, associate was "assessed to have ties" to Russian intelligence. The *New York Times* reported this associate was Kilimnik.

eign Agents Registration Act, requiring Americans engaged in advocacy for foreign principals to register with the Justice Department. "I was mad as hell about it," said Ronald Slim, a former CIA analyst who was then advising Yulia Tymoshenko, Yanukovych's chief rival. Slim had registered with the Justice Department for his similar work on her behalf. "I met with the FBI and told them, he's a foreign agent," Slim later said. But the FBI agents were not interested. They told him the Bureau was focused on terrorism and didn't have the resources to pursue this.

With Manafort's guidance, Yanukovych won the 2010 election, beating Tymoshenko by 4.5 points. Afterward, Manafort continued to advise Yanukovych. And when Yanukovych ordered a criminal investigation of Tymoshenko that resulted in her imprisonment, Manafort recruited a top American law firm that would write a report essentially supporting her conviction.

Manafort stuck with Yanukovych through the bloody protests of 2014. A hacked text message from one of his daughters noted that the profits from his Yanukovych work was "blood money." And after Yanukovych fled Kiev, Manafort hooked up with another pro-Russia party, helping it win seats in the parliament—and pocketing about $1 million.

When Manafort's role as a Trump campaign adviser was announced, Alexandra Chalupa, a consultant working for the Democratic National Committee, could barely contain herself. She had been tracking Manafort for years, trying, with little success, to blow the whistle on his Ukrainian dealings to the American media. "This is huge," she texted top DNC officials. "This is everything to take out Trump."

Foremost on her mind was that it had been Manafort's client, Yanukovych, whose government had gunned down protesters during the Maidan protests in 2014. Chalupa was a proud Ukrainian-American, raised by parents who had told her stories about Josef Stalin's brutal collectivization campaign in the Ukraine in the 1930s that starved and killed millions. She saw Putin's modern-day intervention in Ukraine as an extension of the Soviet crimes—and she was determined to expose all the Americans who had helped facilitate corruption and violence in Ukraine.

Over the next few weeks, Chalupa contacted sources in Ukraine and Washington to gather information on Manafort's work for Yanukovych. In late April, she helped organize a small protest in Manafort's hometown of New Britain, Connecticut. Local Ukrainian-American activists gathered on Paul Manafort Drive—named after Manafort's father, who had once been mayor—and demanded that the city rename the street because of the sins of the son. They called on Trump to fire Manafort and denounce Putin for his continuing aggression against Ukraine.

Chalupa's anti-Manafort crusade didn't get much attention beyond the nasty volleys of pro-Ukraine and pro-Russia camps on Twitter. But her efforts did get noticed. Days after the New Britain protest, she received a security message on her Yahoo email account: "Important action required. We strongly suspect that your account has been the target of state-sponsored actors." It was a rare notice that Yahoo's security team reserved for only the most sophisticated attempts to compromise its users' accounts. "This is a very big deal," a Yahoo security officer said at the time.

"I was freaked out," Chalupa recalled. "This was really scary." She was never told whether her account had been penetrated, but she quickly assumed it had. And there was only one group of state-sponsored actors who would have been behind it: the Russians. It confirmed for Chalupa she was on the right track.

Chalupa was encouraging journalists to dig into Manafort's Ukrainian ties and his undisclosed lobbying on behalf of Yanukovych's political party.* And soon enough, a treasure trove of damning material was discovered.

Some of the clues were hiding in plain sight. In 2011, Yulia Tymoshenko—the Ukrainian politician whom Yanukovych had

---

* One of the journalists Chalupa was in touch with was Michael Isikoff of Yahoo News, who she invited to a reception for visiting Ukrainian journalists at the Ukrainian embassy.

defeated in the 2010 presidential election—had filed a civil lawsuit in federal court in New York that accused her political opponents of having operated a U.S.-based racketeering enterprise. The suit alleged that Manafort had colluded with Dmitry Firtash, a Putin-connected Ukrainian natural gas magnate and a Yanukovych ally, to launder hundreds of millions of dollars in ill-gotten gains from Ukrainian gas interests through a "labyrinth" of companies in Panama, Cyprus, and Europe—and into real estate ventures in New York City.

Firtash was another questionable character. In 2008, he had told the U.S. ambassador in Kiev that years earlier he had to obtain the approval of Semion Mogilevich, a notorious alleged Russian mobster, to get into business. But he denied having a close relationship with the gangster.

That same year, according to documents filed in the lawsuit by Tymoshenko's lawyers, Manafort had met with Firtash in Kiev to discuss a proposal for the oligarch to invest $100 million in a global real estate fund. As part of the arrangement, Firtash would pay $1.5 million in management fees to a firm owned by Manafort and a real estate executive named Brad Zackson, who had once been a manager for the Trump Organization under Fred Trump, Donald's father.

There was no indication that this deal with Firtash was ever consummated. But other documents in the Tymoshenko lawsuit showed that Manafort had also discussed a more ambitious project with Firtash: an $850 million deal to purchase the Drake Hotel in Manhattan and turn it into a luxury tower—a project to be partly financed by Deripaska.

This tower project never materialized either, apparently one of many victims of the financial crisis and real estate crash that fall. And the Tymoshenko lawsuit was dismissed in 2015 on the grounds that the racketeering acts alleged had primarily taken place overseas and were not in the jurisdiction of the federal courts. In 2014, Firtash was arrested in Austria, following his indictment in Chicago for an alleged foreign bribery scheme involving the purchase of titanium in India.

About this time, Manafort's partnership with Deripaska was turning ugly. A decade or so earlier, Manafort and his business associate, Rick Gates, had set up a fund with Deripaska to invest in deals in Ukraine, Russia, and elsewhere. As part of the arrangement, Deripaska's firm, called Surf Horizon, paid $7.35 million in management fees to Manafort and Gates. One of the deals entailed investing $18.9 million to buy a Ukrainian telecommunications company. In late 2014, Deripaska initiated legal action in the Cayman Islands demanding that Manafort and Gates account for what had happened to the funds for this deal.

This Ukrainian telecommunications deal was endlessly complex, but for a reason. Surf Horizon's petition maintained the entire project was an elaborate tax dodge. Manafort had created multiple cutout entities in Cyprus for this venture, and the investment was structured as a series of loans to avoid taxation, the court filings claimed.

According to Deripaska's complaint, the money disappeared. When Deripaska's lawyers made repeated requests for audit reports, the lawsuit claimed, they got no response. "It appears that Paul Manafort and Rick Gates have simply disappeared," Deripaska's lawyers wrote in a petition to the Cayman Islands court.

Manafort and Gates had not disappeared. By the spring of 2016, both were working for Trump's campaign. Manafort's dispute with Deripaska was publicly reported at this time—initially by Yahoo News—but the full significance of Manafort's ties to the Russian oligarch did not register. The man Trump had brought in to help guide his presidential campaign was being pursued—to the tune of millions of dollars—by one of Putin's closest business cronies.*

In the weeks after Manafort became a top Trump campaign official, he sought to use his new status to leverage his standing with Deripaska and make his money problems go away. That spring, he sent emails to Kilimnik, his loyal deputy in Kiev, telling him

---

* In January 2018, Deripaska filed a lawsuit in New York state court against Manafort and Gates, claiming they had defrauded him in the Ukrainian cable deal.

to make sure that Deripaska knew that Manafort had become an influential adviser to a candidate who could land in the White House. Manafort was quite eager to make certain that Deripaska was aware of his new status.

"I assume you have shown our friends my media coverage, right?" Manafort wrote Kilimnik. "Absolutely," he responded from Kiev. "Every article." In another email, Kilimnik reported that a Deripaska aide had been forwarding news stories about Manafort to the Russian billionaire. "Frankly, the coverage has been much better than Trump's," Kilimnik wrote. "In any case it will hugely enhance your reputation no matter what happens."

Manafort was looking to put his work for Trump to financial advantage. Referencing his campaign position, he emailed Kilimnik, "How do we use to get whole. Has OVD operation seen?" (OVD were Deripaska's initials.) As of the previous December, Manafort owed millions to shell companies based in Cyprus that were linked to Deripaska. Manafort did not spell out what he had in mind regarding getting "whole." But he certainly was exploring how to exploit his Trump connection for personal gain.

Manafort was also aiming to keep his Russia-related machinations under wraps. When the *Washington Post* sent a list of questions to the Trump campaign about Manafort's relationship with Deripaska, Manafort instructed Hope Hicks, a campaign spokesperson, to disregard the request. Manafort was using his campaign position to fix his financial relationship with an oligarch close to Putin. That, he knew, had to remain secret.

At this point, Manafort did succeed in preventing his Russian and Ukrainian dealings from becoming a campaign issue. And on May 19, 2016, Trump, closer to becoming the presumptive Republican presidential candidate, promoted Manafort and named him his campaign's chairman and chief strategist.

CHAPTER 8

"How the fuck did he get on the list?"

On March 21, 2016, Donald Trump sat down at the offices of the *Washington Post* for a meeting with the newspaper's editorial board. For the first question, publisher Fred Ryan asked Trump to name his foreign policy advisers.

Trump knew this was coming. For weeks, J. D. Gordon, a campaign aide who had once been a Pentagon spokesman at the Guantanamo detention camp, had been struggling to assemble a Trump national security team, reaching out to former Bush administration officials, conservative academics, and former Pentagon generals without much luck. One of them, recently retired Marine Corps Gen. John Kelly, didn't even return his phone calls. "None of them wanted anything to do with us," he later explained.

But by the time of the *Post* editorial board interview, Sam Clovis, an Iowa radio talk show host who was now the campaign's cochairman, had managed to cobble together a slapdash list of largely obscure figures. Trump read them off to the newspaper's editors and reporters: Walid Phares, a Fox News counterterrorism analyst; Joseph Schmitz, a former Pentagon inspector general; and Keith Kellogg, a retired Army lieutenant general. And there were two names almost nobody had heard of. One was Carter Page. Trump pointed out he was a "PhD." The other was George Papadopoulos. Trump called him "an energy and oil consultant, excellent guy."

None of the Trump advisers had served in senior policymaking positions in previous administrations. None had any serious foreign policy credentials. And two had checkered backgrounds. Phares had once been a close adviser to a Lebanese Christian warlord accused of operating hit squads against Shia Muslims during that country's bloody civil war. Schmitz, after leaving the Pentagon, had become chief counsel to Blackwater, the controversial security firm headed by Erik Prince. Its employees had been charged with gunning down unarmed Iraqi civilians during a massacre at a Baghdad traffic circle in 2007.

Page and Papadopoulos were curious choices. Page had opened Merrill Lynch's Moscow office in 2004 and went on to advise and invest in Gazprom, the natural gas conglomerate mostly owned by the Russian government. In recent years, he had pursued various deals involving Russia, often impeded by the U.S. economic sanctions that he denounced. In 2014, he had written an article blaming NATO for provoking Putin.

The twenty-eight-year-old Papadopoulos had a surprisingly skimpy résumé. He had graduated from DePaul University in 2009 and had worked as an unpaid intern and researcher at the Hudson Institute, a conservative think tank in Washington. On his Linked In profile, he listed one of his credentials: participating as a U.S. representative in a Model UN program. A skilled networker, he had served briefly as an adviser on the presidential campaign of Ben Carson—and had parlayed that into a stint with the Trump effort.

After the list was released, Steve Bannon, then the publisher of the alt-right website *Breitbart News*, called up a friend in the Trump campaign. "These people are a bunch of clowns," he told him. As for Papadopoulos, Bannon asked, "How the fuck did he get on the list?"

Page and Papadopoulos were unknown in the United States, but their new roles were keenly noticed in Russia. Page would soon be asked to give a major speech at a prestigious Moscow university whose board chairman was Russia's deputy prime minister. And Papadopoulos would be courted by a professor from Malta and a mysterious Russian woman. As the FBI would come to suspect, Page and Papadopoulos were being cultivated by cutouts for Russian intelligence, as part of a sophisticated operation to infiltrate and influence the Trump campaign.

On March 24, 2016, three days after Trump first mentioned Papadopoulos' name to the *Washington Post* editorial board, the young policy adviser met for lunch in London with Joseph Mifsud, a professor of diplomacy at the University of Stirling in Scotland. Mifsud was a native of Malta who had boasted about his contacts with high-level Russian officials. He had first met Papadopoulos in Italy a week and a half earlier. According to Papadopoulos' later account, the professor took "great interest" in him once he learned he was joining Trump's foreign policy team. For his part, Papadopoulos thought that if he could cozy up to an academic with ties to Russian officials, that would boost his standing within the campaign.

At their lunch in London, Mifsud introduced Papadopoulos to an attractive Russian woman. He said she was "Putin's niece." The professor noted she was well wired in the Kremlin.*

After the lunch, Papadopoulos emailed Clovis and several other campaign officials to report he had met with this pair and discussed arranging "a meeting between us and the Russian leadership to discuss U.S.-Russia ties under President Trump." Clovis responded that he would "work it through the campaign." But he was pleased. He had already told Papadopoulos that a main foreign policy focus of the Trump campaign was to improve U.S. relations with Russia. "Great work," Clovis emailed Papadopoulos.

A week later, on March 31, Papadopoulos attended the first meeting of the Trump campaign foreign policy committee in a conference room at the Old Post Office in Washington—then under construction to become the new Trump International Hotel. With

---

* Papadopoulos later learned this woman, whose name has been reported in various news reports as "Olga Vinogradova" and "Olga Polonskaya," was not Putin's niece.

Trump presiding, the members introduced themselves. When it was his turn, Papadopoulos mentioned he had contacts in the United Kingdom who could set up a meeting between the GOP contender and Putin. The reaction was mixed. Retired Navy Rear Adm. Charles Kubic, who had just joined the foreign policy team, said this was not a good idea, given that Russia was still under sanctions for its intervention in Ukraine. Gordon, who attended the meeting, later said that Alabama Senator Jeff Sessions, Trump's senior foreign policy adviser, shot down the idea and suggested there should be no further discussion of it. More significant, though, may have been Trump's reaction. "He didn't say yes, he didn't say no," Gordon recalled. "He heard him out." But Papadopoulos later told investigators he believed Trump gave him encouragement. According to sources familiar with Papadopoulos' account, Trump said the idea was "interesting" and looked at Sessions, as if he expected him to follow up, and Sessions nodded in response. (Sessions later said he had "no clear recollection" of this exchange.)

Whatever was said at the meeting, Papadopoulos did not stand down. In mid-April, Mifsud, through email, introduced Papadopoulos to Ivan Timofeev, a program director at the Russian International Affairs Council, a government-funded think tank. The professor described Timofeev as close to officials within the Russian Ministry of Foreign Affairs. Papadopoulos proceeded to have a series of conversations via Skype and email with Timofeev about organizing a meeting between Russian government officials and Trump representatives.

In one email, Papadopoulos, who had edited the outline of Trump's first major foreign policy speech, told Timofeev that the address—in which Trump would call for better relations with Russia—was "the signal to meet."

Around then, things got more interesting. At an April 26 breakfast at a London hotel, Mifsud told Papadopoulos that he had just returned from Moscow, where he had met with high-level Russian officials and had learned that the Russians had obtained "dirt" on Hillary Clinton. "The Russians had emails of Clinton.... They have thousands of emails," Mifsud told Papadopoulos.

It was unclear what emails Mifsud was talking about. The personal emails Clinton said she had destroyed? Or another batch of emails from another source? By now, two different Russian hacking groups had penetrated the DNC, and one of them had also stolen thousands of messages from John Podesta's personal email account. But none of this was publicly known at the time.

The day after the breakfast, Papadopoulos reported back to Stephen Miller, a top campaign policy official: "Have some interesting messages coming in from Moscow about a trip when the time is right." Three days later, he thanked Mifsud for his continued efforts to set up a Trump-Putin meeting. "It's history making if it happens," he wrote.

Papadopoulos was taken with the idea of making history, and he was right in the thick of what could be important behind-the-scenes, world-changing events. And in May, during a night of heavy drinking at the Kensington Wine Room in London, he gabbed to an acquaintance: Alexander Downer, the top Australian diplomat in Britain. Papadopoulos had been introduced by an Israeli embassy official to another Australian diplomat, and somehow that had led to the get-together with Downer.

After several rounds of drinks, Papadopoulos told Downer that the Russians had political dirt on Clinton. The information registered with Downer—but not enough for him to do anything with it. Maybe it was just bar talk.

In the following weeks, Papadopoulos kept emailing campaign officials—including Manafort and campaign manager Corey Lewandowski—to note Russia was interested in hosting Trump or other campaign representatives, including Papadopoulos himself. At one point, Manafort forwarded a Papadopoulos email to another official, noting that Trump "is not doing these trips." But he added, "It should be someone low level in the campaign so as not to send any signal." The wording suggested Manafort was open to some form of contact between the Trump campaign and Moscow.

Papadopoulos never stopped his efforts. For the next several months, he pursued an "off the record" meeting between campaign representatives and Putin's office. At one point, he suggested he make the trip to Russia himself, and Clovis gave him the green light. As it turned out, Papadopoulos never did fly to Moscow. But Carter Page did, taking a trip that would be of interest to the FBI.

The overtures to Papadopoulos were not the only Russian attempt to forge a relationship with the Trump campaign. And one of those efforts came through a broader Russian initiative to gain influence within the American conservative movement.

It was an operation that Rick Hohlt, a veteran Washington lobbyist and top Republican Party fundraiser, had stumbled across two years earlier when he was invited to a private dinner at a Nashville restaurant during the annual convention of the National Rifle Association.

The guest of honor at this dinner was Alexander Torshin, a pudgy deputy governor of Russia's central bank, who was a high-ranking member of Putin's United Russia Party. Torshin was an odd figure to be the toast of the NRA: He was then the target of a Spanish investigation into Russian money laundering. (A wiretap had captured a Russian mobster referring to Torshin as his "El Padrino," or godfather.)

Hohlt was puzzled. Why was the NRA hosting a Russian emissary close to Putin? Torshin, he learned, had become a lifetime member of the NRA and was close friends with David Keene, a former NRA president. But Hohlt was more curious about the presence of a woman who was introduced as Torshin's personal assistant—Maria Butina, a tall, striking redhead who, in flawless English, regaled NRA leaders about her own hunting prowess and her work setting up a gun rights organization in Russia.

Hohlt had run across Butina at the annual Conservative Political Action Conference (CPAC) the previous February. Hohlt was struck by how overly solicitous she was. Could they be friends on Facebook? she asked him. How could they stay in contact? The balding, bespectacled Hohlt, well into his sixties, was not accustomed to this much attention from an attractive young woman. "All I can think was, what the fuck is this all about?" Hohlt recalled.

Torshin and Butina were a duo who kept popping up at

conservative gatherings—NRA conventions, CPAC conferences, and National Prayer Breakfasts in Washington. In July 2015, weeks after Trump had announced his candidacy, Butina showed up at FreedomFest, a conservative evangelical event, in Las Vegas and questioned the new GOP candidate about his stance on Russia during a Q and A session.

"I'm from Russia.... Do you want to continue the politics of sanctions that are damaging both economies?" she asked. "Or do you have any other ideas?" Trump had not yet spoken about this issue as a candidate. "I know Putin," Trump said, during a five-minute-long response. "Putin has no respect for President Obama. Big problem. Big problem." Obama's policies had driven Russia to ally itself more closely with China and this was a "horrible thing" for the United States. "I believe I would get along very nicely with Putin, OK? I don't think you'd need the sanctions. I think we'd get along very well." Thanks to Butina, the Russians now had Trump on the record opposing the sanctions despised by Moscow.

Much later, Trump's campaign advisers would watch the video of this encounter and wonder about it. Steve Bannon raised it with RNC chair Reince Priebus. How was it that this Russian woman happened to be in Las Vegas for that event? And how was it that Trump happened to call on her? And Trump's response? It was odd, Bannon thought, that Trump had a fully developed answer. Priebus agreed there was something strange about Butina. Whenever there were events held by conservative groups, she was always around, he told Bannon.

In the spring of 2016, Torshin and Butina made a direct play to gain influence with the Trump campaign. One of their emissaries was a conservative activist and NRA member named Paul Erickson, who had escorted Butina to CPAC the year before. In May, Erickson sent an email to Rick Dearborn, a senior campaign official and Sessions' chief of staff, under the subject line "Kremlin connection." In the message, he offered to serve as a "back-channel" between the Trump campaign and Putin. Without mentioning them by name, Erickson apparently was proposing to be the go-between connecting Torshin and Butina with the Trump campaign.

"Putin is deadly serious about building a good relationship with Mr. Trump," Erickson wrote. "He wants to extend an invitation to Mr. Trump to visit him in the Kremlin before the election."

Erickson's email spelled out Putin's reason for wanting to boost Trump's campaign. "The Kremlin believes that the only possibility of a true reset in this relationship would be with a new Republican White House," he wrote. "Ever since Hillary compared Putin to Hitler, all senior Russian leaders consider her beyond redemption."

Erickson suggested that the upcoming NRA convention in Louisville would be the ideal opportunity for "first contact" between his Russian friends and the Trump camp. Trump was due to be a featured speaker. And Torshin and Butina would be attending.

Yet another conservative activist, Rick Clay, reached out to the Trump campaign on their behalf, suggesting that Trump talk with Torshin at the NRA event. In an email to Dearborn, Clay described Torshin as "a very close friend of President Putin." Torshin's goal was to arrange a summit in Moscow with Trump and the Reverend Franklin Graham that would highlight the persecution of Christians around the world.

"Please excuse the play on words but this is HUGE!" Clay wrote Dearborn. "The optics of Mr. Trump in Russia with Franklin Graham attending an event of over 1000 World Christian Leaders addressing the Defense of Persecuted Christians accompanied by a very visible meeting between President Putin and Mr. Trump would devastate the Clinton campaign's effort to marginalize Mr. Trump on foreign policy and embolden him further with evangelicals."

Clay's email to Dearborn was forwarded to Jared Kushner, who raised a red flag. He told Dearborn to "pass on this," adding, "a lot of people come claiming to carry a message.... Most likely these people then go back home and claim they have special access to gain importance for themselves. Be careful."

Nevertheless, Torshin did get invited to a private dinner in Louisville with NRA officials. And there he met and spoke briefly with Donald Trump Jr.

* * *

That spring, another national security figure—far more prominent than Page, Papadopoulos, or the others on the campaign's foreign policy advisory team—had entered Trump's orbit: retired Army Lieut. Gen. Michael Flynn.

Flynn had been director of the Defense Intelligence Agency under Obama. A brash and outspoken maverick, Flynn had once been a protégé of Army Gen. Stanley McChrystal. As the chief intelligence officer for McChrystal's Joint Special Operations Command, an elite counterterrorism unit, Flynn had been widely credited with shrewdly exploiting all facets of military intelligence—extracted from computer laptops, cell phones, drone flights, and detainee interrogations—to help quell the Sunni insurgency in Iraq. He later won accolades overseeing intelligence for counterterrorism operations in Afghanistan. But as DIA director, Flynn's disregard for bureaucratic protocol proved his undoing. Amid widespread complaints of mismanagement and repeated clashes with senior Pentagon officials, Flynn was forced to resign in August 2014—an experience that deeply embittered him.

In the months after being fired, Flynn began dropping hints to journalists and others that the real reason for his dismissal was that he had tried to blow the whistle on the Obama White House's disregard of intelligence reports warning of the rise of ISIS. Flynn, though, was unable to point to much evidence that the DIA had provided such reports. But his claims, coming in the aftermath of the gains by ISIS in Iraq and Syria, endeared him to conservative critics of the administration's antiterrorism policies. Soon Flynn was echoing one of their chief critiques: that Obama's failure to denounce "radical Islamic extremism" had undermined the effort to crush ISIS.

After several appearances on Fox News and elsewhere, Flynn was invited to Trump Tower to brief the GOP candidate. Trump and Flynn hit it off, and, according to a close associate of the retired general, came to view themselves as "brothers in the foxhole" doing battle with the liberal media and the Democratic establishment. By late spring, Flynn was being widely mentioned as a future director of national intelligence in a Trump presidency. There was even speculation he could be Trump's vice presidential running mate.

Flynn was fierce, hawkish, and tough-minded, but a dove when it came to Russia; he saw Putin as a potential ally in the fight against Islamic extremism. In December 2015, Flynn was invited to speak in Moscow at a celebration of the tenth anniversary of RT, the Russian government propaganda outlet. A press release announcing his upcoming appearance astonished Pentagon officials. The presence of a retired high-ranking U.S. military officer at such an event—when the U.S. government was imposing stiff sanctions on Putin's government—would be viewed as a huge propaganda coup for the Russians. One of Flynn's former deputies pleaded with him not to go. "Please, sir, don't do this," said Simone Ledeen, a military intelligence officer who worked for Flynn and was a family friend. "It's not just you. You're a retired three-star general. It's the Army. It's all of the people who have been with you, all of these analysts known as 'Flynn's people.' Don't do this to them. Don't do this to yourself."

But Flynn decided to go anyway—and would be well compensated. The Russians would pay him $45,000 and provide first-class tickets and hotel rooms for him and his son.

At the event, in an interview onstage with RT anchor Sophie Shevardnadze, Flynn spoke about the need for Russia and the United States to put aside differences and work more closely in the fight against Islamic extremism. "The United States can't sit there and say, 'Russia, you're bad,'" Flynn said. "And Russia can't sit there and say, 'The United States, you're bad.'...This is a funny marriage we have, Russia and the United States. But it's a marriage. What we don't need is for that marriage to break up."

That night, Flynn attended a gala dinner where he was seated at the VIP table next to Putin. (Sitting across from him at the table was Green Party presidential candidate Jill Stein.) At the end of the dinner, Putin took to the stage and congratulated RT on its success. Flynn, along with the other guests, rose in applause.

In April 2016, a hack of sorts hit Putin. More than 11 million files from the world's fourth biggest offshore law firm, Mossack Fonseca, were given by anonymous source to a German newspaper, which then shared them with media outlets around the world. Dubbed the Panama Papers, the material revealed how world leaders and wealthy individuals across the globe used offshore accounts to hide money and avoid taxes. The documents disclosed that relatives and friends of Putin made and hid millions of dollars in transactions that presumably were enabled by their ties to the Russian president. The documents showed that Sergei Roldugin, a professional cellist and a close Putin friend, was linked to offshore companies with cash flows of up to $2 billion.

Putin's name did not appear in the records. But these revelations certainly bolstered the case he was running a kleptocracy. Putin took the matter personally—and, once again, he blamed the United States. He claimed that "officials and state agencies in the United States are behind all this." And he declared the release of these documents was an attempt "to weaken us from within, make us more acquiescent and make us toe their line."

For Putin, here was more evidence to buttress his belief Washington was scheming against him. But his accusations of American plots had become routine, and this one set off no alarms within the Obama administration.

Neither did an intelligence report that came in a few weeks later. U.S. intelligence intercepted a conversation in which an officer in the GRU, the Russian military intelligence service, boasted that the GRU was about to strike Hillary Clinton in an act of revenge for what Putin believed was her role in the anti-Putin protests of 2011. The GRU, this officer said, was preparing to cause chaos in the U.S. election.

A report based on this intercepted conversation was circulated within U.S. intelligence circles. But it prompted no significant concern. It was as if no one in the U.S. government could imagine what was about to come.

In late May, Robby Mook was briefed about the disturbing news— still a tightly kept secret—that the DNC had been penetrated by Russian hackers. "Oh shit," he thought. "I wonder what they got."

He was upset he had not been told sooner. The DNC's top officials by this point had known their system had been breached for about a month. Yet, heeding CrowdStrike's and the FBI's requests for absolute secrecy, they had said nothing to their colleagues at Hillary for America, the official name of the Clinton campaign.

It was fair to assume that the hackers who mounted a successful intrusion of the DNC might have done the same with the Clinton campaign. The campaign IT team immediately checked its logs over and over to ensure there had been no break-ins. This was already the ever-present nightmare that Shane Hable, the campaign's IT chief, and his colleagues lived with. Every day, they thought, this would be the day: a system hacked, documents destroyed or stolen.

Mook knew that political outfits and campaigns were often targeted by foreign intelligence. The widespread assumption was that these breaches were mounted by the Russians, the Chinese, and others to obtain inside information on policies and personnel decisions in government. But now Mook questioned if something else might be afoot. He immediately wondered if this might have something to do with the Trump campaign.

As Mook saw it, Trump's hiring of Russia-friendly advisers and his repeated sympathetic comments about Putin were inexplicable. More evidence had come on April 27, when Trump gave his first major foreign policy speech at an event sponsored by the Center for the National Interest, a Washington think tank, at the Mayflower Hotel. In the address, Trump vowed to improve relations with Russia. Among the honored guests—at a small private reception before the speech and prominently seated in the first row—was Sergey Kislyak, the Russian ambassador.* Mook and other Clinton campaign advisers became increasingly convinced there was something bizarre about all this—that there was some sort of sinister connection between Trump and the Russians that was hiding beneath the surface.

---

* At the reception before the speech, Sessions talked with Kislyak. Intelligence intercepts would pick up Kislyak reporting to his superiors that he and Sessions had discussed campaign matters and policy topics important for Moscow. Jared Kushner also met Kislyak at this reception.

Mook decided to think like a spy and wondered if the campaign could mount what he called a "honeypot" operation. The Clinton team would plant phony information about Clinton or the campaign within the DNC computer system and wait to see if the Trump campaign or its allies later made public use of it. If they did, it would prove that the Trump camp was in league with the Russians. Then the Clinton campaign could pounce and expose Trump's secret partnership with Moscow.

Mook raised the idea with Marc Elias, the campaign's lawyer. But they both decided it was harebrained. The planted nugget would have to be so tantalizing or salacious that the Trump campaign couldn't resist putting it into play. And they both realized that were they to try anything of the sort—and the Trump campaign took the bait and disseminated the false story—the Clinton campaign could have a tough time convincing voters the information was indeed fake. The whole operation could backfire. The honeypot went nowhere.

On a more practical level, Mook reacted to the DNC breach by implementing new cybersecurity procedures. The campaign intensified the warnings it relayed to its employees about phishing emails. Mook ordered campaign officials not to open attachments received from outside the campaign's email system. Mook was already concerned that consultants for the campaign could easily be hacked and provide hackers a pathway into the campaign's computer system. Anyone doing any work for the campaign was assigned an official hillaryclinton.com account. "I said, 'Let's get everyone inside our fortress,'" Mook recalled.

Mook had no idea that the Russians had penetrated Podesta's email. They were already inside the fortress.

CHAPTER 9

"If it's what you say I love it."

Rob Goldstone and Emin Agalarov were back. Three years earlier, they had helped Trump pull off his successful Miss Universe event in Moscow, which nearly led to the building of a Trump Tower in the Russian capital. In 2015, Trump welcomed them into his office while he was listening to a rap song about himself. Now the flamboyant PR man and the jet-setting Azerbaijani pop star were inserting themselves into Trump's latest and grandest venture—his presidential campaign. And they came bearing a secret message: The Putin regime wanted to help Trump win the White House.

"Good morning," read an email from Goldstone that arrived in Donald Trump Jr.'s inbox at 10:36 A.M. on June 3. "Emin just called and asked me to contact you with something very interesting."

Goldstone's message presented an unusual offer:

> The Crown prosecutor of Russia met with [Emin's] father Aras this morning and in their meeting offered to provide the Trump campaign with some official documents and information that would

incriminate Hillary and her dealings with Russia
and would be very useful to your father.

This is obviously very high level and sensitive
information but is part of Russia and its government's support for Mr. Trump—helped along by Aras
and Emin.

What do you think is the best way to handle
this information and would you be able to speak to
Emin about it directly? I can also send this info
to your father via Rhona [Graff, Trump's longtime
secretary] but it is ultra sensitive so wanted to
send this to you first.

There was good reason for Trump Jr. to take this seriously. Aras
Agalarov had been a trusted business partner of the Trumps and
had serious juice in the Kremlin. And according to Goldstone, this
scheme was being orchestrated by one of the Putin government's
top officials. He had mistakenly called him the "crown prosecutor"—there had been no crown in Russia since Czar Nicholas II
was overthrown—but he was referring to Russia's prosecutor general, Yury Chaika, a staunch Putin loyalist.

The message was extraordinary: an explicit overture from the
Russian government to help elect Trump president. And Trump Jr.
was eager to hear more.

Seventeen minutes later, he replied to Goldstone, "If it's what
you say I love it." He raised the possibility of the Trump campaign
using this information later in the summer and said he wanted to
speak to Emin before proceeding. Trump Jr. was on the road and
asked if Emin could do a call in a few days.

Three days later, Goldstone emailed Trump Jr. about "this Hillary info," and Trump Jr. replied and asked if Emin could talk right
then. Within the hour, Goldstone located Emin. He was on stage
performing in Moscow. But Goldstone told Trump Jr. that Emin
would call him in about twenty minutes. The two men spoke, and
afterward Trump Jr. emailed Goldstone, "Rob thanks for the help."
A plan was in place.

The following day, June 7, Goldstone sent Trump Jr. another email noting he had been asked by Emin to schedule a meeting in the coming days between Trump Jr. and "the Russian government attorney who is flying over from Moscow." In response, Trump Jr. told Goldstone a meeting could take place at his office in Trump Tower—and that Paul Manafort and Jared Kushner would be present.

On June 8, Trump Jr. sent his entire email chain with Goldstone to Manafort and Kushner, apparently as a reminder to show up at the meeting that was now scheduled for the next day. This meant that three of Trump's most important confidants had been informed that Putin's regime wanted to assist Trump covertly by sharing information on Clinton. The subject heading on Trump Jr.'s email made clear what the meeting was about: "Russia—Clinton—private and confidential."

What was Trump Jr. hoping to get from Moscow? The emails setting up this encounter had not indicated what the Russians had. But within the campaign, there certainly was the suspicion—or hope—that Russia might be able to deliver the goods on Clinton. Weeks earlier, Papadopoulos had been told that the Russians had "dirt" on her that included "thousands of emails." And soon after that, Dan Scavino, the campaign's social media chief, posted a tweet declaring the Kremlin was sitting on twenty thousand emails from Clinton's private server. (The tweet was based on a hoax pushed by two conspiracy theory websites.) Whatever Goldstone was bringing them, Trump and his top aides fervently believed that somewhere out there were secrets about Clinton that if exposed would sink her campaign.

On the afternoon of June 9, Goldstone escorted a small entourage—one Russian and two former Russian citizens—into the lobby of Trump Tower in New York City. They were given badges, waved through without anybody asking for any identification, and directed to the twenty-fifth floor.

The most important of these visitors was Natalia Veselnitskaya, an attorney from Moscow who didn't speak English. A former prosecutor in the Moscow region, she ran a substantial law firm with thirty employees. Her clients included large state-owned corporations—which meant she represented Kremlin interests. She also once represented the FSB in a case involving property in Moscow. She was a tough and perhaps dangerous opponent to have.

Several years earlier, Andrei Stolbunov, a Moscow attorney running a Russian anticorruption organization, learned this, when he tangled with her after a company owned by Pyotr Katsyv, the wealthy former transportation minister of the Moscow region, seized the property of one of Stolbunov's clients, a machinery firm located on valuable land near the main Moscow highway. To fight back, Stolbunov's group posted information online about the seizure—how armed goons working for Katsyv had shown up, beaten the owners, and physically taken over the factory. Soon Stolbunov found himself summoned to a Moscow prosecutor's office, where he was ordered to work out a settlement of the dispute with the Katsyv-controlled company's lawyer, Veselnitskaya.

After the meeting, in the corridor, Veselnitskaya, according to Stolbunov, told him that if he did not cease his campaign against Katsyv, he would end up in jail. "We have the power and we will do everything to win this battle," she told him. What do you mean, you have the power? Stolbunov wanted to know. "We are working with officials in the prosecutor's office and the FSB," she replied. Soon two of Stolbunov's colleagues were indeed imprisoned for supposedly conspiring to extort money from Katsyv. And then in 2013, Stolbunov was charged in the same alleged extortion plot. He fled Russia for the United States, where the Obama administration granted him political asylum.

At the time of the Trump Tower meeting, Veselnitskaya was once again representing the Katsyv family. This time, the client was Katsyv's son, Denis Katsyv, whose Cyprus-based company, Prevezon Holdings, had been charged by U.S. attorney Preet Bharara's office with laundering proceeds from the $230 million Russian tax fraud exposed by Sergei Magnitsky and funneling this money into purchases of New York real estate.

The case was political dynamite for Putin; it grew out of the allegations that had led to the Magnitsky Act—the sanctions law that had prompted the Kremlin to cut off adoptions of Russian babies by American families. Veselnitskaya had hired a major U.S. law firm, Baker & Hostetler, to represent Katsyv and Prevezon in the U.S. court case. At the same time, she had a broader, pro-Kremlin mission: She was directing an aggressive Russian lobbying campaign against the Magnitsky Act. With the help of Rinat Akhmetshin, a savvy Russian-American lobbyist in Washington who had once served in a Soviet military intelligence unit, she had set up a Delaware entity called the Human Rights Accountability Global Initiative Foundation to mount this lobbying campaign—a top priority of the Putin government.

Veselnitskaya was in New York City on June 9 to attend a court hearing in the Prevezon case. And she had come to the United States carrying a dense memo labeled "confidential" that laid out Moscow's case against the Magnitsky Act. The language in the document was crude and over the top: The law was an injustice that was reigniting a "new round of the Cold War" between Russia and the United States. It assailed Bill Browder, the businessman who had crusaded for the law's passage, as a "crook who walked all over the whole Congress." The memo was nearly identical with one that Chaika, the Russian prosecutor general, had shared with a sympathetic Republican congressman, Dana Rohrabacher, two months earlier.

For the meeting at Trump Tower, Veselnitskaya had brought along her translator and Ike Kaveladze, the U.S.-based executive of Aras Agalarov's company, who years earlier had been implicated in an investigation of Russian money laundering. Also with her was Akhmetshin—whose presence, he later maintained, was merely happenstance. He had come to New York to see his cousin in a play, and Veselnitskaya invited him to join her for lunch. When he showed up—in jeans and a T-shirt—she told him she had a meeting at Trump Tower and he should come along.

Once on the twenty-fifth floor, Veselnitskaya, Goldstone, and the others were escorted into a cavernous conference room. "So what brings you here?" Trump Jr. asked, as they settled into their chairs around the conference table. "I hear you've got some interesting information."

"Yes," Veselnitskaya replied. And she launched into a lengthy discourse about Browder, his company in Moscow, and the fraud she claimed it had committed against the Russian government. She pointed out that its largest investors were three billionaire brothers named Dirk, Robert, and Daniel Ziff, who were major funders of the Democratic Party. The juicy material was covered in one terse paragraph of the memo she brought with her: The Ziff brothers "financed the two Obama election campaigns. It cannot be ruled out that they also financed Hillary Clinton campaign." The Ziff brothers' funds, she claimed, were tainted, and some of their "dirty money" had gone to Democratic lawmakers and possibly Clinton.

As she spoke, Manafort for a while pecked away on his smartphone, taking notes. But to Veselnitskaya, it appeared that he then nodded off. Kushner arrived late—and then looked restless. Trump Jr. seemed confused and a bit frustrated. It was not clear what compromising information about Clinton she was bringing them.

"Can you show how it goes to Hillary?" he asked.

"I don't know," said Veselnitskaya, speaking through her translator. "I don't know. I'm just a Russian lawyer."

Trump Jr. pressed again. "But you can't show how it goes to Hillary?"

No, Veselnitskaya replied. That was beyond the information she had.

At this point, Trump Jr. seemed deflated, according to Akhmetshin's later account to investigators. Trump Jr., Manafort, and Kushner had taken time out of their jam-packed days to attend this meeting with a Russian emissary because Goldstone, conveying a message from Aras Agalarov, had promised them secret Russian information on Clinton. But there was nothing here that could be used against Clinton.

Veselnitskaya pressed ahead with a lecture on the Magnitsky Act and how Browder had fabricated key details about what had happened to his company in Russia. Kushner emailed an assistant: "Can u pls call me on my cell? need excuse to get out of meeting."

Trump Jr. later claimed that he interrupted Veselnitskaya and gently suggested that questions about the Magnitsky Act could be revisited once his father was elected.

Toward the end of this twenty- to thirty-minute session, Akhmetshin could see it had gone south, and he sought to bail out his friend. The Trump camp should focus on the adoption controversy, he said. "This could be a great campaign issue," he suggested. "Americans want to adopt babies from Russia." And many who do were conservative and religious—exactly the audience that would be supportive of Trump's candidacy.

His effort went nowhere. Trump Jr. and the others did not seem to care much about Russian adoptions. "They couldn't wait to get out of there," Akhmetshin later told investigators. After the meeting Kushner texted Manafort: "Waste of time."

Though the meeting might have been a bust for the Trump intimates, it established a connection of sorts between the Trump campaign and Moscow. And Trump's senior advisers now had new reason to believe that Putin's regime wanted Trump to win and was willing to act clandestinely to boost his chances. The campaign did not report this private Russian outreach to the FBI or any U.S. government agency. ("It's not illegal to listen," Trump Jr. later said.) Russian government officials could have well interpreted that as a signal that Trump would not mind or protest if Moscow took other actions to benefit the Republican candidate. The Russians had offered to help, and Trump's campaign had demonstrated a willingness to take what Moscow had to offer.

In early June, State Department officials huddled around their computers to watch an astonishing video that had just arrived from Moscow. It captured a violent attack outside one of the entrances to the U.S. embassy compound. An embassy officer was dropped off by a taxi. Seconds later, a uniformed FSB guard jumped out of a booth, grabbed the American, and slammed him to the ground. A few feet from the door to the complex, the American struggled to break free. But the Russian remained on top of him, pinning the American to the concrete. It took the U.S. officer about twenty seconds to squirm, kick, and struggle his way to the entrance. When the door automatically opened, he managed to position his feet against a sidewall and, using all his strength, pushed his way through the door, with the FSB man still on top of him. He eventually escaped the guard's grip and was safe on American soil. But his shoulder was broken, and he soon was flown out of the country to receive medical attention.

Secretary of State John Kerry watched the video aboard a plane flying back to Washington—and was furious. When assistant secretary Victoria Nuland and her staff viewed it at Foggy Bottom, they were in disbelief. "Everybody that saw it was horrified," recalled one official. "It brought this to a new level where we had to do a public response."

The video clearly depicted an unprovoked attack on compound property, and was an outright violation of international law prohibiting local nationals from entering diplomatic property without permission. Kerry contacted Lavrov to complain. The Russians were claiming this American had tried to run away from a security checkpoint—or that the American had assaulted the FSB guard. The video did not show any of that. This was unacceptable, Kerry told Lavrov.

The minute-long episode seemed the culminations of years of escalating harassment of U.S. diplomats in Russia—the breaking into of apartments, the defacement of property, the FSB tails on their families. Yet there was an awkward problem regarding how to respond: The assaulted American was officially listed as a U.S. diplomat, but he was actually a CIA officer. He had lost his FSB tail while out and about in Moscow, and the Russians had clobbered him to teach him a lesson.

The conventions of diplomacy and espionage compelled nations to not acknowledge a well-known secret: Governments routinely granted diplomatic cover to their intelligence officers overseas, and these spies worked out of embassies. Raising a public ruckus and slapping a serious punishment on Moscow for this egregious and violent breach of norms and international law would call attention to CIA activity in Russia.

Still, the incident triggered an internal debate within Obama's national security team. Hardliners, including Nuland and Celeste Wallander (who were backed up by Vice President Joe Biden), believed it was finally time to stand up to Putin. Nuland had a saying about the Russians: "They're going to keep punching until they hit bone." She began developing options for a forceful response. She wanted to expel Russian diplomats (many of whom doubled as spies) and shut down one of two sprawling dachas the Russians used as a retreat for their diplomats in the U.S. The one Nuland targeted, on the Eastern Shore of Maryland, had been transformed into a giant intelligence collection post. The building had kept expanding over the years, with chimneys erected on the roof that U.S. officials suspected were disguising electronic listening posts aimed at picking up signals along shipping lines into the U.S. naval base at Norfolk. Two units Nuland had set up in the State Department's Europe division—the Russia Information Group, which tracked Russian disinformation, and the Malign Influence Group, which concentrated on Russian covert actions—circulated more creative ideas aimed at exposing Russian disinformation campaigns. One proposal was to cut U.S. government contracts with Kaspersky Lab, a Russian cybersecurity firm whose founder, Eugene Kaspersky, had graduated from a KGB academy.

But Susan Rice, now Obama's national security adviser, was not on board. "If you egg [the Russians] on, this will escalate," Rice argued during an NSC conference call. As angry as he was, Kerry, too, did not favor a harsh reaction. He was not eager to advertise the U.S. embassy was a base of CIA operations. And he was striving to hammer out a deal with Lavrov to end the horrendous Syrian civil war—an effort that some officials within his own department increasingly viewed as a fool's errand.

This debate exposed a fault line within the Obama administration over how to deal with Russia. The argument this time was about a single act of Russian harassment. Yet within months, administration officials would be at odds in a similar way over a much graver and more consequential Russian attack.

CHAPTER 10

"WikiLeaks has a very big year ahead."

Awave of apprehension—almost panic—swept through the Democratic National Committee's Capitol Hill headquarters on the afternoon of Friday, June 10. The entire staff of more than one hundred employees was ordered into the Lew Wasserman Conference Room at 4 P.M. sharp. Attendance was mandatory, no interns or guests allowed. Many staffers assumed they were about to be the victims of a mass firing, part of a widely anticipated takeover of the DNC by the Clinton campaign—a move that would be in keeping with the transition that routinely occurs when a candidate becomes the presumptive nominee.

Instead, Lindsey Reynolds, the chief operating officer, delivered a sobering but cryptic message to the standing-room-only crowd about something else. A few weeks earlier, James Clapper, the director of national intelligence, had publicly said that unnamed foreign actors were targeting both political parties, and he had cautioned campaigns to be on guard. In light of this warning, Reynolds told the group, the DNC had to update its computer security system. Everybody was to turn in their laptops and devices immediately. No exceptions. And nobody could use their DNC email until further notice.

"Take the weekend off," she told them. And don't breathe a word of this to anybody, she added: "You can't tell your friends. You can't tell your mother. You can't tell your dog."

The staff was baffled. Hand in all devices and take the weekend off at the height of campaign season? Something had to be going on. But Alexandra Chalupa, the DNC consultant tracking Manafort, had no doubt what was happening: The DNC had been breached. "It was the Russians," she told her colleagues.

In the weeks since CrowdStrike had detected the break-in—and confirmed that the FBI warnings had been accurate—the cybersecurity firm had been working feverishly to expel the intruders and secure the DNC's system, without tipping off the hackers. (DNC officials wanted to be sure that no mention of Reynolds' directive would go through a DNC email, because that might alert the Russians.) The job was being completed this weekend. The DNC also had brought in outside consultants to plot a PR strategy for handling the news of the hack. They had decided it would be best to go public, rather than have the story leak out. And it didn't hurt that the story would advance a narrative that benefited the Clinton campaign and the Democrats: The Russians were interfering in the U.S. election, presumably to assist Trump.

Going public about the breach was a dicey move. CrowdStrike's experts had determined that the Russians encrypted files before swiping them from the DNC's computers. They could tell the hackers had targeted the DNC's opposition research folders, but no one at CrowdStrike or the DNC was quite sure what else the hackers had pilfered. And there was the question: What would the Russian intruders do with the DNC files? Were they only spying on the DNC, or would they release material and use it against the Democrats? And if the DNC had no idea what had been stolen, it would be almost impossible to prepare for what might lay ahead. In one of the PR strategy sessions, Luis Miranda, the DNC communications chief, posed a question: "What do we say when people ask if this is the biggest political burglary since Watergate?" Don't worry, someone said. Nobody will ask that.

* * *

On June 14, the *Washington Post*—which had been briefed on the breach by the DNC and CrowdStrike—broke the news with a front-page story headlined, "Russia Government Hackers Penetrated DNC, Stole Opposition Research on Trump." The article by Ellen Nakashima was a true bombshell, reporting that Russian hackers had "so thoroughly compromised the DNC's system that they also were able to read all email and chat traffic." The story noted that Russian cyber spies had also targeted the Clinton and Trump campaigns. "The depth of the penetration reflects the skill and determination of the United States' top cyber-adversary as Russia goes after strategic targets, from the White House and State Department to political campaign organizations," Nakashima wrote.

But the article was incomplete. The DNC, according to Nakashima's report, maintained that no important financial or personal information had been stolen. This would soon be proven wrong. And the story cited DNC leaders saying they were "tipped" about the hack in late April. "When we discovered the intrusion, we treated it like the serious incident it is and reached out to Crowd-Strike immediately," DNC chair Wasserman Schultz told the newspaper. The DNC officials, though, did not disclose that their IT department had been informed by the FBI of a possible breach seven months earlier.

The *Post* story did include a response from the Kremlin. Not surprisingly, the Russians denied everything. "I completely rule out a possibility that the [Russian] government or the government bodies have been involved in this," Dmitry Peskov, the Kremlin's spokesman, said.

The *Post* described the intrusions as "traditional espionage," an attempt by Russian intelligence services to "understand the policies, strengths and weaknesses of a potential future president—much as American spies gather similar information on foreign candidates and leaders." That was how the penetration was initially seen within the Obama White House. Its senior national security officials hardly viewed this break-in as an emergency or any-thing out of the ordinary. Susan Rice knew Moscow and Beijing habitually tried to hack government and nongovernment entities. To her, this seemed like the usual cyber espionage, secret snooping with the intent to collect bits of information on the potential next president—not fundamentally different from what American spies try to do all the time.

But there were warning signs in the initial revelation to signal this might be something more than that. After the *Post* article hit, CrowdStrike released a report entitled "Bears in the Midst," iden-tifying the two sets of Russian state hackers, Cozy Bear and Fancy Bear, as the intruders. The presence of Fancy Bear—the group of cyber actors associated with the GRU, Russia's military intelligence service—was a red flag. In recent years, there had been an increase in aggressive Fancy Bear attacks that went beyond standard espio-nage. Fancy Bear hackers, using the same implants and malware as had been discovered inside the DNC, had a history of creating phony online personas—with such names as "Cyber Caliphate" and "Anonymous Poland"—that stole data and then leaked it to the public. In June 2014, it had penetrated the Ukrainian Central Election Commission's network, destroying data and posting fake election results on its website. In February 2015, it had launched a ferocious attack that seized control of the computer system of TV5Monde, a major French television network, shutting down its broadcasting channels. For this assault, the Fancy Bear hackers had posed as ISIS terrorists whose images suddenly popped up on TV5Monde's website.

These were not acts of espionage. They were nasty Russian influence operations, aimed at demoralizing and confusing the tar-get audience. After the DNC hack was revealed, there was immedi-ate speculation on the blogs of cybersecurity firms: Was this what the Russian hackers were intending?

The Trump campaign first responded to the news of the hack by accusing the DNC of committing a hoax. The day after the *Post* story appeared—six days after Trump Jr., Kushner, and Manafort had met with a Russian emissary as part of what they were told was a secret Russian scheme to assist Trump—the Trump campaign issued a statement: "We believe it was the DNC that did the 'hacking' as a way to distract from the many issues facing their deeply flawed candidate and failed party leader." In other words, the hacking was not even real.

This was the beginning of what would be the Trump camp's refusal to acknowledge the Russians were intervening in the U.S. presidential election. Trump's senior advisers revealed nothing indicating they had recently been told the Kremlin secretly wanted to help Trump become president.

The day following the *Post* story, the leaks began—and confirmed the worst fears of cybersecurity researchers who suspected more than espionage was afoot.

A hacker going by the name Guccifer 2.0 appeared out of the blue online and took credit for the DNC hack and posted some of the stolen material. The moniker was a reference to an infamous Romanian hacker named Guccifer, who was now in an American prison and who had claimed to have hacked into Clinton's personal email server. (He later told the FBI he had not.)

In a blog post, Guccifer 2.0 mocked CrowdStrike for concluding the job was the work of sophisticated Russian cyberspies. The hacker insisted that he was the one who had filched thousands of documents from the DNC. He posted a DNC opposition report on Trump, which was a long compilation of material already in the public record. Guccifer 2.0 scoffed at DNC chair Wasserman Schultz's claim that no financial documents had been stolen from the DNC and highlighted a spreadsheet of DNC donors. (These contributions were a matter of public record.) And he published hundreds of other documents, including what appeared to be a planning document from Clinton's early days as secretary of state.

None of the material was stop-the-presses stuff. But Guccifer 2.0 signed off with an ominous message: "The main part of the papers, thousands of files and mails, I gave to WikiLeaks. They will publish them soon.... Fuck the Illuminati and their conspiracies!!!!!!!!!"

* * *

The next day, June 16, a delegation from the DNC—Amy Dacey, the DNC chief executive; Michael Sussmann, the outside lawyer; and CrowdStrike's Shawn Henry—entered FBI headquarters for a meeting with Jim Trainor, the assistant FBI director in charge of the Bureau's cyber division. Trainor was an earnest twenty-year FBI veteran who had worked in counterintelligence. He had helped handle the "illegals" case—the Russian spies rolled up by the Bureau six years earlier. His calm and friendly demeanor did little to tamp down the simmering tensions at this meeting. Dacey demanded to know why the FBI had not informed top DNC officials earlier and had only interacted with a low-level contractor. "We told the DNC leadership," Trainor responded, with a wave of his hand. "I have it in my notes."

Dacey bristled. "I don't know who you think the leadership is," she shot back. "The chairwoman [Wasserman Schultz] and I are the leaders—and we weren't notified. We didn't know anything about this."

Trainor dismissed her complaint. "I have my reporting on this," he replied. "We're confident about this."

But Trainor did confirm CrowdStrike's conclusions: The breach was indeed a Russian hack. The evidence was compelling, he told the DNC delegation. Sussmann wanted to know if the Bureau would be willing to state that publicly and put the weight of the FBI behind the CrowdStrike conclusion. The Bureau was cautious in assessing blame in such matters. In the cyber world, attribution was a tricky business. And if the FBI attributed blame, that would mean the U.S. government was leveling a serious accusation—in this case, against a foreign power. This was well above Trainor's pay grade. The FBI didn't do public attributions. "That's a call for the White House," Trainor said. "We'll pass along your request."

Guccifer 2.0's reference to WikiLeaks caused some U.S. intelligence officials to suspect there was a Russian connection. WikiLeaks had catapulted to worldwide fame and notoriety five years earlier as a pro–transparency and whistleblowing site when it published hundreds of thousands of classified U.S. government documents and

State Department cables that had been leaked by an Army intelligence analyst named Bradley Manning. The subsequent dump of these documents infuriated U.S. government officials, none more so than Secretary of State Hillary Clinton, who denounced the release as "an attack on the international community" that had endangered lives and would "tear at the fabric" of responsible government.

Though WikiLeaks and its founder, Julian Assange, were initially hailed by some on the left as courageous truth tellers, U.S. intelligence officials took a darker view. They suspected there was some sort of link between him and Moscow. In 2012, Assange was given his own show on RT, the Russian government propaganda channel. The next year, he dispatched one of his lawyers to help Edward Snowden, the NSA contractor who stole and leaked thousands of classified documents about U.S. surveillance programs, when Snowden fled from Hong Kong to Moscow. In Russia, Snowden was granted asylum by Putin's government, and Assange later took credit for having urged Snowden to head to Moscow.

The white-haired, charismatic, and PR-savvy Assange was now a wanted man. Obama's Justice Department had launched a criminal investigation of him for the release of the Manning material. In 2010, Sweden attempted to extradite him from England on sexual assault charges. Assange denied the accusations and claimed this was part of an American plot to silence him. Eventually, he skipped bail and sought asylum in the Ecuadorian embassy in London in August 2012, and he had been stuck there ever since.

Still, Assange regularly gave interviews and issued tweets denouncing U.S. officials, most relentlessly Hillary Clinton. "A vote today for Hillary Clinton is a vote for endless, stupid war," he wrote in February 2016. He blamed her for the ongoing mess in Libya. And he added, "Hillary's problem is not just that she's a war hawk. She's a war hawk with bad judgment who gets an unseemly emotional rush out of killing people. She shouldn't be let near a gun shop, let alone an army. And she certainly should not become president of the United States." As did Putin, Assange seemed to carry a grudge against the woman who was about to become the Democratic presidential nominee.

In early June, Assange had appeared, via a video link, at a Moscow conference and lambasted Clinton. He was intent on stopping her, and this was no secret. Days later—right before the DNC breach became public—he told a British interviewer, "We have upcoming leaks in relation to Hillary Clinton. . . . WikiLeaks has a very big year ahead."

In the weeks after the initial dump, Guccifer 2.0 would post much more material. The caches included personal information on DNC donors, fundraising documents from the Democratic Congressional Campaign Committee (the Democratic outfit known by its abbreviation DCCC and focused on House races), internal records from the Clinton campaign, and emails from the Clinton Foundation. The load also included Clinton campaign memos outlining possible responses to political attacks against Clinton. Guccifer 2.0 revealed the DNC plans for the "counter convention" it intended to hold in response to the GOP convention in Cleveland in mid-July. There were thousands and thousands of pages.

In blog posts and tweets, Guccifer 2.0 taunted Clinton, the Democrats, CrowdStrike, and other cyber sleuths. The hacker insisted he was a man from Romania. ("I've never met a female hacker of the highest level," he wrote. "Girls, don't get offended. I love you.") He cited Assange and Snowden as "modern heroes." He referred to Clinton as a "bought and sold" phony and Trump as "sincere in what he says," though he denounced Trump's throw-'em-out immigration policy.

The insular and global world of cybersecurity techies immediately zeroed in on Guccifer 2.0. Who was he really?

Matt Tait, a young British-based cybersecurity researcher who tweeted anonymously under the handle @Pwnallthethings, was initially skeptical that Guccifer 2.0 was a Russian creation—or that the entire hack had been directed from Moscow.

But he dug into the metadata of the DNC documents being released by Guccifer 2.0 and noticed that they had been opened in a program using the Russian language option. Then he spotted another clue: The user name of one of the computers employed by the hackers contained a reference to Felix Dzerzhinsky, a Soviet revolutionary who had created Lenin's secret police, the forerunner of the KGB and later the FSB. And he noted the quality of Guccifer 2.0's English varied greatly, suggesting this was a collective persona, not an individual. That convinced Tait: It was indeed the Russians. On Twitter—where various cybersecurity mavens were trading thoughts and theories about the DNC hack—Tait tweeted, "LOL. Russian #opsec fail."

Another cyber-intelligence expert, Thomas Rid, a professor at King's College in London, soon uncovered a damning clue. He had followed Russian hacking for years. One episode he had studied closely was the penetration of the German parliament in May 2015—an attack German intelligence had attributed to the Russians. He knew that another researcher had identified the malware implants used in the German penetration and had posted that computer code online. CrowdStrike had done the same for the DNC breach.

For a cybersecurity detective, finding a malware implant is akin to a police officer discovering a gun or set of burglar's tools at a crime scene. Rid wrote a program that could search both sets of data. He quickly had a hit: a command-and-control IP address used in the cyberattack against the Bundestag had also been used in the DNC operation. Here was more proof. This evidence also tied the DNC break-in to other Russian hack attacks, including those against NATO, Georgia, and a human rights group in Syria.

For Rid, Tait, and other experts, the case was strong that the Russians were behind both the hack and the dumps. But so far the U.S. government had said nothing.

The DNC hack and the Guccifer 2.0 releases were yet one more headache for the Clinton campaign. By June, Clinton had essentially vanquished Sanders, after a long and bitter primary battle. But it wasn't quite over. The Sanders campaign was hinting at extending the nomination contest by trying to convince party officials to dump Clinton and vowing a fight over the party platform. Clinton and her aides needed to find a way to win over Sanders voters embittered with the Democratic establishment after watching their maverick candidate defeated by a party favorite many of them considered a corporate shill.

In the middle of coping with all these challenges, Mook ordered the establishment of a working group within the campaign to handle the Guccifer 2.0 releases. Glen Caplin, a young New York political operative who specialized in research and communications, was put in charge. His brief on the campaign was to handle what he called "the dumpster fires." He had spent much of the last year dealing with the Benghazi and email server controversies. His people combed through each release of the DNC documents looking for damaging material and fielded the flood of queries from reporters.

Mook was worried that the DNC breach would spell deeper problems. In response to the DNC hack, the campaign had publicly declared its computer system had not been compromised. But Hillary for America had submitted data to a DNC analytics program that had been penetrated. Mook instructed campaign officials not to discuss this. If word got out that any Clinton campaign data had been compromised by the DNC hack, it could create the impression that the campaign itself had been infiltrated and that her operation was not competent. Worse, talk of any penetration of the Clinton campaign could be conflated with the allegations regarding Clinton's use of a personal email server and fuel the speculation that Clinton's private email server had been breached. Clinton was due to be questioned soon by the FBI in this ongoing probe. Mook was hoping to keep the campaign far from the DNC hack fallout.

For Clinton and her aides there was no question about what was going on: The Russians were meddling in the election to influence its outcome. This was a Russian plot to get Trump elected. "We believed this to our core," Caplin later said. In early June, while giving a speech on national security, Clinton had ripped into Trump for praising "dictators like Vladimir Putin." She added, "I'll leave it to the psychiatrists to explain his affection for tyrants." Now she did not know if there was a direct connection between Trump's kind words for Putin and the DNC hack, but she and her aides suspected as much. With the releases of the stolen material, Clinton and her advisers became more convinced they were the targets of a Russian operation far more serious than cyber espionage. Was it personal? Was Putin gunning for her? Clinton told aides she believed that the Russians saw her as the front-runner and were looking to destabilize the election.

The Clintonites devised a strategy for shaping the story. This was not about the documents coming out, they told reporters. This was about Russia interfering in U.S. democracy. Asked by journalists about the DNC hack and the released material, Caplin and other campaign aides refused to discuss details of the documents Guccifer 2.0 was dumping. They kept insisting the Russians were responsible for the DNC hack and were bent on influencing the outcome of the presidential race. Political reporters, not surprisingly, focused on the juicy tidbits flowing out every few days. For many journalists, the campaign line seemed like self-serving spin.

The Guccifer 2.0 releases—even if the material was not explosive— did start to move the needle inside the White House. The Russian operation was now more than routine cyber espionage. Never before in an American election had hacked political material been weaponized this way. Clearly, the hackers and Guccifer 2.0 were out to damage a major presidential candidate. This was a new form of high-tech information warfare.

At the White House, a trio of Obama's most senior aides— Rice, White House chief of staff Denis McDonough, and homeland security adviser Lisa Monaco—took charge of the administration's response. An order was sent to the intelligence community: Tell us what's going on here. The president wanted to know more. Obama and his top aides had been observing Trump's comments about Russia and Putin for months and had found them confounding.

Now with this cyberattack—probably initiated by Russia—his top aides were much more concerned.

Deliberations within the White House about the matter were closely held—much more so than with other sensitive topics. Obama and his senior people did not bring other national security staffers into the discussions. "There were cryptic conversations about what was going on, and whether at any point we would attribute it to the Russians," a White House official recalled.

Within weeks, the DNC hack story fizzled out. The documents Guccifer 2.0 published had no major and direct influence on the campaign. (The same was true for another website called DCLeaks.com, which was also releasing stolen emails.) But a big problem remained for the campaign: Mook and other Clinton aides had good reason to suspect there was more to come.

As Caplin's research team pored over Guccifer 2.0 releases, it had discovered that the caches included documents that did not originate with the DNC. One of these was a memo sent from Marc Elias to Podesta, Mook, and Dennis Cheng, the campaign finance director. The memo itself was mundane, involving a fundraising legal technicality. But the campaign could find no sign that the document had ever been circulated within the DNC computer network. It seemed most likely purloined from Podesta's email account.

No one yet knew Podesta's email had been compromised. But top Clinton officials now feared there could be other dumps—and not just from the DNC. Podesta's role as campaign chairman was to oversee the organization and manage the often-competing elements of the unwieldy and conflict-ridden community of Clinton friends, allies, consultants, and hangers-on. His emails would include documents from the heart of Clinton World with headline-worthy material that might derail their efforts.

Yet the Clinton aides concluded there was little they could do about this. "I didn't take six weeks off to review the sixty thousand emails in my in-box," Podesta later said. But every time

Guccifer 2.0 released a new batch, the campaign searched for Podesta material.

"There was a constant fear that something big would happen," Shane Hable, the campaign's chief information officer, recalled. "Every day, we wondered if this will be the day it hits. We just kept on waiting for whatever it would be."

CHAPTER 11

"I have to report this to headquarters."

Early in June, two men met for lunch at an Italian restaurant in Terminal 5 of London's Heathrow Airport. They shared a deep passion: uncovering and countering the corruption and misdeeds of Putin's regime.

On one side of the table was Christopher Steele, the British spy who had handled the Litvinenko case a decade earlier. In his early fifties, Steele still looked the part—a dapper dresser with pale blue eyes and a somber, no-nonsense demeanor. Across the table was Glenn Simpson, a tall, scruffy American with an intense manner. They were kindred spirits, each fixated on the machinations of the Kremlin. The fifty-two-year-old Simpson had once been a renowned investigative journalist at the *Wall Street Journal*. One of his specialties was scoops revealing that powerful Russian oligarchs and organized crime figures had hired Washington lobbyists and lawyers to exert influence in the nation's capital. In 2009, he had quit the paper to form a modest-sized private investigative and research service in Washington.

The firm, which he later named Fusion GPS, handled jobs for political and corporate clients in the United States and abroad—always under the cloak of secrecy. Simpson once described what his company did as "journalism for rent." It often was hired by corporations entangled in bitter regulatory or legal disputes, such as Herbalife, a supplement company accused of essentially being a pyramid scheme, and Theranos, a health care tech start-up that issued questionable claims about its pioneering blood-testing technology. The firm's mission often was to ward off damaging media stories and investigate the critics of its controversial clients. In 2012, Fusion GPS was hired to do opposition research on Mitt Romney for Barack Obama's reelection campaign. As had become standard practice in the shadowy world of "oppo" research, the Obama campaign's payments to Fusion GPS were never publicly disclosed; the money paid to the investigative firm was reported on campaign disclosure reports as legal bills to the campaign's law firm, Perkins Coie.

More recently, Fusion GPS had assisted an American law firm defending Prevezon, the Russian-owned company accused in the United States of laundering money. This was the case that had spurred Congress to pass the Magnitsky Act—the law imposing sanctions on Russian officials engaged in human rights abuses. Simpson's job was to dig up material that could be used to discredit Browder. In an odd twist of fate, this had placed Simpson and his firm on the same side as Natalia Veselnitskaya, the Russian attorney who represented Prevezon and who had been sent by the Agalarovs to meet with Trump Jr., Manafort, and Kushner in Trump Tower. But even still, Simpson had maintained his focus on Putin's Mafia state. As Simpson often said, he had "an interest, bordering on an obsession, with Russian kleptocracy and organized crime."

On such matters, Steele was the man to see.

Steele was no longer with British intelligence. But he was still in the spy business—as a private contractor. While in MI6, Steele had become friendly with a high-ranking colleague named Chris Burrows, who specialized in counterterrorism. In 2009, they each left MI6 and did what many spies do; they entered the private intelligence business. Together they formed a firm called Orbis Business Intelligence, which was designed to capitalize on Steele's vast knowledge of Russia and the interrelationships there between business and politics. On its website, Orbis boasted, "Our core strength is our ability to meld a high-level source network with a sophisticated investigative capability. We provide strategic advice, mount intelligence-gathering operations and conduct complex, often cross-border investigations." Steele and Burrows were spies for hire.

Steele was the heart of the operation, Burrows its salesman. Steele, who possessed a phenomenal memory, was a master of vacuuming up huge amounts of information and analyzing material. While Burrows marveled at Steele's ability to recollect facts, he believed himself better at intuition—at understanding sources and assessing their motives and credibility. One of the firm's assets that Burrows pitched to clients was Steele's deep understanding of how the Russians used *kompromat*—compromising information usually obtained through furtive means—as a weapon in politics, diplomacy, and business.

Right away, Orbis was a success—in part because it did far more than spit out reports based on public record data searches, which was the mainstay of many of its competitors. It conducted operations, much as spy services did. In one case, the company was hired by a British insurance company operating in Russia that was being harassed by Russian tax collectors. Steele discovered the reason: The son of the chief Russian regulator had a rival business. So he put in motion an operation. Through his contacts, Steele let it be known to senior Russian officials that if the harassment did not stop, word about this would be spread to other multinational companies, threatening future investments in the region. The harassment stopped. This was a successful exercise in what Burrows called "covert influence."

In 2010, Steele and Burrows landed a major assignment: to support the English Football Association's bid to host the soccer World Cup in 2018. It was an intensely competitive process. Senior British officials and Prince Charles were directly involved in lobbying FIFA, the international soccer federation, for the tournament. At the same time, the Obama administration was pushing for the U.S. to be awarded the 2022 World Cup.

When FIFA selected Russia for 2018 and Qatar for 2022, the Brits and the Americans were outraged—and convinced the decision was the result of corruption that included payoffs. Steele had picked up intelligence that Putin was using friendly oligarchs to slip bribes to FIFA board members. When recounting the FIFA story to colleagues, Steele said, "We had a burning sense of injustice. This was the most corrupt international organization in the world."

He rang up an FBI agent named Mike Gaeta, whom he had recently met at a conference in Oxford. Gaeta specialized in Russian organized crime and was then assigned to the New York field office.

I have got some material I'd like to show you, Steele told him. Gaeta was interested, and soon Steele was flying to the United States for meetings with FBI officials in New York and Washington, D.C., to share intelligence he had collected about the unsavory connections of various FIFA officials.

He gave the FBI intelligence reports that amounted to a dossier on FIFA corruption. One especially damning piece of evidence was a 2005 photograph Steele had uncovered showing Sepp Blatter, the longtime FIFA president, laughing and clinking glasses at a Moscow nightclub with Alimzhan Tokhtakhounov, the alleged Russian organized crime boss known as the "Little Taiwanese." Tokhtakhounov was on the Bureau's "most wanted" list, a fugitive from U.S. justice who had been indicted in 2002 for allegedly scheming to fix the Winter Olympics figure skating competition that year to ensure a gold medal for Russia. The indictment was announced by James Comey, then a U.S. attorney. (Tokhtakhounov would be indicted again in 2013 for allegedly protecting a high-stakes, trans-Atlantic gambling ring, which operated in Trump Tower and laundered tens of millions of dollars for Russian oligarchs through shell companies in Cyprus.)

Steele's reports helped spur a wide-ranging, years-long investigation that ultimately led to multiple indictments against FIFA figures by federal prosecutors in Brooklyn. Blatter wasn't charged, but he was forced to resign. Steele had established himself as a trusted source for the FBI.

He soon did the same with the U.S. State Department. In the spring of 2014, Steele, retained by a private business client, was producing reports on the Ukrainian crisis. He thought they might be of interest to Washington and reached out to Jonathan Winer, a senior official at Foggy Bottom who once had done lobbying work for Mikhail Khodorkovsky, now an exiled Russian oligarch and Putin foe. Winer notified Victoria Nuland that he had a source with good contacts in Russia and Ukraine. Would she be interested? Yes, she said, and after reviewing a few of Steele's reports, she told Winer to "keep them coming." But Nuland, concerned that the material could be intercepted by Russian hackers, asked Winer to place them into a secure State Department classified computer system before forwarding them to her.

Between May 2014 and February 2016, Steele sent Nuland 120 Orbis reports about political and diplomatic developments in Russia and Ukraine. The memos covered efforts to evade the Western sanctions and activities of various oligarchs. The material—which included information on Russian plans and intentions—seemed generally on the mark, Nuland thought. "His stuff was 75 to 80 percent accurate," she later said. "At times, I thought he had gotten spun up by a source. But in general, they were congruent with what I was seeing."

By the spring of 2016, Steele was now deemed a valuable supplier of intelligence to two agencies of the U.S. government: the FBI and the State Department bureau in charge of Russia policy.

For years, Fusion and Orbis had cooperated on various ventures. And in the Heathrow airport, Simpson explained that he had a new assignment for Steele, should he choose to accept it.

Simpson and his firm had been investigating Donald Trump for months. Initially, his client for this project was the Washington Free Beacon, a conservative website funded by billionaire hedge-fund kingpin Paul Singer, a lucrative Fusion GPS client. The website and Singer had been part of the conservative never-Trump movement that aimed to prevent the mogul from bagging the Republican nomination. Now that was essentially a lost cause, and they saw no reason to keep paying Simpson to conduct opposition research on Trump.

But Simpson had wanted to keep the Trump project going. So he and his partner, another former *Wall Street Journal* reporter named Peter Fritsch, had pitched Marc Elias, the Democratic lawyer who served as both the chief counsel for the Clinton campaign and the Democratic National Committee. In April, Elias and Simpson worked out a deal: Fusion GPS would be retained by Elias's firm, Perkins Coie, with the investigators' fees and expenses paid by the Clinton campaign and the DNC. Once again, the arrangement would be obscured on campaign disclosure reports filed with the Federal Election Commission: The payments to Fusion GPS were reported as legal fees to the law firm. Over time, more than $1 million in Hillary for America and DNC funds would be paid to Fusion GPS in fees and expenses. Yet many of the top officials at the Clinton campaign and the DNC were not aware of the arrangement and what Fusion GPS was up to. When, months later, Donna Brazile, then the interim DNC chair, picked up rumors about the firm's research in Russia, she confronted Elias and demanded an explanation. He brushed her off, according to Brazile, and said, "You don't want to know."

It was ironic that Simpson was the Clinton campaign's chief undercover oppo man. He had no sympathy for Clinton or most of the people around her, starting with her husband. Simpson had spent a good chunk of his career as a journalist investigating the Clintons. In 1996, Simpson broke big stories about the flood of foreign money from China, Indonesia, and elsewhere that poured into Democratic Party coffers to boost Bill Clinton's reelection campaign. In his first front-page piece on the subject, Simpson and co-author Jill Abramson wrote that the Asian cash flow highlights "a subject that doesn't get much discussion: How foreign influence seeps into the American political system."

More recently, Fusion GPS had tracked wealthy foreign donors who had pumped money into the Clinton Foundation in what looked to Simpson to be an effort to influence and win favors from Clinton's State Department. "I had no interest in working for

Hillary fucking Clinton," Simpson privately told friends. "I covered these people, Hillary and Bill Clinton, for years. They were an old-fashioned political machine."

For Simpson, Trump was now the bigger and more sinister threat. His multiple bankruptcies, his past ties to mob figures, his questionable business dealings that had resulted in repeated lawsuits alleging fraud—all of this alarmed Simpson. And there were other things he was curious about: Ivanka Trump and Jared Kushner's social relationship with a Russian oligarch named Roman Abramovich and Donald Trump's extensive loans from Deutsche Bank, which had been accused of being part of a Russian money-laundering scheme. But it was Trump's trips to Russia that intrigued him the most. He knew that Trump had gone to Moscow repeatedly, but nothing had ever come of it other than the Miss Universe pageant. Simson thought this was puzzling. Who had Trump been trying to do business with? What had gone wrong? Simpson asked if Steele would be willing to investigate. His brief to Steele was simple: "Tell me what he's been doing over there."

Simpson at this point knew something else that he did not share with Steele during their lunch at Heathrow. As a Democratic Party contractor, he had been briefed on the Russian hack of the DNC—a development that was not yet public. It raised the possibility the Russians might be seeking to influence the election on behalf of Trump. Simpson was not yet at liberty to share what he knew. He was extremely cagey about what he told Steele. But Simpson was hoping that Steele—whose firm had investigated Russian influence operations in western Europe—could pick up some intelligence on what the Russians were doing in the election.

Steele was game. Orbis had ongoing projects in Russia for clients involved in commercial litigation. He figured he could easily hand this new assignment to his contacts in Russia whom he paid to search out information and prepare reports. (Steele himself was known to the Russians and could not operate there.) Simpson and Steele agreed to a thirty-day contract—with an option to renew. Steele would be paid about $30,000 a month.

Steele got in touch with one of his chief sources in Russia—or, as he called him, the "collector"—and instructed him to start seeking information on Trump. Steele guarded the collector's identity as a top secret. But Simpson understood that the collector was a Russian émigré living in the West who traveled frequently to Moscow and was acquainted with well-informed Russian professionals and officials. He was Steele's undercover operative, working his own Russian sources for whatever nuggets they might yield.

Two weeks or so later, Steele flew to meet his chief collector in a European city. As Steele listened and took notes, he could scarcely believe what he was hearing. His collector, relaying what he had been told by his contacts, informed Steele that the Russians had been targeting and cultivating Trump for years and had even gathered *kompromat* on him, specifically tales of weird sexual indiscretions that the collector said "were an open secret" in Moscow. Steele was horrified. "I thought I had heard and seen everything in my career," he told associates.

Steele immediately notified Simpson. He had "absolute dynamite," Steele said, mentioning the sexual *kompromat*.

"I'm going to need a report," Simpson said. "You should write it up."

Steele quickly composed a three-page memo that would become one of the most famous and controversial private intelligence reports of all time.

At the top and bottom of each page, Steele typed, "CONFIDENTIAL/SENSITIVE SOURCE," and the memo, dated June 20, began with a four-point summary. The first point was the broadest one: "Russian regime has been cultivating, supporting and assisting TRUMP for at least 5 years. Aim, endorsed by PUTIN, has been to encourage splits and divisions in western alliance." Next, Steele noted, "So far TRUMP has declined various sweetener real estate business deals offered him in Russia in order to further the Kremlin's cultivation of him. However he and his inner circle have accepted a regular flow of intelligence from the Kremlin, including on his Democratic and other political rivals."

The third point was potentially the most explosive: "Former top Russian intelligence officer claims FSB has compromised TRUMP through his activities in MOSCOW sufficiently to be able to blackmail him. According to several knowledgeable sources, his conduct in Moscow has included perverted sexual acts which have been arranged/monitored by the FSB."

The final point was about Trump's rival: "A dossier of compromising material on Hillary CLINTON has been collated by the Russian Intelligence Services over many years and mainly comprises bugged conversations she had on various visits to Russia and intercepted phone calls rather than any embarrassing conduct. The dossier is controlled by Kremlin spokesman, PESKOV, directly on PUTIN's orders. However it has not as yet been distributed abroad, including to TRUMP. Russian intentions for deployment still unclear."

In the following two pages, Steele went into details. He characterized his collector's sources without naming them. He described Source A as a senior Russia foreign ministry official and Source B as a former top Russian intelligence officer still active within the Kremlin. Both had each recently told a "trusted compatriot"—the collector—that Moscow had been running an operation for years to cultivate and co-opt Trump and that this project was "supported and directed" by Putin.

According to Source C, a senior Russian financial official, the Trump operation was part of Putin's overall plan to sow disunity within the United States and the trans-Atlantic alliance. This source reported having heard Putin express his desire to return to the nineteenth-century style of "Great Power" politics in which nations would pursue their own interests rather than an ideals-based international order.

Source A, Steele reported, had confided that the Kremlin had been providing Trump and his team valuable intelligence on Clinton. The memo noted that Putin's "cultivation operation" had included offering Trump lucrative real estate development deals in Russia. But, Steele wrote, "for reasons, unknown, TRUMP has not taken up any of these."

Then came the salacious details that would forever color the report. Steele alleged that Russian intelligence had been able "to exploit TRUMP's personal obsessions and sexual perversion in order to obtain suitable '*kompromat.*'" Source D, described as "a close associate of TRUMP who had organized and managed his recent trips to Moscow," claimed that "TRUMP's (perverted) conduct in Moscow included hiring the presidential suite of the Ritz Carlton Hotel, where he knew President and Mrs. OBAMA (whom he hated) had stayed on one of their official trips to Russia, and defiling the bed where they had slept by employing a number of prostitutes to perform a 'golden showers' (urination) show in front of him. The hotel was known to be under FSB control with microphones and concealed cameras in all the main rooms to record anything they wanted to."

Another source cited in the memo claimed this bizarre event was believed to have transpired in 2013. (That was when Trump was in Moscow for the Miss Universe contest.) Steele reported that one of his Russian operatives had spoken to a female staffer at the hotel who "confirmed" the story. And Source B, the former Russian intelligence officer still connected to the Kremlin, asserted that Trump's "unorthodox behavior in Russia over the years had provided the authorities there with enough embarrassing material on the now Republican presidential candidate to be able to blackmail him if they so wished."

When Burrows, Steele's partner, reviewed the memo, he nearly gagged. "What the fuck!" Burrows said to Steele during a testy conversation. "What the fuck is a golden shower? I never heard of it."

Burrows feared Steele was sensationalizing his material. "Why did you put the word 'perverted'" in there?" Burrows asked.

"Because that's what he said," Steele replied, referring to the collector, who was his primary source.

"But does it have to be in there?" Burrows asked.

"You're being judgmental," Steele answered.

Burrows feared the political consequences of circulating such a document. "It's *une patate chaude,*" he told his colleague. French for "hot potato." Are you sure about this? Burrows asked.

"That was what the source said to me," Steele replied, referring again to the collector, whose information was at best secondhand. "I'm as sure as I can be."

Steele's perspective was undoubtedly influenced by the FSB's rich history of using sexual *kompromat*—and its key role in Putin's rise to power. In 1999, Russia's prosecutor general, Yuri Skuratov, was mounting an aggressive investigation into evidence of corruption of President Boris Yeltsin's inner circle. Among those implicated was Yeltsin's chief political adviser, his own daughter. Then a Russian television station aired a blurry black-and-white videotape showing two young women—described on the broadcast as prostitutes— cavorting in various states of undress with an older man who resembled Skuratov. A scandal erupted and within a couple of weeks, the authenticity of the tape was validated by no less an authority than the director of the FSB: Vladimir Putin. Skuratov was later fired— and by then an ever-grateful Yeltsin had designated Putin as his successor as Russia's president.

The Skuratov video had all the trademarks of an old KGB operation frequently used during the Cold War to blackmail visiting diplomats and businessmen. And it remained an active part of the FSB playbook. In July 2009, a Russian news website was provided a video showing a portly British diplomat, James Hudson, frolicking with two blonde prostitutes during a visit to a brothel. The site posted the video under the headline "Adventures of Mr Hudson in Russia." It was enough to end Hudson's adventures. No sooner was it posted than the British diplomat was forced to resign—a new example of how *kompromat* remained a clear and present danger to all prominent visitors to Russia.

But the fact that the FSB used sexual *kompromat* was not evidence that it had been employed against Trump. There was nothing in his report indicating how Steele's anonymous sources knew or could have known about the alleged "golden showers" incident involving Trump. The wording was vague. Source D was said to have been present at the hotel. But did this source witness the incident inside Trump's hotel room, speak directly to one of the prostitutes, or see the alleged tape? The memo provided no answers, and similar questions could be raised about the claims of Steele's other sources who purported to confirm the incident.

If accurate, this memo could be the most consequential piece of opposition research in U.S. history. But Burrows later privately described the report as akin to preliminary intelligence reporting—information not analyzed, vetted, or ready for distribution. "It was not meant to be definitive," Burrows said. "It was a report that needed to be explored further. This was not gospel. It was raw product."

Simpson could barely wait for Steele's report. Steele had forwarded it on a thumb drive with a passcode via Federal Express. It was supposed to arrive in Washington on the morning of June 24, Steele's birthday. That day, he was celebrating with his wife, taking a stroll at Wisley, a Royal Horticultural Society garden outside London. It was also a momentous time in Britain—the day after the Brexit vote that had turned the country upside down.

Simpson was getting anxious. The FedEx package had not arrived. He kept calling Steele, interrupting his day off, to ask, "Where is it?" Simpson had to fend off a burst of paranoia. Had it gotten lost—or had Russian intelligence intercepted the package? The explanation for the delay ended up being mundane. The buzzer to Simpson's office—in an unmarked office building near Washington's Dupont Circle—was not working. The next day, FedEx delivered the thumb drive.

As soon as he read the memo, Simpson realized it could potentially blow up the election. But he also knew it was fraught with problems. He had not asked Steele to probe Trump's personal conduct. Yet now he had these outlandish allegations in writing. How could they be proven? Who would believe it? He thought Steele was more worked up over this piece of the report than he was. But that was natural; Steele was the *kompromat* expert. And he saw Steele's focus on Trump's supposed sexual acts as a reflection of his proper British reserve. "Chris is basically a Boy Scout," Simpson later testified. More le Carré than Fleming.

Simpson would later learn from Steele the identity of Source D, the main source for the "golden showers" allegation. It was Sergei

Millian, the Belarusian American businessman who in the mid-2000s said he was retained to locate Russian customers for Trump properties in the United States. Like all of those who had spoken to Steele's collector, Millian was an unwitting source; he had no idea his conversation with the collector would be passed along to Trump's political foes.

For Simpson, Millian was now an investigative target. He tipped off ABC News, which conducted an on-air interview with Millian, in which he said Trump "likes Russia, because he likes beautiful ladies—talking to them, of course."

The memo had described Millian as a Trump intimate, but there was no public evidence he was close to the mogul at that time or was in Moscow during the Miss Universe event. Had Millian made something up or repeated rumors he had heard from others to impress Steele's collector? Simpson had his doubts. He considered Millian a big talker. (For his part Millian subsequently insisted on Russian television, "I don't have any compromising information [on Trump], neither in Russia nor in the United States, nor could I have.")

Steele's faith in the sensational sex claim would fade over time. Much later, after this report and follow-up memos would become infamous, Steele would say that he believed 70 to 90 percent of the broad assertions of his reporting—that Russia had mounted a campaign to cultivate Trump and had colluded with the Trump campaign—was true. (Burrows would assess the level of accuracy at 70 to 80 percent.) As for the likelihood of the claim that prostitutes had urinated in Trump's presence, Steele would say to colleagues, "It's fifty-fifty."*

When Simpson first received Steele's report, however, the main question was how to corroborate the more consequential allegations about a Trump-Russia connection. Some of the material in the report was hard to believe. Simpson assumed a lot of it would

---

* Steele would later wonder if there was a connection between Trump's 2013 visit with Emin Agalarov and Rob Goldstone to the Las Vegas nightclub, The Act, which sometimes featured women urinating on each other, and the golden showers story in his first memo. But he didn't know.

be wrong. While the lurid stories were practically impossible to verify, the other big-picture claims—the Russians had been trying to cultivate Trump and there had been secret information sharing between the Trump camp and Moscow—might be true and confirmable and possible ammunition for Trump's foes.

Neither Simpson nor Steele were aware of recent events that would later lend weight to some of these claims. Trump just months earlier had been in the middle of a potentially lucrative deal to build a Trump Tower in Moscow. One of his foreign policy advisers, George Papadopoulos, had been in regular contact with Russian sources in an attempt to set up a meeting between Trump and Putin. And days before Steele began his inquiries, Trump's top advisers had met with a Russian delegation at Trump Tower seeking derogatory information from the Kremlin on Hillary Clinton.

Soon after sending Simpson the memo, Steele made an unnerving suggestion: They should share this report with the FBI. Steele believed this information—a presidential candidate possibly being compromised by Putin's regime—was too important to reserve as confidential campaign oppo research. "This is a grave national security threat," he told Simpson. The former MI6 man explained that he felt obligated to report it.

Simpson immediately saw that this could create a problem. If he brought this information to the FBI, such a move could be portrayed as a partisan effort to manipulate the Bureau and instigate an investigation of a political rival. Should that become public, it would be political suicide for the Clinton campaign. Moreover, Clinton remained under investigation by the FBI in the email server case. Too many Clinton officials did not trust the Bureau. There was no way the campaign would want to approach the FBI with such dicey material. He told Steele to hold off.

But in a series of calls, Steele kept pushing. This was intelligence, he argued, which needed to be shared with the appropriate government officials. "I wouldn't even know who to call," Simpson said at one point. Steele replied, "Oh, I know who to call."

Finally, Simpson relented. He knew this was a momentous step, but he had his doubts. Still, he could justify it. "I thought it was a possible crime in progress," he later testified. After all, what if a research project turned up advance knowledge of a terrorist plot? Of course, he would call the cops. In this case, it appeared possible that a foreign intelligence service was covertly manipulating the American election. Steele was now free to tell the FBI. And Simpson said not a word about this to Elias.

Steele called Michael Gaeta, his FBI contact on the FIFA case. "I've got something you should see," he said. "I can't discuss it over the phone. You have to come here. Believe me, Mike, you have to come to London."

There were a few hoops Gaeta had to jump through. He was assigned to the U.S. embassy in Rome. The FBI checked with Victoria Nuland's office at the State Department: Do you support this meeting? Nuland, having found Steele's reports on Ukraine to have been generally credible, gave the green light.

Within a few days, on July 5, Gaeta arrived and headed to Steele's office near Victoria station. Steele handed him a copy of the report. Gaeta, a seasoned FBI agent, started to read. He turned white. For a while, Gaeta said nothing. Then he remarked, "I have to report this to headquarters."

CHAPTER 12

"As for the Ukraine amendment, excellent work."

On the morning of July 5—the same day Steele was meeting with Gaeta—all work stopped at Clinton headquarters. Staffers crowded around television sets. There was absolute silence. Within moments, the fate of Hillary Clinton's quest for the presidency could be decided.

In a conference room at the FBI headquarters, James Comey, the tall and imposing FBI chief, strode to a podium. Comey, a Republican, had been appointed head of the Bureau by Obama three years earlier. As a deputy attorney general and U.S. attorney, he had developed a reputation as a straight shooter. In a now-famous incident, he had rushed to a hospital room in 2004, where then–Attorney General John Ashcroft lay ill, to stop senior Bush White House aides from pressuring Ashcroft to reauthorize a domestic warrantless wiretapping program that Comey and other officials believed was illegal. The event cemented Comey's reputation as a principled law enforcement officer who truly was above politics.

Standing in front of the flags of the United States and the FBI,

Comey was about to announce whether the FBI would recommend the indictment of a presidential candidate.

Comey started off acknowledging this was an unprecedented moment. The Bureau never revealed its findings in such a manner. Typically, if an FBI investigation resulted in an indictment, the charges themselves would stand as the main statement on the case. And if there were no indictment, under Justice Department rules, the Bureau would not comment on what it had or had not uncovered. But Comey explained that due to the "intense public interest" he was going to provide more than the usual details. He noted that he had not coordinated or reviewed what he was about to say with the Justice Department—of which the FBI was a part—or any other element of the U.S. government.

Comey did not explain that one reason he was taking this action on his own was that he and his senior aides had been chafing about Attorney General Loretta Lynch's role in the Clinton email server probe. The previous September, as Comey was preparing to testify before Congress, Lynch had ordered him to refer to the Clinton email inquiry as a "matter," not an investigation. It was a directive that Comey viewed as absurd and designed to conform with Clinton's own misleading talking points that the FBI's criminal probe was merely a "security review." ("I guess you're the Federal Bureau of Matters now," one national security prosecutor cracked after the meeting.) And in late June, Lynch had met with Bill Clinton when he had boarded her airplane while they both were on the tarmac at a Phoenix airport. Their half-hour chat, Lynch later said, was "primarily social," about golf and grandchildren. The encounter caused a storm of criticism, given that Hillary Clinton was still under investigation by Lynch's department. "I wish I had seen around that corner and not had that discussion with the former president, as innocuous as it was, because it did give people concern," Lynch said a few days later. In response to the uproar, Lynch announced she would accept the recommendations of career prosecutors and the FBI on the Clinton case, whatever they were.

Comey also did not reveal his concern about something else. Months earlier, the FBI had obtained a purported Russian intelligence document citing a supposed DNC email that suggested Lynch would not let the Clinton investigation go too far. Though there were questions about the document's validity—and whether the email was real—Comey feared that the Russian document could leak and cast a further cloud over any decision the Justice Department made about Clinton's server.

It was the job of Justice Department prosecutors, not the FBI, to render the final decision on whether criminal charges would be brought in any investigation. But in this instance, Comey chose on his own to leave the Justice Department out of the picture and publicly announce the FBI's recommendation himself. He began to read a statement he and his senior staff had been drafting and redrafting for weeks.

At the lectern, Comey explained all the steps the Bureau had taken during its probe. Agents, he reported, had searched through millions of email fragments on one of Clinton's personal servers. The Bureau had reviewed the thirty thousand emails she had returned to the State Department and found 110 emails on 52 email chains that contained classified information at the time they were sent. Seven of those chains involved matters that were at the "Top Secret/Special Access Program" level. This contradicted Clinton's repeated claim that she had not used the private email server to transmit classified information. Another two thousand emails contained information that was later determined to be classified. The Bureau found several thousand work-related emails that were not in the group of messages Clinton had returned to the department. Comey suggested that Clinton's lawyers did a shoddy job in reviewing her emails for State Department–related messages.

In the Brooklyn headquarters, hearts began to sink. Classified information, missing emails—it appeared Comey was going to announce an indictment. That would be it. Some of her aides believed the campaign was finished.

Comey began to sum up his conclusions: "Although we did not find clear evidence that Secretary Clinton or her colleagues intended to violate laws governing the handling of classified information, there is evidence that they were extremely careless in their handling of very sensitive, highly classified information." It was a damning—and extraordinary—statement for the FBI director to make. The Clintonites staring at television screens could not tell where Comey was heading.

Then there was the question of whether foreign powers had intercepted Clinton's emails—a pressing national security issue. The Bureau did not find direct evidence that her server had been hacked, but Comey noted that Clinton had used her personal email extensively while traveling overseas, including "in the territory of sophisticated adversaries." He added: "Given that combination of factors, we assess it is possible that hostile actors gained access to Secretary Clinton's personal email account."

Finally, Comey remarked that the FBI had not found evidence that Clinton had engaged in willful misconduct or sought to obstruct justice—key factors in any decision to prosecute. "Although there is evidence of potential violations of the statutes regarding the handling of classified information," he said, "our judgment is that no reasonable prosecutor would bring such a case."

Clinton was in the clear. A cheer erupted in the Brooklyn campaign office. Top aides huddled afterward and wondered if they should challenge Comey on his biting statements criticizing Clinton's conduct. After a brief deliberation, they decided it would be counterproductive. Did they want to put Clinton, whose integrity was a campaign issue, in a direct confrontation with the head of the FBI? His statement was a split decision, but one they could live with.

It seemed that the email server episode was over. But another FBI inquiry—into Donald Trump's campaign—was about to begin.

When the first Steele memo arrived in FBI headquarters that same week, it got the attention of the Bureau's counterintelligence division. The officials there knew about Steele's track record providing reports that were helpful in the FIFA soccer corruption investigation. They also knew from the outset that Steele had an agenda and that he was likely working for the Democrats. But this was not a deal breaker, according to one senior official who reviewed Steele's report at the time. FBI agents were used to receiving intelligence from informants with agendas or grudges. Gang leaders and drug cartel bosses dime out their competitors, and agents and prosecutors are happy to take the information if it checks out and helps them make a case. "It was a concerning document," recalled the senior official. "Of course, we took it seriously."

Within days, a rambling and boring lecture in Moscow ratcheted up the Bureau's concerns.

In the spring, Carter Page, the little-known energy consultant who had been named a Trump adviser, had been invited by the rector of the prestigious New Economic School in Moscow to deliver a speech there. Although a private university, the school had direct ties to the Kremlin: Arkady Dvorkovich, Russia's deputy prime minister, was the chairman of its board. Page asked Trump campaign official, J. D. Gordon, for permission to travel to Russia for the event.

Gordon was essentially Page's handler on the campaign, and his relationship with Page was not a smooth one. Page wanted high-level access and to be part of senior-level strategizing. In May, he had sent an email to Gordon suggesting Trump visit Russia "to raise the temperature a little bit." (No campaign official jumped at this suggestion.) Page also wrote policy papers for the campaign, but only one was accepted. The subject: energy and hydraulic fracking. When Trump made an energy speech in North Dakota, Page flew to Bismarck for the event. Yet none of his material was used. Page was irate. "Nothing I gave you was in the speech," Page subsequently complained to Gordon. "Not my problem," Gordon told him.

Page had grandiose ideas about his future role in a Trump administration. "In his heart of hearts," Gordon later said of Page, "he wanted to be U.S. ambassador to Moscow."

When Page told Gordon that he wanted to go to Moscow for a speaking engagement, Gordon thought to himself, "No flipping way. This is a really dumb idea. I'll get my face ripped off." He refused to forward his speech request form. But the energy consultant would not take no for an answer and went over Gordon's head.

In an email, he appealed to Corey Lewandowski, then Trump's campaign manager. Lewandowski said okay—but Page would have to travel to Moscow in his private capacity, not as a representative of the Trump campaign.

On July 7, Page appeared onstage in an auditorium at the New Economic School in Moscow to deliver a talk on U.S.-Russian economic relations. At the start of his presentation, Page insisted he was speaking only as a private citizen and a business executive.

Russian officials could be forgiven for believing that Page was bearing a message from Trump. After all, Trump had repeatedly spoken about improving relations with Russia and getting along with Putin. And Page was known as something of a Putin fan. In a 2014 blog post, after Obama had added Igor Sechin, the chairman of Rosneft, the state-owned oil company, and a close Putin ally, to the sanctions list, Page had declared, "Sechin has done more to advance U.S.-Russian relations than any individual in or out of government from either side of the Atlantic over the past decade." And at a June meeting of Washington foreign policy experts with the Indian prime minister, Page stunned the crowd by praising Putin as stronger and more reliable than Obama.

Now, before the two hundred or so college students who had gathered in the auditorium at the school, Page, reading off his laptop in a painful monotone, described U.S.-Russian economic interactions. Soon into the lecture, some students looked as if they were having trouble staying awake.

But Page's message was provocative for an adviser to a Republican presidential candidate. He denigrated U.S. policymakers for their "hypocritical focus on ideas such as democratization, inequality, corruption, and regime change" when dealing with Russia. He called for Washington to put aside its "critical tone" and "intolerance"—to not fixate on corruption—and, instead, to exploit "opportunities to build upon mutual interest" with Russia. He decried that the West "unnecessarily perpetuated Cold War tendencies." He was urging Washington to not get hung up on the Putin regime's human rights abuses, lack of transparency, political repression, and culture of corruption. Mutual respect, he contended, would yield mutual benefits. At least, the deals and the money would flow.

It was a theme that the Putin establishment, no doubt, relished. At least one influential Russian openly embraced Page's appearance in Moscow. Alexander Dugin, a Kremlin-connected political scientist known as the "mad philosopher"—who had urged Russians to "kill, kill, kill" Ukrainians—promoted Page's lecture. A big fan of Trump and a hard-core ultranationalist, Dugin had produced a series of videos hailing the Republican candidate. Now he praised Page for promoting "an alternative for the U.S.," and, on Tsargrad, a TV station he founded, he broadcast Page's lecture live.

While in Moscow, Page declined to tell a Reuters reporter whether he would be meeting with anyone from the Russian government. But Page did speak after his speech—briefly, he later said—with Dvorkovich, the deputy prime minister who chaired the board for the school. And afterward Page sent the campaign a memo noting, "Dvorkovich expressed a strong support for Mr. Trump and a desire to work together toward devising better solutions in response to the vast range of current international problems." Page also met with Andrey Baranov, the head of investor relations for Rosneft, which was subject to U.S. sanctions. And he boasted to the campaign that he had been in contact with top Russian officials during this trip, emailing Gordon that he would soon send a "readout" about his trip "regarding some incredible insights and outreach I've received from a few Russian legislators and senior members of the Presidential administration here."

Page's speech may have been a snooze. But his time in Moscow caught the attention of the FBI. That was in large part because he had been known to the Bureau's spy catchers for at least three years.

In 2013, Page had attended an energy symposium in New York City and met a Russian diplomat named Victor Podobnyy. The Russian gave Page his business card and his email addresses. Over the following months, Page and Podobnyy corresponded and met occasionally. Page freely shared with the Russian his thoughts on the energy industry, and he passed along documents related to the energy business. The Russian hinted that he had connections in the Russian government that could help Page obtain contracts.

Page had been suckered. Podobnyy was a Russian intelligence officer working for the SVR, Moscow's foreign intelligence service. He was part of a three-man spy ring that had been handed the assignment of gathering information related to potential U.S. sanctions against Russia, American efforts to develop alternative energy, and other economic topics.

Podobnyy did not think too highly of Page. During a conversation with one of his spying comrades that was intercepted by U.S. intelligence, Podobnyy called Page an "idiot" who "wants to earn lots of money." He noted that Page often flew to Moscow, and he remarked that it was easy to fool Page, noting "his enthusiasm works for me." Podobnyy told his colleague that he was feeding Page "empty promises" and described his recruitment method this way: "You promise a favor for a favor. You get the documents from him and tell him to go fuck himself."

FBI agents, though, were on to the Russians, and in June of that year two agents interviewed Page about his contacts with Podobnyy. He told them he had passed to Podobnyy only publicly available materials and excerpts from lectures he was giving while teaching a course at New York University.

In 2015, the FBI broke up this espionage operation and brought charges against one of the spies, Evgeny Buryakov, who had been posing as a Russian banker. (Podobnyy and the other Russian in the ring each were protected because they had been working undercover as diplomats, and they quickly left the United States.) Buryakov was eventually sentenced to thirty months in prison.

Page had not been accused of any wrongdoing—and his peripheral role did not become public. But the operation placed him on the FBI's radar screen. And his trip to Moscow in July 2016 rang a bell within the Bureau, raising concerns about whether one of Trump's foreign policy advisers was being manipulated by the Kremlin.

In mid-July, the Republicans descended upon Cleveland for their national convention. There was little drama left in the GOP race.

Earlier talk of a Republican effort to block Trump's ascension at the convention had evaporated. The party was now Trumpified. Delegates roamed the streets of the city wearing HILLARY FOR PRISON 2016 T-shirts. And Republican lobbyists—the denizens of the "rigged system" and the "swamp" Trump excoriated—held receptions and resigned themselves to Trump being their nominee. Mainstream Republicans shared the consensus of the politerati: This political novice running a dark campaign brimming with anger (if not bigotry) was unlikely to succeed in November. The party would have to grin and bear its way until the election—and then find a new path forward.

Trump's curious relationship with Putin and Russia was never advertised from the podium inside the Quicken Loans Arena. But questions about the Trump campaign's ties to Moscow were lurking in the background.

On the afternoon of July 18, the opening day of the convention, Michael Flynn, now Trump's high-profile national security adviser, came to the Yahoo News booth for an interview with chief investigative correspondent Michael Isikoff. Flynn was there to promote *The Field of Fight*, a new book he had written with Michael Ledeen, a hard-line neoconservative. In the book, Flynn called for ramping up the war against jihadi terrorism and more forcefully confronting the mullahs in Iran. And he took a tougher line on Russia than he had before, slamming Moscow for supporting the Iranian regime. At the end of the interview, Isikoff raised an issue Flynn was not eager to discuss: his December 2015 trip to Moscow for the tenth-anniversary celebration of RT, the Russian propaganda channel, where he had sat at the VIP dinner table next to Putin.

The interview grew testy.

Isikoff: Were you paid for that event?
Flynn: I . . . you'd have to ask the folks I went over there to . . .
Isikoff: Well I'm asking you. You'd know if you were paid.
Flynn: Yeah, I went over as a speaking event. It was a speaking

event. What difference does that make? Yeah, somebody can go, oh, he's paid by the Russians.

Isikoff: Well, Donald Trump has made a lot of the fact that Hillary Clinton has taken money from Wall Street, Goldman Sachs.

Flynn: Well I didn't take any money from Russia, if that's what you're asking me.

Isikoff: Well then, who paid you?

Flynn: My, my speaker's bureau. Ask them.

That afternoon, a story about the interview was posted on the Yahoo website, highlighting Flynn's trip to Russia. Flynn shot Isikoff an email: "Of all we spoke about today, the headline is my speaking engagement in Russia? That's not news of any substance. Did you really read my book and see how much I took Russia to task?"

That evening, Flynn gave a stem-winder of a speech to the convention. He led the raucous crowd in fierce cheers of "Lock her up!" as he vilified Clinton for putting "our nation's security at extremely high risk with her careless use of a private email server."

He declared, "If I did a tenth, a tenth of what she did, I would be in jail today."

On the third evening, Indiana Governor Mike Pence, whom Trump had chosen as his running mate, excoriated Clinton and Obama for being feckless caretakers of national security. One sign of their weakness, he insisted, was "feigning resets with Russia." He vowed that Trump would "stand with our allies." Yet that same night, Trump signaled the opposite. In an interview with the *New York Times*, he said he might not honor the NATO obligation to protect fellow members of the alliance if they were attacked. This was major news and exactly what Putin wanted to hear. Trump was arguably conveying to Russia that he might accept aggression from Moscow.

When Trump delivered his acceptance speech, he said nothing about Russia or Putin. He stuck to his usual script, presenting a dystopian view of a United States overrun with crime and endangered by illegal immigration. He blasted Clinton for committing "terrible, terrible crimes." The man who months earlier had secretly tried to land a deal in Moscow claimed that Clinton had raked in "millions of dollars trading access and favors to special interests and foreign powers." He proclaimed, "I am your voice."

There were few surprises during the official proceedings. Far more intriguing was what was going on behind the scenes. During the week of the convention, several Trump associates met with Sergey Kislyak, the longtime Russian ambassador to the United States, at a conference co-sponsored by the State Department and conservative Heritage Foundation. Sessions delivered the keynote address for that event. Afterward, he chatted with Kislyak and other ambassadors. Subsequently, the Russian ambassador reported back to Moscow that the two had discussed Trump's positions on policy matters of concern to the Russian government. U.S. intelligence captured Kislyak sharing this news with his superiors back home.

J. D. Gordon and Carter Page also had a chance to chat with Kislyak. At an evening reception that was part of this conference, Kislyak spoke briefly with Gordon, as Page stood by. The discussion, according to Gordon, centered on improving U.S.-Russia ties. "It's important to have better relations between the U.S. and Russia," Gordon told the ambassador. "We should cooperate against jihadi networks." Kislyak, while nibbling on chicken satays, nodded in agreement. So too did Page.

These encounters with Kislyak attracted no public notice at the time. But there was a Russia-related controversy at the convention that did draw attention. And it started the week before during a bitter fight over the party platform's plank on Ukraine.

The GOP platform committee was holding one of its last meetings in Cleveland to finish up the policy document that would be presented to the delegates at the convention for their approval. Gordon was assigned the task of monitoring the process to ensure that no national security-related amendments at odds with Trump's positions ended up in the platform.

Enter Diana Denman, a onetime aspiring actress and a veteran

Texan GOP activist. She considered herself a proud Reagan Republican and had come to Cleveland as a delegate for Ted Cruz, the Texas senator who had placed a distant second to Trump in the nomination battle. In 1998, Denman had served as an election observer in Ukraine, and since then she had identified with the democratic (and anti-Russian) forces in that country.

As a member of the platform committee's national security subcommittee, she introduced an amendment condemning "Russia's ongoing military aggression in Ukraine." Her measure called for maintaining and possibly intensifying sanctions against Russia. And it proposed "providing lethal defensive weapons to Ukraine's Armed Forces." (Ukraine had been asking the United States for arms. Despite support from some officials in the Pentagon, Obama had rejected the idea and favored sending nonlethal assistance.)

Immediately, Denman could tell something was wrong. Two men who were watching from the side quickly stood up and headed over to Steve Yates, the head of the Idaho GOP who was cochairing the national security subcommittee, and began discussing the language of her amendment.

Denman joined the group and asked, "Who are you? What's the problem?" One of the men was Gordon. Are you a staffer? Denman asked. No, he said, he was with the Trump campaign. The wording of her amendment, Gordon told her, had to be "cleared." With whom? Denman demanded to know. "New York," he said, according to Denman. She snapped back, "Do you have a problem with people who want to be free?"

Gordon realized the amendment could be a problem. "You didn't have to be a rocket scientist to know that arming Ukraine was not consistent with Trump's position," he later said. It was Gordon's job to make sure Trump's views were reflected in the platform—and that there wouldn't be headlines along the lines of "GOP Platform Committee Rebukes Trump."

Gordon urged Yates to push the pause button, explaining he had to talk to other campaign officials about this. He called John Mashburn, the campaign's policy director, telling him he needed to get to the meeting immediately. Another campaign aide called Dearborn, a senior campaign official, to deliver the same message. Dearborn showed up, hopping mad. "Why are you calling me?" he demanded to know. Gordon explained the situation, and Dearborn agreed that the amendment had to be killed.

A new version of the amendment was crafted and approved. It still called for maintaining and possibly increasing sanctions on Russia until Ukraine's territorial integrity was restored. But the reference to supplying weapons to Ukraine was gone.

The Trump aides thought they had dodged a bullet. The campaign certainly did not need a controversy at the convention that would call attention to Trump's unconventional stance toward Putin. But that's what it got.

On the first day of the convention, the *Washington Post* revealed what had happened during the platform meeting, reporting the "Trump campaign worked behind the scenes last week to make sure the new Republican platform won't call for giving weapons to Ukraine to fight Russian and rebel forces, contradicting the view of almost all Republican foreign policy leaders in Washington." This boosted an inconvenient storyline for the campaign: that Trump was too cozy with Putin. Moreover, this prompted media attention regarding Manafort and his years of profitable work for Yanukovych and the Party of Regions. There was, though, no evidence that Manafort had been involved.

After the platform battle, Page shot Gordon an email: "As for the Ukraine amendment, excellent work."

In mid- and late July, Christopher Steele sent new reports to Glenn Simpson based on his conversations with his collector. They were as alarming as his first memo. One of the reports focused on Russian state-sponsored hacking. It asserted the FSB was using "coercion and blackmail" to recruit hackers as part of a massive campaign to target Western governments and corporations. Russia's secret police had achieved "significant operational success" by inserting malware into cheap Russian IT games.

Another memo cited further evidence of an "extensive conspiracy" between Trump's campaign and the Kremlin that had been sanctioned at the "highest levels" of the Russian government. This conspiracy, the report said, was being managed within the Trump campaign by Manafort. It claimed there was an "agreed exchange of information" in which Trump's team was "using moles within DNC and hackers in the U.S." to provide intelligence to Russia. It made further claims about Trump's efforts to do business in Russia. It asserted that while the real estate mogul had explored the market in St. Petersburg as well as Moscow, in the end he had to "settle for the use of extensive sexual services there from local prostitutes rather than business success."

A third report focused on Page's trip to Moscow. It claimed that the Trump adviser had held "secret meetings" in Moscow. One of them purportedly was with Igor Sechin, the president of Rosneft, the giant Russian state-owned gas company, who as a Putin intimate had been sanctioned by the Obama administration over Russia's intervention in Ukraine. According to Steele's report, Sechin had raised the issue of future U.S.-Russia energy cooperation in exchange for lifting Western sanctions on Russia.

Another secret meeting, the memo alleged, was with a Kremlin official named Igor Diveykin, who supposedly told Page about a dossier of *kompromat* that the Kremlin had compiled on Hillary Clinton and "its possible release to the Republican's campaign team." Page later adamantly denied he held any of the secret meetings described in the memos (but admitted he had met with Andrey Baranov, the investor relations chief at Sechin's company).

As with Steele's first report, none of the sources in the memos were identified. Steele later told associates one of the sources for the information was the paramour of a Kremlin insider. In short, it was pillow talk.

CHAPTER 13

"Next they're going to put polonium in my tea."

The tweet that shook the 2016 election popped up at 7:26 A.M. EST on July 22. It was the Friday before the Democratic National Convention, and delegates from across the country were heading to Philadelphia to nominate Hillary Clinton for president. "Are you ready for Hillary?" asked the tweet from Julian Assange's WikiLeaks. "We begin our series today with 20 thousand emails from the top of the DNC."

For weeks, Democratic Party officials and others had been anxiously waiting to see if the Russian hackers who had broken into the DNC would do any more with the documents they had stolen. The suspected Russian front, Guccifer 2.0, had posted some DNC documents but none had been terribly damaging. Yet there had been an ominous forewarning: Guccifer 2.0 had claimed he had given "the main part of the papers, thousands of files and mails" to WikiLeaks. Now Assange and WikiLeaks were proving Guccifer 2.0 right. Two hours after that tweet, they posted a trove of hacked DNC emails in one of their biggest political document dumps ever.

If the primary purpose of Russian information warfare operations, as outlined in the Gerasimov doctrine, was to sow confusion and exploit divisions within the adversary, the WikiLeaks release could not have worked better. From the moment WikiLeaks disseminated the DNC emails, it was clear this dump would feed the anger among Bernie Sanders supporters—and incite insurrection at the Democratic convention. Several emails showed top DNC officials favoring Clinton, privately deriding Sanders staffers, and swapping ideas to undercut the Vermont senator's campaign.

In one email, Wasserman Schultz referred to Jeff Weaver, Sanders's campaign manager, as a "damn liar." In another, she responded to a Weaver vow to continue the Sanders campaign until the convention and noted, "He is an ASS."

One especially embarrassing email chain began with Brad Marshall, the DNC's chief financial officer, proposing to other DNC officials a line of attack regarding Sanders' religious beliefs, or lack thereof. He wrote: "Can we get someone to ask his belief. Does he believe in a God. He had skated on saying he has a Jewish heritage. I think I read he is an atheist. . . . My Southern Baptist peeps would draw a big difference between a Jew and an atheist." Clearly, he was suggesting something of a smear job. In the email thread, Dacey, the DNC's chief executive officer, replied, "AMEN." ("I picked the wrong word and I regretted it," Dacey later said. "I was just trying to shut down the conversation.") And in a May 21, 2016, message to Luis Miranda, the DNC communications director, Mark Paustenbach, his deputy, raised an idea for a story they could pitch to a political reporter: "Wondering if there's a good Bernie narrative for a story, which is that Bernie never ever had his act together, that his campaign was a mess."

There was no evidence the DNC ever acted on either of these ideas. But it didn't matter. By the time Sanders delegates arrived in Philadelphia, they were damn mad. "It was kind of like a punch in the gut," Robert Becker, the Sanders campaign floor manager for the convention, recalled. "It was the tenor and tone of some of those emails. These weren't volunteers chittering and chattering. This was the leadership of the party. I was literally offended. And to have them mock the Bernie campaign? It was like, what the fuck have you guys built over the last year?"

And Trump was more than happy to fuel the flames. "Leaked e-mails of DNC show plans to destroy Bernie Sanders," he tweeted. "Mock his heritage and much more. On-line from Wikileakes, really vicious. RIGGED." In another tweet, he gleefully asserted, "The Wikileaks e-mail release today was so bad to Sanders that it will make it impossible for him to support her, unless he is a fraud!"

This was the last thing the Clinton campaign needed at the moment its primary goal was to bring a divided party together.

As the campaign's senior officials huddled about how to respond, they had little doubt about what was going on and who was behind it. "We viewed it as a conscious effort to divide the party at a key party gathering," said Jake Sullivan, now Clinton's top national security adviser. "Our reaction was we were under attack by the Russians." And when campaign manager Mook talked to Clinton about the release of the DNC emails, she told him she was convinced it was Putin's payback against her. "Next they're going to put polonium in my tea," she joked. She was referring to another Russian intelligence operation: the 2006 assassination of Alexander Litvinenko.

Luis Miranda himself was enraged. The DNC communications chief was driving back to Washington, D.C., from the convention in Cleveland when WikiLeaks began dumping the DNC emails. His emails made up more than half of the cache posted; much of the rest came from members of the DNC's fundraising team. He was the main target, his privacy violated, his communications made public. (The DNC lawyers at Perkins Coie found it puzzling that the hackers had not swiped and released emails from Dacey and other senior DNC officials.)

At rest stops and Starbucks along the way, Miranda encountered reporters also returning from the GOP convention, and they were asking him about individual emails. Miranda saw that many, though not all, of the emails fueling the DNC-screwed-Sanders argument had come from the past May. That was after the DNC in late April had discovered that Russian hackers had violated its network and before CrowdStrike had booted out the intruders in early June. Miranda wondered why the cybersecurity experts had waited six weeks to turn off the network. To him, it seemed as if the DNC and CrowdStrike had watched burglars freely roam in and out of the network, pilfering material for weeks—without warning DNC staffers that their communications were open to theft. Though the DNC's lawyers believed CrowdStrike's remediation effort had been conducted as quickly as possible—and that the DNC brass had no choice but to keep the infiltration a secret from its employees—Miranda couldn't get over a key fact: Many of the most damaging emails in the WikiLeaks dump had been swiped after the DNC already knew it had been hacked.

The timing was especially cruel for Miranda and his DNC colleagues. It was in May that party professionals were most annoyed at Sanders. By then, Clinton had achieved a lock on the nomination. As they saw it, Sanders' refusal to bow out and endorse Clinton was the petulant self-indulgence of a vain man who didn't care about party unity. It was no surprise that the emails from this stretch reflected their frustration with Sanders and his campaign staffers. But the timing of when these damning emails had been written got lost in the commotion they were causing.

Within the Clinton campaign, there was debate about how far they should go in responding to the WikiLeaks dump. All the senior staff wanted to get the word out that this was a Russian hit job. CrowdStrike and other cybersecurity experts had concluded that. But Mook—who by now had been briefed by campaign lawyer Marc Elias on some of the contents of the explosive Steele memos—wanted to go further. He proposed saying that the Russians were using WikiLeaks as part of a plot to elect Trump. "Everything is telling us that this is true, so what are we waiting for?" Mook argued to his colleagues.

Other Clinton officials were reticent and pushed back. "No one wanted to come off sounding crazy," recalled Mook. "It was hard to believe. It was Tom Clancy–ish and fictional." The Clinton aides agreed that Mook and others doing interviews could continue asserting that Moscow was intervening in the election—but they would stop short of saying it was for the benefit of Trump.

The only problem was the media wasn't buying it either way. On Sunday morning, Mook appeared on CNN's *State of the Union*. As soon as host Jake Tapper asked him about the DNC emails and the party's treatment of Sanders in the primaries, Mook turned toward Russia: "Experts are telling us that Russian state actors broke into the DNC, stole these e-mails. And other experts are now saying that the Russians are releasing these e-mails for the purpose of actually helping Donald Trump."

So much for the campaign guidance. But Mook had other evidence to cite. He pointed to the weakening of the Ukrainian plank at the GOP convention and Trump's declaration that he might not honor the United States' NATO commitments. "When you put all this together," he said, "it's a disturbing picture. And I think voters need to reflect on that."

Tapper pressed Mook for proof: "What evidence is there that the Russians were behind this in terms of the hacking or in terms of the timing by WikiLeaks?" Mook referred to the cybersecurity experts who had reached this conclusion. "But," Tapper countered, "it is a very, very strong charge that you're leveling here. You're basically suggesting that Russians hacked into the DNC and now are releasing these files through WikiLeaks to help elect Donald Trump."

Later in the show, Tapper turned to Trump Jr. and asked him to respond to Mook's charge. Trump's son lit into Mook: "Well, it just goes to show you their exact moral compass. I mean, they will say anything to be able to win this. I mean, this is time and time again, lie after lie…There's nothing wrong with a fair fight, Jake. I don't mind a fair fight, but these lies and the perpetuating of that kind of nonsense to try, you know, gain some political capital is just outrageous and he should be ashamed of himself."

Manafort took a similar line that morning on another show. He insisted Mook's assertions about the Russians were "pure obfuscation" on the part of the Clinton campaign. Asked if there were any ties between Trump, Manafort, the campaign, and Putin's regime, Manafort replied, "That's absurd. And, you know, there's no basis for it."

"Next they're going to put polonium in my tea."

By now, Trump Jr. and Manafort had good reason to believe the Russians were keenly interested in helping the Trump campaign. Both men, along with Trump son-in-law Jared Kushner, had met the previous month at Trump Tower with a delegation from Moscow they were told would have "official documents" incriminating Hillary Clinton. Manafort had also been emailed about the contacts that Papadopoulos had with Russian cutouts trying to arrange a meeting between Putin and Trump. And Manafort had his own Russian to deal with. He was trying to placate Oleg Deripaska, the billionaire oligarch tight with Putin, who was pursuing him in a legal action in the Cayman Islands for an accounting of the millions of dollars they had jointly invested in the ill-fated Ukrainian cable deal. Three weeks earlier, Manafort had emailed his Russian business associate, Konstantin Kilimnik, with an idea about how to hold Deripaska at bay: Offer to provide him inside information about the Trump campaign. "If he needs private briefings we can accommodate," he emailed Kilimnik on July 7.

The material dumped by WikiLeaks did not show the vast DNC conspiracy to undercut Sanders that the media coverage suggested. Yet the brush was so dry, it took only a few emails to set it ablaze. And the fire ignited quickly. The anger among Sanders supporters—on Twitter, in the media, and in hotel lobbies in Philadelphia—was red-hot. Many demanded Wasserman Schultz and the rest of the DNC senior staff be fired. Mook and other Clinton aides quickly realized—and feared—the convention could be overwhelmed by this conflict and the ensuing chaos. For them, the hacked DNC emails posed an existential threat.

On Saturday, July 23, two days before the convention would open, Mook had several conversations with Wasserman Schultz. It was time for her to go, he told her. Long before the WikiLeaks dump, Clinton's top advisers had not been satisfied with her leadership of the DNC—nor had White House officials. Now the Clinton team worried that the convention could blow up. Yet as much as Mook pushed Wasserman Schultz to resign, she resisted. She demanded that she first speak to Obama. She did—and he, too, pushed her. At last, Wasserman Schultz relented and announced she would step down. (Longtime Democratic activist Donna Brazile would replace her on an interim basis.) Wasserman Schultz was the first direct victim of the Russian information operation.

It was not enough to quell the storm. At a breakfast meeting of the Florida state delegation on Monday morning, Wasserman Schultz was booed and heckled by Sanders delegates. The protesters held signs that read "Email." She had to be whisked away by a squad of police officers.

That afternoon, in a cavernous ballroom in the convention center, Sanders delivered a rousing speech. As he hit all the usual themes—end big-money politics, restore the middle class, stop trade agreements, continue the revolution—his supporters cheered wildly. But when he declared they must band together to defeat the "bigotry" of Trump by electing Clinton, Sanders was drowned out by a chorus of boos and anti-Clinton chants. "Not with her!" delegates shouted.

For Mook and the others, it looked as if the convention could collapse in a flood of acrimony. They feared that hundreds of Sanders delegates, enraged by the released DNC emails, would shout down pro-Clinton speakers during the convention's prime-time hours and even hiss and hoot at Clinton during her acceptance speech. To prevent outright open warfare at the convention, the Clinton and Sanders campaigns merged their convention teams. And the Sanders operation went full throttle to persuade, coax, and cajole delegates to not disrupt the proceedings.

The first night, Sanders delegates did boo speakers. But Sanders delivered a forceful speech declaring that the best way for his supporters to advance their progressive revolution was to work for Clinton to defeat Trump. And on the second night, Sanders, at the end of the roll call vote, moved to hand Clinton the nomination by acclamation—a gesture of support.

Those actions appeared to quiet the possible uprising of Sanders delegates. Bitterness among the Sanders delegates did linger for the rest of the convention—with many of them continuing to cite the hacked emails as evidence their champion had been unfairly obstructed by a corrupt political establishment. But Clinton's coronation proceeded free of any further commotion.

The Clinton campaign had survived the initial Russian attack. But Clinton and her advisers assumed there was more to come. They determined that to withstand whatever was next from Moscow, they had to keep the Russian intervention in the spotlight. So one afternoon during the convention, Jennifer Palmieri and Jake Sullivan grabbed a golf cart and went on a tour of the television networks' operations, which were set up in big air-conditioned tents in the parking lots of the Wells Fargo Center. Their mission was to convince the execs, editors, and anchors that they should devote more attention to the Russian intervention.

Palmieri was a veteran political operative who had served in the White House and had two decades of experience working with political reporters. She knew them all. Sullivan was a national security expert who had been a top deputy to Clinton at the State Department. He had also been a lead negotiator for the Obama White House in the talks that yielded the Iran nuclear deal.

At CNN, they sat down with network chief Jeff Zucker and several correspondents. At Fox News, Bret Baier was part of the session. There was a big group of execs and reporters at the meeting with NBC and MSNBC.

At each stop, Sullivan and Palmieri presented the case that the Russians were covertly attacking the election. They noted that intelligence community officials were telling reporters on background—not for public attribution—that Russian intelligence had pulled off the DNC hack.

The pair walked the journalists through Trump's past links to Russia. They pointed to the GOP's platform shift on Ukraine. They detailed the Manafort ties. Sullivan explained how Moscow had conducted active measures in the past. This was, Sullivan and Palmieri insisted, a national security issue.

"The response," Sullivan later said, "generally was, 'That's interesting.' And they looked at us like we were wearing tin-foil hats." Palmieri recalled it this way: "The reaction was, 'Okay, now tell us about the emails." As she later put it, "We did not succeed."

Sullivan and Palmieri realized that the campaign's response to the dumped emails—we're not going to discuss the contents of stolen material, and we're blaming the Russians—did not sit well with reporters. Nor did it sit well with the Sanders delegates, many of whom, like reporters, were still keenly focused on the content of the emails, not where they came from. "When that [Russia] argument was being made," Nomiki Konst, a Sanders campaign surrogate and delegate, later said, "it just reinforced that nobody wanted to take responsibility. The Clinton campaign had it ingrained in them, not to take responsibility, but to deflect."

When Mook went on television and claimed Moscow had hacked the DNC to influence the election and benefit Trump, White House officials cringed. They knew the public evidence indicated Russian intelligence was to blame for the DNC breach. And the initial confidential reports from the intelligence community—often called the IC by people within it—confirmed this. But Mook's statement posed a problem because Obama and the administration were not willing at this stage to publicly back up the Clinton camp's assertion.

Weeks earlier, the White House had instructed the IC to find out who or what was behind the DNC hack and the Guccifer 2.0 leaks. The preliminary judgments had come in, yet there was still no firm official consensus within the IC. (Often different intelligence agencies would reach varying conclusions on such matters—or establish different levels of confidence in a conclusion—and it would take time and perhaps more information to iron out the differences.)

By now, Obama was intensely concerned the Russians were messing with the presidential race. "We were worried, given the Russian history of meddling in elections." McDonough, Obama's chief of staff, recalled. "There was no misunderstanding in the White House on Putin's view of the West. We were not surprised at a Russian intention to screw with elections around the world."

In the years since Putin had returned to the presidency in 2012, McDonough later remarked, the White House had watched Russia demonstrate a greater "willingness to push the envelope" when it came to confronting the United States, "and it alarmed us."

But Obama didn't want to get ahead of the intelligence community. He told his aides that the White House had to take its lead from the intelligence agencies on this politically sensitive matter. Otherwise, the administration could be accused of playing politics with national security. Everyone knew who Obama was supporting in the race. And Obama realized how easy it would be for Trump to claim the White House was exploiting—or faking—intelligence to help Clinton, were he to lean too far into this controversy. "We could never get in front of the IC," a senior White House official later explained. "We would be accused of doctoring the intel and politicizing it—to affect an election."

Consequently, when Obama was first publicly queried about the WikiLeaks dump and any Russian link, he tried to help Clinton as much as he could—without placing the U.S. government seal of approval on the campaign's Russian accusations. Asked by NBC News's Savannah Guthrie if Russia was trying to interfere, Obama replied that the FBI was still investigating but added that "experts have attributed this to the Russians." He continued, "What I do know is that Donald Trump has repeatedly expressed admiration for Vladimir Putin." When pressed on whether Putin would try to influence the 2016 presidential campaign, Obama remarked, "Anything's possible."

This frustrated the Clinton campaign. Couldn't Obama—the campaign's best asset—tell the nation what was happening? Without the U.S. government blaming the Russians for the hacks and the document dumps, Clinton and her aides were out on a limb. Their statements could be easily dismissed as desperate political spin or unfounded hysteria—or both.

Democrats on the Hill also wanted more out of Obama. If the Russians were targeting their presidential candidate, they believed voters needed to know. On the third day of the convention, Representative Adam Schiff and Senator Dianne Feinstein, the top-ranking Democrats on the House and Senate intelligence committees, sent Obama a public letter noting that if Moscow had engineered the WikiLeaks dump, "the episode would represent an unprecedented attempt to meddle in American domestic politics—one that would demand a response by the United States." They asked Obama to consider declassifying and releasing intelligence "assessments regarding the incident, including any that might illuminate potential Russian motivations for what would be an unprecedented interference in a U.S. Presidential race."

Their letter didn't prompt the Obama White House to do anything different. The next day, White House press secretary Josh Earnest stuck to a careful script: "I just don't want to say anything that could be perceived even as having some kind of influence over the course of that [FBI] investigation [of the DNC hack]....I recognize there's been an analysis done that has indicated that the Russians are likely to blame, but that is not a conclusion that the FBI has chosen to publicize at this point."

Once again, Clinton campaign officials were exasperated. In their view, the White House was not helping.

About this time, the FBI received a startling message that had been passed from the Australian government: Papadopoulos back in May had told its top diplomat in Britain the Russian government had dirt on Clinton. In the wake of the WikiLeaks dump, this information seemed ominous. And it spurred the FBI to take a closer look at the ties between Trump's campaign and the Russians.

The Bureau already had in its possession the initial Steele memo, with its harrowing allegation of a Trump-Moscow conspiracy. And Page's trip in early July to the Russian capital was suspicious. The hack of the DNC—and the subsequent releases by Guccifer 2.0 and DCLeaks, both deemed to be Russian intelligence fronts—was another piece. Then there was Manafort. The Ukrainian government had recently asked the bureau for help in tracking payments to Manafort from the pro-Russia Party of Regions. The FBI also had received intelligence from friendly spy services, including the Dutch and the British, about the Russian hack, as well as contacts between Trump associates and Russia.

With the Papadopoulos report in hand, Comey's FBI made a fateful decision: It launched a counterintelligence investigation into possible links between the Trump campaign and the government of Vladimir Putin. This would be one of the Bureau's most highly guarded secrets.

Even while the FBI was beginning its probe, the U.S. intelligence community was slow to come around to the enormity of what was happening. The fact that the Russians had apparently decided to release—or weaponize—the documents it had stolen was an escalation that made the DNC hack much different than what had happened when the Chinese penetrated the computers of the Obama and McCain campaigns in 2008. But the significance of this was not immediately grasped at the highest levels of the IC.

Director of National Intelligence James Clapper was speaking the week of the Democratic convention at the Aspen Security Forum—an annual conference at which the country's top current and former national security officials appeared. To the surprise of many in the audience, Clapper seemed dismissive of the importance of the DNC hack. No one should be "hyperventilating," Clapper said. He then added sarcastically: "I'm shocked somebody did some hacking. That's never happened before." Clapper was even nonplussed about the idea Russia was seeking to disrupt the election, saying that this "isn't terribly different than what went on in the heyday of the Cold War."

Clapper's comments found a receptive audience—in Moscow. RT, the Russian-controlled English-language media outlet, embraced Clapper's skepticism, publishing a story headlined, "US Intel Head Calls for End to 'Hyperventilation' Over Russia's Alleged Role in DNC Hack." The top U.S. intelligence official had just doused the Clinton campaign's claims with cold water and helped Moscow's top propaganda shop.

Unlike the White House, Trump was not reluctant to say what he thought about the Russian allegations. On the first day of the

Democratic convention, Trump weighed in on the Clinton team's effort to make the WikiLeaks dump about Russia and him. He tweeted, "The new joke in town is that Russia leaked the disastrous DNC e-mails, which should never have been written (stupid), because Putin likes me." On ABC's *This Week*, he denied having any relationship with Putin. (He did not mention his recent attempt to develop a tower project in Moscow with the approval of Putin's government.) And Trump said his campaign had nothing to do with softening the Republican Party platform on arming Ukraine. On *Meet the Press*, Manafort also denied any campaign involvement in that platform fight. They each were dissembling.

Speaking at a press conference in Doral, Florida, on July 27, Trump made one of the most remarkable statements of his entire campaign. He doubted the Russians had hacked the Democrats, he said. "Nobody knows who it is," he told reporters. But if it had been the Russians, he had a message for them about the deleted Hillary Clinton emails: "I will tell you this—Russia, if you're listening, I hope you're able to find the thirty thousand emails that are missing. I think you'll probably be rewarded mightily by our press."

For months, the media and the Democrats had been speculating whether there was any behind-the-scenes connection between Trump and Russia. But here was a clear and unmistakable message from Trump to the Kremlin. Trump had just invited a foreign adversary to hack his political rival.

CHAPTER 14

"We've been told to stand down."

In mid-February 2015, Gen. Alexander Bortnikov, director of Russia's FSB, showed up in Washington uninvited. Without consulting the Obama administration, the Kremlin had selected Bortnikov to serve as chief of a Russian delegation to the White House summit on Countering Violent Extremism. This was awkward. The White House had planned the gathering as a high-profile event that would highlight global cooperation to combat the spread of radical jihadi propaganda. But Bortnikov's presence was not what administration officials had in mind. Seven months earlier, the European Union had blacklisted the FSB director, sanctioning him for his role in the Kremlin decision-making that led to Russia's invasion of Ukraine. EU officials were livid—and complained to U.S. officials they had been sandbagged. They were being asked to exchange policy ideas with a man they had labeled an international pariah. "Nobody wanted him there," Ned Price, NSC communications director, recalled.

In the middle of this dispute, CIA director John Brennan took the unusual step of inviting Bortnikov to visit him in his office on the seventh floor of CIA headquarters. As difficult as it was to have the chief of Russia's secret police at a White House summit, many of the agency's Russia hands believed it was even more unseemly to welcome him to the CIA.

"We have to be really careful about the message being sent," Steve Hall, the director of the CIA's Russia House, told Brennan.

"Yeah, yeah, I get all that," Brennan replied. "But we deal with a lot of nasty people around the world." Brennan thought it was useful to stay in contact with Bortnikov because he was particularly close to Putin. Brennan had cleared the invitation with the White House. He and Obama wanted to press the FSB chief for help in dealing with the Syrian crisis and counterterrorism efforts against the Islamic State.

Hall, who had met Bortnikov during his days as CIA station chief in Moscow a few years earlier, greeted the FSB chief at the CIA's entrance, and escorted him into the main hallway, where they met Brennan. Hall didn't relish the assignment. In Brennan's office, both spy chiefs stuck to their standard talking points. Brennan won no new commitments from Bortnikov. But Hall, who sat in on the session, sensed a certain smugness on Bortnikov's part. "I'm sure he expected people like Steve Hall to be saying, 'Don't have this thug in your office,'" Hall recalled. "He realized, just by sitting in that office, he'd already won."

More than a year later, on August 4, 2016, Brennan was on the phone with Bortnikov, for a regularly scheduled call, with the main subject once more the war in Syria. By this point, Brennan had had it with the Russian spy chief. Brennan's pleas for help in defusing the Syrian crisis had gotten nowhere. And after they finished discussing Syria—again, with no progress—Brennan addressed two other issues not on the official agenda.

First, Brennan raised Russia's harassment of U.S. diplomats— an especially sensitive matter at Langley after the undercover CIA officer was beaten outside the U.S. embassy in Moscow two months earlier. The continuing mistreatment of U.S. diplomats, Brennan told Bortnikov, was "irresponsible, reckless, intolerable and needed to stop." And, he pointedly noted, it was Bortnikov's own FSB "that has been most responsible for this outrageous behavior."

Then Brennan turned to an even more sensitive issue: Russia's interference in the American election. Brennan now was aware that a few months after he had welcomed Bortnikov to the CIA, Russian hackers had begun their cyberattack on the Democratic National Committee. We know you're doing this, Brennan said to the Russian. He pointed out that Americans would be enraged to find out Moscow was seeking to subvert the election and that such an operation could backfire. Brennan warned Bortnikov that if Russia continued this information warfare, there would be a price to pay. He did not specify the consequences.

Bortnikov, as Brennan expected, denied Russia was doing anything to influence the election. This was, he groused, Washington yet again scapegoating Moscow. Brennan repeated his warning. Once more Bortnikov claimed there was no Russian meddling. But, he added, he would inform Putin of Brennan's comments.

This was the first of several warnings that the Obama administration would send to Moscow. But the question of how forcefully to respond would soon divide the White House staff, pitting the National Security Council's top analysts for Russia and cyber issues against senior policymakers within the administration.

At the end of July, it had become obvious to Brennan that the Russians were mounting an aggressive and wide-ranging effort to interfere in the election. He was also seeing intelligence about contacts and interactions between Russian officials and Americans involved in the Trump campaign. By now, several European intelligence services had reported to the CIA that Russian operatives were reaching out to people within Trump's circle. Brennan wondered whether Moscow had the cooperation of anyone within Trump's camp.

Brennan spoke with Comey and Adm. Mike Rogers, the head of the NSA, and asked them to dispatch to the CIA their experts to form a working group at Langley that would review the intelligence and figure out the full scope and nature of the Russian operation. Brennan was thinking about the lessons of the 9/11 attack. Al Qaeda had been able to pull off that operation partly because U.S. intelligence agencies—several of which had collected bits of intelligence regarding the plotters before the attack—had not shared the material within the intelligence community. Brennan wanted a process in which NSA, FBI, and CIA experts could freely share with each other the information each agency had on the Russian operation—even the most sensitive information that tended not to be disseminated throughout the full intelligence community.

Brennan realized this was what he would later call "an exceptionally, exceptionally sensitive issue." Here was an active counterintelligence case—already begun by the FBI—aiming at uncovering and stopping Russian covert activity in the middle of a U.S. presidential campaign. And it included digging into whether it involved Americans in contact with Russia.

While Brennan wrangled the intelligence agencies into a turf-crossing operation that could feed the White House information on the Russian operation, Obama convened a series of meetings to devise a plan for responding to and countering whatever the Russians were up to. The meetings followed the procedure known in the federal government as the interagency process. The general routine is for the deputy chiefs of the relevant government agencies to meet and hammer out options for the principals—that is, the heads of the agencies—and then the principals hold a separate (and sometimes parallel) chain of meetings to discuss and perhaps debate before presenting choices to the president.

But for this topic, the protocols were not routine. Usually when the White House invited the deputies and principals to such meetings they informed them of the subject at hand and provided "read-ahead" memos outlining what was on the agenda. This time, the agency officials just received instructions to show up at the White House at a certain time. No reason given. No memos supplied. "We were only told that a meeting was scheduled and our principal or deputy was expected to attend," recalled a senior administration official who participated in the sessions. (At the State Department, only a small number of officials were cleared to receive the most sensitive information on the Russian hack; the group included John Kerry; Tony Blinken, the deputy secretary of state; Dan Smith, head of the department's intelligence bureau; and Jon Finer, Kerry's chief of staff.)

For the usual interagency sessions, principals and deputies could bring staffers. Not this time. "There were no plus-ones," an attendee recalled. When the subject of a principals or deputies meeting was a national security matter, the gathering was often held in the Situation Room of the White House. The in-house video feed of the Sit Room—without audio—would be available to national security officials at the White House and elsewhere, and these officials could at least see that a meeting was in progress and who was attending. For the meetings related to the Russian hack, Susan Rice ordered the video feed turned off. She did not want others in the national security establishment to know what was under way, fearing leaks from within the bureaucracy.

Rice would chair the principals' meetings—which brought together Brennan, Clapper, Comey, Kerry, Defense Secretary Ash Carter, Homeland Security Secretary Jeh Johnson, Treasury Secretary Jack Lew, Attorney General Loretta Lynch, and Gen. Joseph Dunford, the chairman of the Joint Chiefs of Staff—with only a few other White House officials present, including Denis McDonough, Lisa Monaco, and Colin Kahl, Joe Biden's national security adviser. (Kahl had to insist to Rice that he be allowed to attend so Biden could be kept up to speed.)

Rice's number two, deputy national security adviser Avril Haines, oversaw the deputies' sessions. White House officials not in the meetings were not told what was being discussed. This even included other NSC staffers—some of whom bristled at being cut out. Often the intelligence material covered in these meetings was not placed in the President's Daily Brief, the top secret document presented to the president every morning. Too many people had access to the PDB. "The opsec on this"—the operational security—"was as tight as it could be," one White House official later said.

* * *

As the interagency process began, there was no question on the big picture being drawn up by the analysts and experts assembled by Brennan: Russian state-sponsored hackers were behind the cyberattacks and the release of the swiped material. "They knew who the cutouts were," one participant later said. "There was not a lot of doubt." It was not immediately clear, however, how far and wide within the Russian government the effort ran. Was it coming from one or two Russian outfits operating on their own? Or was it being directed from the top and part of a larger project?

The intelligence, at this stage, was also unclear on a central point: Moscow's primary aim. Was it to sow discord and chaos to delegitimize the U.S. election? Prompting a political crisis in the United States was certainly in keeping with Putin's overall goal of weakening Western governments. There was another obvious reason for the Russian assault: Putin despised Hillary Clinton, blaming her for the domestic protests that followed the 2011 Russian legislative elections marred by fraud. U.S. officials saw the Russian operation as designed at least to weaken Clinton during the election—not necessarily prevent her from winning. After all, the Russians were as susceptible as any political observers to the conventional wisdom that she was likely to beat Trump. If Clinton, after a chaotic election, staggered across the finish line, bruised and battered, she might well be a damaged president and less able to challenge Putin.

And there was a third possible reason: to help Trump. Did the Russians believe they could influence a national election in the United States and affect the results? At this stage, the intelligence community analysts and officials working on this issue considered this point not yet fully substantiated by the intelligence they possessed. Given Trump's business dealings with Russians over the years and his positive remarks about Putin, there seemed ample cause for Putin to desire Trump in the White House. The intelligence experts did believe this could be part of the mix for Moscow: Why not shoot for the moon and see if we can get Trump elected?

"All these potential motives were not mutually exclusive," a top Obama aide later said.

Obama would be vacationing in Martha's Vineyard until August 21, and the deputies took his return as an informal deadline for preparing a list of options—sanctions, diplomatic responses, and cyber counterattacks—that could be put in front of the principals and the president.

As these deliberations were under way, more troubling intelligence got reported to the White House: Russian-linked hackers were probing the computers of state election systems, particularly voter registration databases. The first reports to the FBI came from Illinois. In late June, its voter database was targeted in a persistent cyberattack that lasted for weeks. The attackers were using foreign IP addresses, many of which were traced to a Dutch company owned by a heavily tattooed twenty-six-year-old Russian who lived in Siberia. The hackers were relentlessly pinging the Illinois database five times per second, twenty-four hours a day, and they succeeded in accessing data on up to two hundred thousand voters. Then there was a similar report from Arizona, where the user name and password of a county election official was stolen. The state was forced to shut down its voter registration system for a week. Then in Florida, another attack. One NSC staffer regularly walked into the office of Michael Daniel, the White House director of cybersecurity, with disturbing updates. "Michael," he would say, "five more states got popped." Or four. Or three. At one point, Daniel took a depth breath and told him, "It's starting to look like every single state has been targeted."

"I don't think anybody knew what to make of it," Jeh Johnson later said. The states selected seemed to be random; his Department of Homeland Security could see no logic to it. If the goal was simply to instigate confusion on Election Day, Johnson figured, whoever was doing this could simply call in a bomb threat. Other administration officials had a darker view and believed that the Russians were deliberately plotting digital manipulations, perhaps with the goal of altering results.

Michael Daniel was worried. He believed the Russians' ability to fiddle with the national vote count—and swing a national U.S.

election to a desired candidate—seemed limited, if not impossible. "We have three thousand jurisdictions," Daniel subsequently explained. "You have to pick the county where the race was going to be tight and manipulate the results. That seemed beyond their reach. The Russians were not trying to flip votes. To have that level of precision was not feasible."

But Daniel was focused on another parade of horribles: If hackers could penetrate a state election voter database, they might be able to delete every tenth name. Or flip two digits in a voter's ID number—so when a voter showed up at the polls, his or her name would not match. The changes could be subtle, not easily discerned. But the potential for disorder on Election Day was immense. The Russians would only have to cause problems in a small number of locations—problems with registration files, vote counting, or other mechanisms—and faith in the overall tally could be questioned. Who knew what would happen then?

Daniel even fretted that the Russians might post online a video of a hacked voting machine. The video would not have to be real to stoke the paranoids of the world and cause a segment of the electorate to suspect—or conclude—that the results could not be trusted. He envisioned Moscow planning to create multiple disruptions on Election Day to call the final counts into question.

The Russian scans, probes, and penetrations of state voting systems changed the top secret conversations under way. Administration officials now feared the Russians were scheming to infiltrate voting systems to disrupt the election or affect tallies on Election Day. And the consensus among Obama's top advisers was that potential Russian election tampering was far more dangerous. The Russian hack-and-dump campaign, they generally believed, was unlikely to make the difference in the outcome of the presidential election. (After all, could Trump really beat Clinton?) Yet messing with voting systems could raise questions about the integrity of the election and the results. That was, they thought, the more serious threat.

Weeks earlier, Trump had started claiming that the only way he could lose the election would be if it were "rigged." With one candidate and his supporters spreading this notion, it would not take many irregularities to spark a full-scale crisis on Election Day.

Obama instructed Johnson to move immediately to shore up the defenses of state election systems. On August 15, Johnson, while in the basement of his parents' home in upstate New York, held a conference call with secretaries of state and other chief election officials of every state. Without mentioning the Russian cyber intrusions into state systems, he told them there was a need to boost the security of the election infrastructure and offered DHS's assistance. He raised the possibility of designating election systems as "critical infrastructure"—just like dams and the electrical grid—meaning that a cyberattack could trigger a federal response.

Much to Johnson's surprise, this move ran into resistance. Many of the state officials—especially from the red states—wanted little, if anything, to do with the DHS. Leading the charge was Brian Kemp, Georgia's secretary of state, an ambitious, staunchly conservative Republican who feared the hidden hand of the Obama White House. "We don't need the federal government to take over our voting," he told Johnson.

Johnson tried to explain that DHS's cybersecurity experts could help state systems search for vulnerabilities and protect against penetrations. He encouraged them to take basic cybersecurity steps, such as ensuring voting machines were not connected to the internet when voting was under way. And he kept explaining that any federal help would be voluntary for the states. "He must have used the word *voluntary* fifteen times," recalled a Homeland Security official who was on the call. "But there was a lot of skepticism that revolved around saying, 'We don't want Big Brother coming in and running our election process.'"

After the call, Johnson and his aides realized encouraging local officials to accept their help was going to be tough. They gave up on the idea of declaring these systems critical infrastructure and instead concluded they would have to keep urging state and local officials to accept their cybersecurity assistance.

Johnson's interaction with local and state officials was a warning for the White House. If administration officials were going to enlist these election officials to thwart Russian interference in the voting, they would need GOP leaders in Congress to be part of the endeavor and, in a way, vouch for the federal government. Yet they had no idea how difficult that would be.

At the first principals meeting, Brennan had serious news for his colleagues: The most recent intelligence indicated that Putin had ordered or was overseeing the Russian cyber operations targeting the U.S. election. And the IC was now certain that the Russian operation entailed more than spy services gathering information. It now viewed the Russian action as a full-scale active measure.

This intelligence was so sensitive it had not been put in the President's Daily Brief. Brennan had informed Obama personally about this, but he did not want this information circulating throughout the national security system.

The other principals were surprised to hear that Putin had a direct hand in the operation and that he would be so bold. It was one thing for Russian intelligence to see what it could get away with; it was quite another for these attacks to be part of a concerted effort from the top of the Kremlin hierarchy.

But the secret source in the Kremlin, who two years earlier had regularly provided information to an American official in the U.S. embassy, had warned that a massive operation targeting Western democracies was being planned. The development of the Gerasimov doctrine was another indication that full-scale information warfare against the United States was a possibility. And there had been the intelligence report in May noting that a GRU officer had bragged of a payback operation that would be Putin's revenge on Clinton. But these few clues had not led to a consensus at senior government levels that a major Putin-led attack was on the way.

At this point, Obama's top national security officials were uncertain how to respond. As they would later explain it, any steps they might take—calling out the Russians, imposing sanctions, raising alarms about the penetrations of state systems—could draw greater attention to the issue and maybe even help cause the disorder the Kremlin sought. A high-profile U.S. government reaction, they worried, could amplify the psychological effects of the Russian attack and help Moscow achieve its end. "There was a concern if we did too much to spin this up into an Obama-Putin face-off, it would help the Russians achieve their objectives," a participant in the principals meeting later noted. "It would create chaos, help Trump, and hurt Clinton. We had to figure out how to do this in a way so we wouldn't create an own-goal. We had a strong sense of the Hippocratic Oath: Do no harm."

A parallel concern for them was how the Obama administration could respond to the Russian attack without appearing too partisan. Obama was actively campaigning for Clinton. Would a tough and vocal reaction be seen as a White House attempt to assist Clinton and stick it to Trump? They worried that if a White House effort to counter Russian meddling came across as a political maneuver, that could compromise the ability of DHS to work with state and local election officials to make sure the voting system was sound. (Was Obama too worried about being perceived as prejudicial or conniving? "Perhaps there was some overcompensation," a top Obama aide said later.)

As Obama and his top policymakers saw it, they were stuck with several dilemmas. Inform the public about the Russian attack without triggering widespread unease about the election system. Be proactive without coming across as partisan and bolstering Trump's claim the election was a sham. Prevent Putin from further cyber aggression without prompting him to do more. "This was one of the most complex and challenging issues I dealt with in government," Avril Haines, the NSC's number two official, who oversaw the deputies meetings, later remarked.

The principals asked the Treasury Department to craft a list of far-reaching economic sanctions. Officials at the State Department began working up diplomatic penalties. And the White House pushed the IC to develop more intelligence on the Russian operation so Obama and his aides could consider whether to publicly call out Moscow.

At this point, a group of NSC officials, committed to a forceful response to Moscow's intervention, started concocting creative

options for cyberattacks that would expand the information war
Putin had begun.

Michael Daniel and Celeste Wallander, the NSC's top Russia
analyst, were convinced the United States needed to strike back
hard against the Russians and make it clear that Moscow had
crossed a red line. Words alone wouldn't do the trick; there had
to be consequences. "I wanted to send a signal that we would not
tolerate disruptions to our electoral process," Daniel recalled. His
basic argument: "The Russians are going to push as hard as they
can until we start pushing back."

Daniel and Wallander began drafting options for more aggressive responses beyond anything the Obama administration or
the U.S. government had ever before contemplated in response
to a cyberattack. One proposal was to unleash the NSA to mount
a series of far-reaching cyberattacks: to dismantle the Guccifer
2.0 and DCLeaks websites that had been leaking the emails and
memos stolen from Democratic targets, to bombard Russian news
sites with a wave of automated traffic in a denial-of-service attack
that would shut the news sites down, and to launch an attack on the
Russian intelligence agencies themselves, seeking to disrupt their
command and control modes.

Knowing that Putin was notoriously protective of any information about his family, Wallander suggested targeting Putin
himself. She proposed leaking snippets of classified intelligence
to reveal the secret bank accounts in Latvia held for Putin's
daughters—a direct poke at the Russian president that would be
sure to infuriate him. Wallander also brainstormed ideas with Victoria Nuland, the assistant secretary of state for European affairs
and a fellow hard-liner. They drafted other proposals: to dump
dirt on Russian websites about Putin's money, about the girlfriends
of top Russian officials, about corruption in Putin's United Russia
party—essentially to give Putin a taste of his own medicine. "We
wanted to raise the cost in a manner Putin recognized," Nuland
recalled.

One idea Daniel proposed was unusual: The United States and
NATO should publicly announce a giant "cyber exercise" against

a mythical Eurasian country, demonstrating that Western nations had it within their power to shut down Russia's entire civil infrastructure and cripple its economy.

But Wallander and Daniel's bosses at the White House were not on board. One day in late August, national security adviser Susan Rice called Daniel into her office and demanded he cease and desist from working on the cyber options he was developing. "Don't get ahead of us," she warned him. The White House was not prepared to endorse any of these ideas. Daniel and his team in the White House cyber response group were given strict orders: "Stand down." She told Daniel to "knock it off," he recalled.

Daniel walked back to his office. "That was one pissed-off national security adviser," he told one of his aides. At his morning staff meeting, Daniel matter-of-factly said to his team it had to stop work on options to counter the Russian attack: "We've been told to stand down." Daniel Prieto, one of Daniel's top deputies, recalled, "I was incredulous and in disbelief. It took me a moment to process. In my head I was like, did I hear that correctly?" Then Prieto spoke up, asking, "Why the hell are we standing down? Michael, can you help us understand?" Daniel informed them that the orders came from both Rice and Monaco. They were concerned that were the options to leak, it would force Obama to act. "They didn't want to box the president in," Prieto subsequently said.

It was a critical moment that, as Prieto saw it, scuttled the chance for a forceful immediate response to the Russian hack—and keenly disappointed the NSC aides who had been developing the options. They were convinced that the president and his top aides didn't get the stakes. "There was a disconnect between the urgency felt at the staff level" and the views of the president and his senior aides, Prieto later said. When senior officials argued that the issue could be revisited after Election Day, Daniel and his staff intensely disagreed. "No—the longer you wait, it diminishes your effectiveness. If you're in a street fight, you have to hit back," Prieto remarked.

* * *

Obama and his top aides did view the challenge at hand differently than the NSC staffers. "The first-order objective directed by President Obama," McDonough recalled, "was to protect the integrity of election." Confronting Putin was necessary, Obama believed, but not if it risked blowing up the election. He wanted to make sure whatever action was taken would not lead to a political crisis at home—and with Trump the possibility for that was great. The nation had had more than two hundred years of elections and peaceful transitions of power. Obama didn't want that to end on his watch.

By now, the principals were into the nitty-gritty, discussing in the Sit Room the specifics of how to respond. They were not overly concerned about Moscow's influence campaign to shape voter attitudes. The key question was precisely how to thwart further Russian meddling that could undermine the mechanics of the election. Strong sanctions? Other punishments?

The principals did discuss cyber responses. The prospect of hitting back with cyber caused trepidation within the deputies and principals meetings. The United States was telling Russia this sort of meddling was unacceptable. If Washington engaged in the same type of covert combat, some of the principals believed, Washington's demand would mean nothing, and there could be an escalation in cyber warfare. There were concerns that the U.S. would have more to lose in all-out cyberwar.

"If we got into a tit-for-tat on cyber with the Russians, it would not be to our advantage," a participant later remarked. "They could do more to damage us in a cyber war or have a greater impact." In one of the meetings, Clapper said that he was worried that Russia might respond with cyberattacks against America's critical infrastructure—and possibly shut down the electrical grid.

The State Department had worked up its own traditional punishments: booting Russian diplomats—and spies—out of the United States and shutting down Russian facilities on American soil. And Treasury had drafted a series of economic sanctions that included massive assaults on Putin's economy, such as targeting Russia's military industries and cutting off Russia from the global financial system. One proposal called for imposing the same sorts of sanctions as had been placed on Iran: any entity that did business with Russian banks would not be allowed to do business with U.S. financial institutions. But the intelligence community warned that if the United States responded with a massive response of any kind, Putin would see it as an attempt at regime change. "This could lead to a nuclear escalation," a top Obama aide later said, speaking metaphorically.

After two weeks or so of deliberations, the White House put these options on hold. Instead, Obama and his aides came up with a different plan. First, DHS would keep trying to work with the state voting systems. For that to succeed, the administration needed buy-in from congressional Republicans. So Obama would reach out to Senate Majority Leader Mitch McConnell and House Speaker Paul Ryan to try to deliver a bipartisan and public message that the Russian threat to the election was serious and that local officials should collaborate with the feds to protect the electoral infrastructure.

Obama and the principals also decided that the U.S. government would have to issue a public statement calling out Russia for having already secretly messed with the 2016 campaign. But even this seemed a difficult task fraught with potential problems. Obama and his top aides believed that if the president himself issued such a message, Trump and the Republicans would accuse him of exploiting intelligence—or making up intelligence—to help Clinton. The declaration would have to come from the intelligence community. The IC was instructed to start crafting a statement. In the meantime, Obama would continue to say nothing publicly about the most serious information warfare attack ever launched against the United States.

Most of all, Obama and his aides had to figure out how to ensure the Russians ceased their meddling immediately. They came up with an answer that would frustrate the NSC hawks, who believed Obama and his senior advisers were tying themselves in knots and looking for reasons not to act. The president would privately warn Putin and vow overwhelming retaliation for any further intervention in the election. This, they thought, could more likely dissuade Putin than hitting back at this moment. That is, they believed the *threat* of action would be more effective than actually taking action.

A meeting of the G20 was scheduled for the first week in September at China. Obama and Putin would both be attending. Obama, according to this plan, would confront Putin and issue a powerful threat that supposedly would convince Russia to back off. Obama would do so without spelling out for Putin the precise damage he would inflict on Russia. "An unspecified threat would be far more potent than Putin knowing what we would do," one of the principals later said. "Let his imagination run wild. That would be far more effective, we thought, than freezing this or that person's assets." But the essence of the message would be that if Putin did not stop, the United States would impose sanctions to crater Russia's economy.

Obama and his aides were confident the intelligence community could track any new Russian efforts to penetrate the election infrastructure. If the IC detected new attempts, Obama then could quickly slam Russia with sanctions or other retribution. But, the principals agreed, for this plan—no action now, but possible consequences later—to work, the president had to be ready to pull the trigger.

CHAPTER 15

"He's got me as the fall guy."

It may have been just a throwaway line. But to former FBI analyst Clint Watts, an offhand comment Paul Manafort made to CNN's Jake Tapper on the morning of August 14 was a sign of something deeply troubling beneath the surface of the 2016 presidential campaign.

Manafort was being grilled about Trump's latest off-the-wall comment—a remark at a rally in Wilmington, North Carolina, about how "Second Amendment people" might have to do something to stop Hillary Clinton's judicial appointments were she to be elected. Was Trump suggesting violence to stop judicial picks? Tapper asked. Not at all, Manafort replied. The fact Tapper was asking at all, he said, was further evidence of news media bias.

"I mean, there's plenty of news to cover this week that I haven't seen covered," he said. "You had the NATO base in Turkey being under attack by terrorists."

A terrorist attack in Turkey? What was Manafort talking about? There had been no such incident. But when Watts, a counterintelligence expert, saw the exchange, he knew immediately what this

was about: a piece of Russian disinformation that had been rico-
cheting around the world on social media sites for weeks.

In late July, RT and Sputnik, the Russian news outlets, had
reported a story about protests at the U.S. air base in Incirlik,
Turkey—where the U.S. military stored nuclear weapons—
claiming that seven thousand armed police had surrounded the
facility in response to a "massive wave of protests" by demonstrators shouting "Death to the U.S.!" The base, the Russian outlets
said, was in lockdown amid fears of an attack, and Sputnik reported
that there was the danger that the nukes could fall into the hands of
"international terrorists." These stories—aimed at stirring tensions
between the U.S. and Turkey—were amplified on RT and Sputnik's Twitter feeds and websites. But they had been overblown: The
protests were peaceful, and U.S. officials said there was no threat
to the security of the air base. The protests had received no major
U.S. media coverage.

But now a mangled version of this Russian propaganda was
being repeated on national television by the campaign chairman
of one of the two major party presidential candidates. "What the
hell?" Watts thought. And later he recalled, "That's when we knew
something weird was going on."

Watts was among a handful of private researchers who, for the past
several years, had been tracking the ways that social media was
being exploited by the United States' enemies. Much of his initial
interest in this subject was spurred by the alarming success ISIS
was having using social media to recruit thousands of young, alien-
ated men to join the fight in Iraq and Syria. But Watts started to see
a pattern of more sophisticated messaging that seemed to be ema-
nating from websites and Twitter accounts based in Russia.

A key moment came in March 2014 when, a few weeks after
Putin annexed Crimea, a strange petition popped up on the White
House website. Written in clunky English by a mysterious character
identified only as "S.V." of Anchorage, it demanded that Alaska be
returned to Russia. As kooky as the idea sounded, the petition suddenly started getting traction. Twitter accounts promoted it; mes-

sages pumping it showed up on Facebook. Within a few weeks, it had gotten nearly forty thousand signatures.

For Watts, it was an eye-opener. As he examined the names on the petition, he noticed that many of them were identical with those on automated Twitter bots that had shown up in other social media campaigns pushing Kremlin propaganda. Some of these bots looked like "honeypot" accounts, featuring photos of attractive looking women to lure in online audiences. He also saw that these accounts were tied to internet hecklers or trolls who fiercely attacked and ridiculed Kremlin critics and promoted Russian talking points to English-speaking audiences.

The pattern that Watts discovered matched what Russian whistleblower Lyudmila Savchuk would reveal about the operations of the Internet Research Agency, the Kremlin-linked troll farm in St. Petersburg. But Watts was frustrated that the issue was not getting more attention among U.S. national security officials. He wrote a short article for a foreign policy think tank's website noting that Facebook and Twitter were "littered with pro-Russian, Western looking accounts" aimed at undermining the credibility of the U.S. government. It got little attention. But soon after it appeared, the FBI contacted him—to tell him had been targeted in a cyberattack.

As a recognized expert on the manipulation of social media, Watts would occasionally be invited to give briefings at the FBI and the CIA. He began alerting his former intelligence colleagues to the ways that the Russian social media effort was increasingly targeting the United States. Russian bots had promoted the Occupy Wall Street movement and later Black Lives Matter, causes of great interest to progressives. Yet they also cheered on the far-right supporters of cattle rancher Cliven Bundy, who was locked in an armed confrontation with federal agents over grazing fees on government-owned land in southeastern Nevada. They played up a U.S. military special forces exercise in southern states called Jade Helm 15—an event that inspired a bizarre conspiracy theory that the Obama administration planned to impose martial law. All of these causes—which cut across ideological lines—were being given wide attention on RT and Sputnik, the Russian propaganda news sites.

This was, Watts concluded, the return of Soviet Cold War active measures with a vengeance—the promotion of divisive and bogus news stories aimed at destabilizing Russia's adversaries, using the new tools of social media. But when he gave his briefings, with charts and slides displaying the Twitter bots and RT stories, he mostly got shrugs from his former colleagues. "I don't think they understood what Russia was trying to do," he subsequently said.

Others within the stove–piped U.S. intelligence community were starting to take notice, however. In 2015, the CIA had floated a proposal for a covert action program to create fake websites to counter Kremlin propaganda and to unleash the NSA to zap websites and servers used to control phony Russian personas. But the plan got little support from senior Obama administration policymakers, in part because they thought that the free flow of information would drown out Russian propaganda. "We believed that the truth shall set you free, that the truth would prevail," Tony Blinken, Obama's deputy secretary of state, later said. "That proved a bit naïve."

For Watts, Manafort's comments that August morning were a wake-up call. It was a sign that Russia's active measures were moving beyond the ideological fringes and now creeping into the mainstream American political dialogue. This, Watts believed, needed to be exposed, and he was determined to do so. But as he and the researchers he worked with would come to learn, there was more—much more—to the Russian effort. It was a campaign that was shrewdly exploiting America's biggest social media companies. And remarkably, almost nobody at the time realized it, not even the companies themselves.

Manafort wouldn't last long. The same day as the CNN interview, the *New York Times* reported that Ukraine's anticorruption bureau had discovered handwritten ledgers showing Yanukovych's pro-Putin party designated $12.7 million in undisclosed cash payments for Manafort between 2007 and 2012. The newspaper noted that Ukrainian investigators had asserted these disbursements were part of an illegal off-the-books system. Ukrainian officials were also probing a collection of offshore shell companies linked to Yanukovych's inner circle and a series of murky transactions. One of these involved the $18.9 million deal to sell Ukrainian cable television assets to a partnership owned by Manafort and Oleg Deripaska—the deal that had prompted the Russian oligarch to file a legal action in the Cayman Islands.

Manafort's lawyer denied he had received such cash payments or been involved with any corruption in Yanukovych's regime. But it didn't matter. Trump's faith in Manafort was already eroding. He was being undermined by a new top adviser: Steve Bannon, an eccentric, rabble-rousing conservative populist. Bannon privately ridiculed the campaign chairman to Trump as an out-of-touch elitist. Bannon made fun of Manafort for wearing Oxford shirts during TV appearances from his summer home in the Hamptons. He compared him to Thurston Howell III, the millionaire castaway on *Gilligan's Island*. Bannon confronted Manafort over the *Times* story. Manafort dismissed it. Trump didn't. "I've got a crook running my campaign," he said when he read it.

Four days after the *Times*' Ukraine story, Trump was about to go onstage at a rally in Charlotte, North Carolina, when he was handed a printout of an AP story that had just been posted. It reported the existence of emails showing that Manafort and his deputy, Rick Gates, had run a "covert Washington lobbying operation" on behalf of Ukraine's pro-Russia political party and noted the two operatives had not disclosed their work as foreign agents "as required under federal law." Trump had finally had it. "Tell Jared to fire him," he snapped at an aide. The next morning at Trump Tower, Kushner did just that. "It will make me look guilty," Manafort protested. There was nothing he could do, Kushner told him. A press release was going out in sixty seconds. It did. Longtime Republican operative Kellyanne Conway was the new campaign manager; Bannon was the campaign's new CEO.

Trump's dismissal of Manafort would make little difference to the FBI. Its counterintelligence investigation into possible links between the Trump campaign and the Russians was just getting underway. On August 15, a meeting of FBI agents working the case was held at the office of deputy director Andrew McCabe. One of those there was a seasoned, senior agent, Peter Strzok.

Strzok was the chief of the FBI's counterespionage section in the Bureau's counterintelligence division. He had been in charge of the FBI's investigation of Clinton's email server and led the questioning of the Democratic candidate in an interview a few days before Comey announced the Bureau would not recommend criminal charges. Strzok was no partisan. He had helped draft Comey's statement describing Clinton's handling of classified information as "extremely careless"—a public verdict critics said was out of bounds for the FBI to make when no charges were being brought. But whatever he thought about Clinton's conduct, Strzok held Trump in contempt. Throughout this period, Strzok was having a relationship with an FBI lawyer named Lisa Page, and in private text messages they described the GOP candidate to each other as an "utter idiot," a "menace," and a "douche." In one exchange, Page texted Strzok, "God trump is a loathsome human." Strzok replied, "He's awful."

In his texts to Page prior to this meeting, Strzok had made clear he saw the FBI's Trump-Russia probe as critical, referring to the campaign's "PERVASIVE CONNECTIONS" with the Kremlin. But in McCabe's office, Page suggested the Bureau could take its time pursuing the probe—and not risk burning sensitive sources— because Clinton was going to win the election.

Strzok took a different view. What if Trump did win? What if people the FBI was now investigating were named to high-level positions? After the meeting, Strzok texted Page, "I want to believe the path you threw out for consideration in Andy's office—that there's no way he gets elected—but I'm afraid we can't take that risk. It's like an insurance policy in the unlikely event you die before you're 40."

Strzok thought a Trump presidency would be a risk. The investigation was the insurance policy.

* * *

Two days after the McCabe meeting, Donald Trump trekked to an FBI field office in New York City, which had a secure conference room. He brought with him Michael Flynn and New Jersey Governor Chris Christie, a former rival for the nomination who had become one of Trump's most prominent supporters. Trump was there to receive his first official intelligence briefing.

These classified sessions were routinely conducted for major presidential nominees. They tended not to offer the candidates information that was highly sensitive. The aim was to provide them updates that went a bit beyond what they could read in newspapers. And Trump, with his comments about Putin, his and his associates' ties with Russia, and his penchant for speaking recklessly, had caused concern within the U.S. intelligence community about whether he could be trusted with sensitive information. His briefing would certainly not be loaded with information the IC did not want leaked or shared.

The feeling was mutual. Trump had done little to create a positive atmosphere for the sessions. Hours before the meeting, an interview with Trump aired in which he said he did not have much trust in current U.S. intelligence officials.

Yet now he was sitting in a room with briefers sent by the intelligence community. Trump, notorious for being impatient with briefings, was presented basic material on security threats and challenges around the world. But during the meeting, Trump was given information that directly affected him. It contradicted what he and his campaign had been saying for weeks. He was told, as Clapper would later confirm, there were direct links between Putin's regime and the hacks and information dumps that had targeted the Democrats and the Clinton campaign. (Clinton, too, received a similar briefing around this time.)

Now Trump and Flynn knew that the U.S. intelligence community was convinced the DNC penetration and the Guccifer 2.0 and WikiLeaks releases were part of a Russian operation—and that this was not, as the Trump campaign had originally claimed, a hoax. Yet this briefing would not stop Trump and his campaign from dismissing assertions of Russian intervention. He didn't trust his briefers. It was the start of what would become a feud between Trump and the U.S. intelligence community that would last throughout the campaign and beyond.

A few days earlier, another Russian strike occurred, showing how extensive Putin's cyberattacks had been. The target was the Democratic Congressional Campaign Committee (DCCC). And the impact of this latest dumping operation—which would include the organization's most important internal memos—would be as disruptive and consequential as anything that had happened so far.

Kelly Ward was the DCCC's executive director. It was her job to get Democrats elected to the House. Even though the DCCC shared the same Capitol Hill office building as the DNC, it was a separate entity from the DNC. And the party brass had not told her that the DCCC, too, had been penetrated by Russian hackers until minutes before the *Washington Post* in mid-June broke the news of the DNC hack. It was only then that Amy Dacey, the DNC's chief executive officer, called to give Ward a heads-up. Ward was at first shocked. Later, she pressed for an explanation. Why hadn't Dacey told her earlier? After all, the DNC had known for weeks the Russians had compromised its computers and those of the DCCC. Dacey said that the DNC couldn't alert the DCCC because CrowdStrike was trying to kick the Russians out without the hackers discovering they had been caught—and couldn't risk any leaks. Now, weeks later, Ward was furious. Democrats didn't trust fellow Democrats?

After learning of the breach, Ward had hired CrowdStrike as well and soon got back a damage assessment: Fancy Bear had wormed its way into twenty-three separate DCCC computers in seven different departments. It had gained access to the committee's main server, hosting 2.5 million documents. (Fortunately for the DCCC, it kept its email on the cloud.) Hayley Dierker, Ward's chief of staff, began working with the FBI's Adrian Hawkins—the same agent who nearly a year earlier had tried to alert the DNC to the Russian hack. She soon learned something astonishing: The Russians had been using servers at businesses in Virginia and Chicago as pass-throughs for the material they were exfiltrating from the DCCC's computers. She would later be told that the businesses weren't co-conspirators. These firms had no idea that the Russians had covertly commandeered their networks to swipe DCCC documents.

On August 12, Ward and Dierker were meeting at FBI headquarters with Jim Trainor, the cyber chief at the FBI, for an afternoon briefing on the Russian attack. (The day before, Trainor had briefed Donna Brazile, the interim DNC chair, and other party officials on the DNC attack.) Michael Sussmann and Shawn Henry of CrowdStrike were also there. The two women did not find the session useful. It felt as if they were being read the Wikipedia page for Fancy Bear. They had gotten no answers to what worried them the most: Which documents did the Russians steal?

Afterward, the two women were having drinks at Asia Nine, a trendy restaurant near the Hoover building, when Dierker got an alert: Guccifer 2.0 had struck again. "It's time for new revelations now," he proclaimed on his website. Some hacked DCCC documents had appeared in earlier dumps, but they hadn't made much of a splash. But now the suspected Russian intelligence front posted a cache of DCCC records that included log-in details for DCCC accounts and a strategy memo for a key congressional race in Florida. But the most immediate problem was that Guccifer 2.0 also released a document listing the phone numbers, email addresses, and home addresses of all Democratic members of the House.

The DCCC quickly set up a war room to deal with this assault. Congress was on recess; most of the members were back in their districts. And now each were vulnerable to protesters—or kooks— who could show up at their residences. The Capitol police dispatched state troopers to many of their homes. Two of them were vandalized. Some representatives immediately began to get abusive and angry calls, texts, and emails. Representative Emanuel Cleaver from Missouri received what he called "an avalanche of mean-spirited phone calls" that came from people using profanity and the N-word, while obscene and racist emails poured into his inbox.

Pelosi the next day sent a letter to all Democratic House members to inform them of this "electronic Watergate break-in." She advised her colleagues to not let family members read incoming texts or answer their phones. Pelosi herself had been victimized. "I have received scores of mostly obscene and sick calls, voicemails, and text messages," she wrote.

Pelosi held an emergency conference call for all members of the Democratic caucus. It was a dispiriting session. Panicky members peppered Pelosi with questions about whether they had to change their cell phone numbers and personal emails. It was every man and woman for themself. "They weren't discussing the greater threat," a participant on the call later said. "They weren't talking about what to do about the Russians."

Guccifer 2.0's dump with the personal data of Democrats was just the beginning. In the following weeks, Guccifer 2.0 orchestrated a series of releases containing some of the DCCC's most sensitive strategy files, field plans, finance documents, and crucial voter data, including the turnout models the DCCC had developed in different districts. The internet persona gave exclusives to political bloggers in some of the districts and select media outlets, including the *Hill*, the *Daily Caller*, and the *Observer*, which was owned by Jared Kushner. The leaked material included internal memos about crucial swing district races in Florida, Pennsylvania, North Carolina, New Hampshire, and elsewhere.

Perhaps the most damaging documents were candid assessments of Democratic candidates, covering their strengths and weaknesses. Guccifer 2.0 released blunt DCCC memos about a Florida primary battle, in which one candidate, Annette Taddeo—the contender the DCCC favored—was described as a "somewhat poor fundraiser" with a reputation as an "inadequate campaigner." Her Democratic rival, Joe Garcia, whom the DCCC believed to be the weaker candidate for the general election, was a "flashback to a corrupt line of politicians" who "embarrassingly" had been caught on a C-SPAN video "picking his earwax and seemingly eating it."

The DCCC releases did not cause as much of a national political fuss as the DNC emails posted prior to the Democratic convention. But they had a direct impact—and may well have succeeded in influencing elections. In the Florida race, Garcia would make use of the dumped material and defeat Taddeo—only to later lose to his Republican rival. Whether by design or by accident, Guccifer 2.0 had revealed material related to some of the most competitive congressional races of 2016. "We felt what they were doing was strategic and targeted," Ward recalled. "The memos they were dumping were about our most important districts."

Ward, Dierker, and other DCCC staffers knew they were being attacked by Russia—and felt they were utterly on their own. Obama wasn't saying anything. The media was barely covering this. Ward and Dierker tried to get their counterparts at the National Republican Congressional Committee to denounce the Russian attack and eschew using the material Moscow had stolen. But there was no interest from the GOP. Instead, the Republicans would use some of the hacked documents as fodder for TV ads. One GOP-leaning Florida blogger, who eagerly solicited Guccifer 2.0 and posted files from the hacker, profusely thanked him for the material.

"I don't think you realize what you gave me," wrote the anonymous blogger known as HelloFLA! "This is probably worth millions of dollars."

"Hmmm. ok. u owe me a million," Guccifer 2.0 responded.

Manafort—long an obsession for Democratic opposition researchers on the Russian trail—was out of the picture. But now the Democrats were focusing on another Trump ally: Roger Stone.

The sixty-four-year-old Stone was a self-professed practitioner of the dark arts of politics. A onetime Nixon aide—his back bore a tattoo of the thirty-seventh president—Stone prided himself on being an all-out political warrior, willing to sling mud or worse at his foes. Stone told reporters his motto was, "Admit nothing, deny everything, launch counterattack." And he did it with relish, trafficking in conspiracy theories. In 2013, he published a book alleging that Lyndon Johnson had killed John Kennedy. As the 2016 campaign got under way, he published another book, *The Clintons' War on Women*, a savage attack on Hillary Clinton for allegedly targeting women who had accused her husband of misconduct. It carried an approving blurb from Trump: "This book on Hillary—really tough...We appreciate Roger Stone...he is one tough cookie."

Stone had been a friend of Trump's for almost forty years, dating back to the days they both were pals of Roy Cohn, the New York mob lawyer and political fixer who had once been Joe McCarthy's chief counsel. Stone had also been Trump's on-again, off-again political adviser. He had been one of the first hires for the presidential campaign, working with Trump through the first half of 2015 to develop his "Make America Great Again" strategy. But in August of that year, Trump fired Stone—though Stone insisted he had quit, frustrated with Trump's tendency to diverge from the main antiestablishment message of his campaign and become embroiled in "controversies involving personalities and provocative media fights."

Still, Stone remained one of Trump's most ardent champions. "I'm the ultimate Trump loyalist," he declared. At the Republican convention, he and Alex Jones, the notorious Infowars conspiracy theorist, headlined a rally of Trump supporters. In front of the modest-sized crowd, Stone called Hillary Clinton "a short-tempered, foul-mouthed, bipolar, mentally unbalanced criminal." It was typical Stone excess.

And Stone seemed still to be plugged into the Trump camp. At the GOP convention, he told one journalist that in between appearing at events where he called for Clinton to be locked up, he had been meeting with Trump campaign staff and discussing strategy.

So Clinton campaign officials kept a close eye on Stone. If the Trump camp was engaged in anything underhanded, they assumed, Stone would part of the scheme. And in early August they picked up a troubling clue that suggested to them he might be in league with WikiLeaks in relation to the Russia operation.

On August 8, Stone gave a speech to a Florida Republican

group in which he claimed that Clinton's emails would emerge and show "stone-cold proof of the criminality of Bill, Hillary, and Chelsea Clinton." When an attendee asked him what Assange was going to do for an October Surprise to affect the election, Stone replied, "Well, it could be any number of things. I actually have communicated with Assange. I believe the next tranche of his documents pertain to the Clinton Foundation, but there's no telling what the October Surprise may be."

Glen Caplin, the Russia oppo man at Clinton headquarters, and some of his colleagues were astonished by Stone's remarks. They saw this as an admission from a longtime associate of Trump that he was in contact with a key player in the Russian attack on their campaign. Shortly after WikiLeaks had put out the DNC emails prior to the Democratic convention, Assange had told CNN that his website expected to release "a lot more material" related to the election. And now a Trump confidant was publicly saying he was in touch with Assange. "The fact that Roger Stone, who was infamous for dirty tricks, had said this was alarming," Caplin later remarked.

Stone had jumped headfirst into the Russia controversy. A few days before his talk in Florida, he had penned a piece for Steve Bannon's *Breitbart*, in which he claimed Guccifer 2.0 was indeed a lone hacker and responsible for the DNC breach, not the Russians. After Twitter suspended Guccifer 2.0's account for posting the personal information of House Democrats, Stone defended the internet persona, calling the move "outrageous" and asking, "Why are those exposing the truth banned?" He hailed Guccifer 2.0 as a "hero." When the account was restored a few days later, Stone exclaimed in a tweet, "Thank You, Sweet Jesus. I've prayed for it."

Guccifer 2.0 was grateful. In one tweet, the hacker (or hackers) addressed Stone and said, "thanks that u believe in the real #Guccifer2." And after Stone posted a link to a story he had written claiming the election could be "rigged" against Trump, the Guccifer 2.0 Twitter account promoted it and said to Stone, "paying u back." Stone and Guccifer 2.0 even traded private messages on Twitter. In one, Stone asked Guccifer 2.0 to promote a story he had written. And in a private tweet to Stone, Guccifer 2.0. said, "i'm pleased to say that u r great man.... please tell me if i can help u anyhow. it would be a great pleasure to me."

Stone also championed WikiLeaks and Assange, and he kept suggesting he knew what WikiLeaks would next be throwing at Clinton. In an interview with Jerome Corsi, a writer for WorldNet-Daily, a right-wing site, Stone boasted that he had directly interacted with Assange and had learned that the WikiLeaks founder possessed a set of the thirty thousand personal emails Clinton had destroyed. "Assange," Stone said, "claims the emails contain enough damaging information to put Hillary Clinton in jail for selling State Department 'official acts' in exchange for contributions to the Clinton Foundation."

This was amazing news—or would be, if true: Assange possessed Clinton's personal emails. Had Assange really told Stone this? Or was Stone seeking to stir the pot and make trouble however he could?

In between posting tweets in which he claimed that Clinton's health was precarious and alleged that the vote-counting machines were going to be rigged against Trump, Stone kept asserting that Assange had Clinton's emails, that they contained "proof of criminal activity," and that "America will have them soon." In an interview with conservative commentator Dana Loesch, Stone said, "I believe Mr. Assange has all of the emails that Huma Abedin and Cheryl Mills—the two top Clinton aides—believed they had destroyed.... So, Assange is going to be very influential in this election."

At the time, it looked to the Clinton staffers—and many others—that Stone might well have an inside track with WikiLeaks and, by extension, the Russians. They were worried more hacked materials—including John Podesta's emails—might yet be coming out. And when Stone tweeted on August 21, "Trust me, it will soon [be] Podesta's time in the barrel," they took notice. Stone's tweet made them wonder if their worst fears might soon come true.

Stone later claimed that he never had communicated directly with Assange—and there was no public evidence to the contrary.

Everything he knew about WikiLeaks' plans, he insisted, he had gleaned from Assange's own tweets, which he then "confirmed" in "multiple conversations" throughout August and September with his "back-channel" to Assange: Randy Credico, a New York radio show host and comic who was an Assange champion.

There was, however, a problem with Stone's story. According to Credico, he had never spoken to Assange until the WikiLeaks founder was a guest on his show on August 25—seventeen days after Stone first claimed to have "communicated" with Assange. Credico, a left-wing activist and Bernie Sanders supporter, had an unlikely friendship with Stone. But he said he "absolutely" never told Stone anything about Assange's plans to release emails damaging to Clinton—because he never knew anything about them. "He's got me as the fall guy," Credico said. "It's ridiculous."*

---

* Asked about Credico's statements, Stone said, "His memory is either selective or faulty."

CHAPTER 16

"Does it even matter who hacked this data?"

No one else was in the room where it happened. Just Obama and Putin and their translators.

In early September, during the G20 summit in Hangzhou, Obama and Putin had what diplomats called a "sidelines" meeting. For this session, no aides were present. It was as private a conversation as possible between the leaders of nuclear superpowers. It went on for an hour and a half. Afterward, the two men left the conference room, each looking somber and grim-faced. They made no statements to reporters. There was no joint press conference.

A senior White House official told reporters the talks were "candid" and "blunt." He said they were primarily devoted to ending the war in Syria, the still-simmering conflict in Ukraine, and, in a vague reference, Russia's "cyber intrusions." The president informed his aides he had delivered the message he and his advisers had crafted: We know what you're doing; if you don't cut it out, we will impose onerous and unprecedented penalties. One senior U.S. government official briefed on the meeting was told the president said to Putin in effect: "You fuck with us over the election and we'll crash your economy."

Putin had denied everything to Obama—and, as he had done before, blamed the United States for interfering in Russian politics. His response was hardly a surprise. Four days earlier, in an interview with *Bloomberg* in Vladivostok, Putin had dismissed the cyberattack on the DNC. "I don't know anything about it, and on a state level Russia has never done this," he said. Then he echoed the arguments of Julian Assange: "Does it even matter who hacked this data? The important thing is the content that was given to the public." Putin, never known for his commitment to transparency in Russia, was now the advocate for the American public's right to know.

If Obama was tough in private, publicly he played the statesman. Asked at a post-summit news conference about Russia's hacking of the election, the president spoke in generalities—and insisted the United States did not want a blowup over the issue. "We've had problems with cyber intrusions from Russia in the past, from other countries in the past," he said. "Our goal is not to suddenly, in the cyber arena, duplicate a cycle of escalation that we saw when it comes to other arms races in the past, but rather to start instituting some norms so that everybody's acting responsibly."

John Podesta, Clinton's campaign chairman, listened intently to Obama's post-G20 press conference and was disappointed. He wanted more out of Obama, not this tepid response—especially on a day when the *Washington Post* was reporting that U.S. intelligence and law enforcement agencies were "investigating what they see as a broad covert Russian operation in the United States to sow public distrust in the upcoming presidential election and in U.S. political institutions."

For weeks, the Clinton campaign had been trying to promote the case that it was under assault from a Russian government that had close ties to its Republican rival. But as Podesta and other campaign officials saw it, Obama's comments hardly spoke to the gravity of the matter. If the president would not publicly acknowledge the Russian role, it placed them at a serious disadvantage. "If Barack Obama had gone out and said the U.S. was under attack and we're going to take action," a top Clinton adviser later said, "it would have had a major impact on how the story was covered. It would have made people sit up and take notice and remove this impediment. After all, if this was a big deal, wouldn't our government be doing something?"

There was one senior U.S. government official willing to speak out about the Russian hack, and it was the last person the Clinton campaign would have expected to come to its rescue: James Comey.

The FBI director had decided he would draft an op-ed to run in either the *New York Times* or the *Washington Post* that spelled out Russia's meddling and explained that this was a new national security threat that the government and the public needed to take seriously. Comey wrote a draft of the article and told officials at the White House he planned to submit it to run the Sunday after the G20 summit. Then some White House aides identified a problem: that Sunday was September 11. Maybe this wasn't the best day for the FBI director to be talking about anything other than the memory of the nearly three thousand Americans killed in the terror attack. Comey pulled back his plans to submit the piece for that weekend. Afterward, White House officials nixed the idea entirely. If the government was going to speak out on this issue, it would do so with one voice through the intelligence community. The piece never ran.

Trump was still dismissing the notion of any Russian involvement. He gave an interview that week to veteran broadcaster Larry King. "I think maybe the Democrats are putting that out," he said, when asked about claims of Russian hacking of the election. "Who knows, but I think it's pretty unlikely." Trump campaign aides would later say the candidate thought the interview would run on King's podcast. In fact, it ran on King's new TV outlet: RT, the Russian propaganda station.

Days after Obama was back from China, he called the four congressional leaders—Mitch McConnell, Paul Ryan, Harry Reid, and Nancy Pelosi—to the Oval Office. The White House had been trying for the past couple of weeks to hold such a session, but

McConnell and Ryan had claimed scheduling conflicts. Obama's aides wondered if the Republicans were ducking the president.

The official White House schedule noted that the purpose of this meeting was for the president to update the lawmakers on the G20 summit. But the real agenda was the Russian operation. All four had been briefed by Brennan and told the available intelligence indicated that the Russians had launched the operation to derail the U.S. election, harm Clinton, and possibly help Trump, and that it was likely this was a plot approved, if not directed, by Putin.

Now, in this meeting, where none of the legislators were allowed to bring aides, Obama explained that he wanted them to come together, put party aside, and, as the top leaders of the United States, issue a joint public statement declaring there was a potential threat to the election and urging state and local officials to work with the federal government to thwart any attempt to tarnish the election. Obama also hoped that the statement would identify Russia as the source of the threat.

But the plea was doomed by the poisonous political atmosphere in Washington. The main obstacle was McConnell. Obama and his top aides viewed the Senate majority leader as an unrelenting partisan. He had blocked the president's initiatives for years and, most recently, wouldn't even allow the Senate to vote on Obama's Supreme Court pick. For his part, McConnell didn't trust Obama and suspected that he and his senior aides were hyping the intelligence to help Clinton.

In the Oval Office meeting, McConnell told the president he thought he was trying to politicize the matter. He wouldn't help him do so by signing off on any bipartisan message. "To our dismay and disbelief McConnell said this was BS, you're just trying to help Hillary Clinton," one senior administration aide later said. Ryan wasn't quite as adamant. Still, it was election season. McConnell realized that if he accepted Obama's request, he would essentially be undercutting his own party's nominee. Any damage to Trump's campaign would also hurt Republican candidates running for the Senate and threaten McConnell's position as majority leader. Trump's refusal to acknowledge the Russian hacking was preventing McConnell from cooperating with Obama.

In the days after the meeting, Jeh Johnson and Lisa Monaco briefed other members of Congress. And McDonough and Monaco attempted to persuade McConnell to change his mind. Ryan, too, tried. He told White House aides that they should let him work on McConnell, saying that maybe he could bring the majority leader around. (Ryan had long functioned as an intermediary between the White House and McConnell.) But McConnell held firm.

By now, the White House was caught in a squeeze. Top Democrats on the intelligence committees were restless. It had been two months since the intelligence community had reached the conclusion that Russia was threatening the election and was behind the WikiLeaks dump at the Democratic convention. Yet the White House had said nothing about it.

Senator Dianne Feinstein, the ranking Democrat on the Senate Intelligence Committee, and Representative Adam Schiff, her counterpart on the House intelligence panel, had both been briefed by Brennan and were distressed. They began pressing the White House to speak out and tell the public what was going on. Feinstein was being egged on by Hillary Clinton, who would occasionally stay at her house in California. Schiff viewed the matter in a larger context: He had been concerned for some time about the administration's failure to publicly attribute cyber hacks to their state sponsors, arguing that this made such attacks a "penalty-free enterprise." He wanted more than just a public statement. He wanted the White House to start talking to European allies about sanctions.

In Feinstein and Schiff's view, this was not something that should wait until after the election. The pair spoke with other Democrats on the Hill, who agreed: The American public had to be told. If the White House would not say anything, Feinstein and Schiff were prepared to issue their own statement holding the Russians accountable.

White House officials were not happy. They were still hoping they could win over McConnell. If two top congressional Democrats spoke out on the issue, it would only reinforce McConnell's view that the whole thing was partisan. McDonough was assigned the task of keeping Feinstein and Schiff bottled up.

McDonough pleaded with the two Democrats to hold off. He conveyed to them the White House belief that a partisan statement attributing the hacks and dumps to the Russians would play into Trump's narrative that the election was rigged and spread uncertainty about the election. He raised other objections: A public statement by them would impede the effort to work with the state and local election officials, especially in red states where suspicions about the administration ran high. He urged Feinstein and Schiff to wait, while the White House kept pressuring McConnell and Ryan to sign on to the letter they wanted to send to the state officials. This whole episode, aides later said, irritated Obama.

Schiff and Feinstein agreed to hold back for a few days. But they soon tired of waiting and, on September 22, released a brief but powerful four-paragraph statement. "Based on briefings we have received," it said, "we have concluded that the Russian intelligence agencies are making a serious and concerted effort to influence the U.S. election." The pair reported that the effort was "intended to sow doubt about the security of our election and may well be intended to influence the outcomes of the election." And they added, "We believe that orders for the Russian intelligence agencies to conduct such actions could come only from very senior levels of the Russian government." They called on Putin to immediately halt the operation.

Before issuing the statement, Feinstein and Schiff vetted it with the intelligence community. They wanted to be sure they would not inadvertently disclose any secret sources and methods. The IC had no objection. Schiff considered this a bizarre situation: The White House was not willing to publicly identify Russia as the culprit, but the intelligence community was allowing two Democratic members of Congress to cite intelligence briefings to do so—and to basically declare Putin was running this operation.

The Feinstein-Schiff statement, with its reference to the briefings they had received, was a clear public signal that U.S. intelligence agencies had concluded Russian intelligence, on Putin's orders, was attempting to subvert an American presidential election. Reporting on the statement, the *Washington Post* noted, "The blunt language goes far beyond the more equivocal characterizations issued by the White House and U.S. intelligence agencies, which have so far been unwilling to explicitly blame Moscow."

Even so, Feinstein and Schiff's effort made barely a ripple. It had been released by two Democratic partisans and did not have the official imprimatur of the U.S. intelligence community. Their letter received relatively little attention. Stories about it ran inside the major newspapers, and it went unmentioned on the network news.

Unable to yet coax a statement out of McConnell, the Obama administration now redoubled its efforts to reach out to local election officials. The idea of vote tampering was still the top concern. In mid-September, Johnson issued his own statement noting DHS had seen "efforts at cyber intrusions of voter registration data maintained in state election systems." He said the DHS was "ready to assist state and local election officials in protecting their systems." Johnson added, "We strongly encourage more state and local election officials to do so."

This was not a message to convince (or scare) anyone into fully cooperating with the federal government. Nor did it convey the apprehension at the top levels of the U.S. government about the nearing election. But it was the best the administration could manage, while waiting for McConnell.

That wait did not pay off. A week after Feinstein and Schiff sounded the alarm, the four leaders of Congress, including McConnell, finally issued a letter. It was not the clear warning the White House had envisioned. The letter was brief. It declared that "states face the challenge of malefactors that are seeking to use cyberattacks to disrupt the administration of our elections." There was no mention of Russia. It urged states "to take full advantage of the robust public and private resources available to them to ensure that their network infrastructure is secure from attack."

"Does it even matter who hacked this data?"

The missive held little sense of urgency. It was not much more than an iteration of the obvious and bland encouragement for states to consider seeking help from DHS. Like the Feinstein-Schiff letter, it made no difference.

In September, Matt Tait, the British cybersecurity expert who had helped expose Guccifer 2.0 as a Russian front, received an odd call from Peter W. Smith, a Chicago-based private-equity executive and veteran Republican activist. (A longtime nemesis of the Clintons, Smith in the 1990s helped fund the research for Troopergate—the story that quoted Arkansas state troopers saying they arranged sexual liaisons for Bill Clinton when he was Arkansas governor.)

Smith was on a quest for the Holy Grail: Hillary Clinton's deleted emails. He told Tait that he had been contacted by someone on the Dark Web—a corner of the internet that is invisible to search engines and allows for anonymous communications, often for illegal transactions. This contact claimed to possess the private emails Clinton had deleted from her server. Smith asked if Tait could help him determine if the emails were authentic.

Tait assumed Smith had reached out to him because he had been going through the thousands of Clinton's State Department emails that were being released in batches by the department each month and tweeting out interesting nuggets. Tait hadn't been looking to score partisan points. He was mostly interested in the emails for insights into Clinton's thinking about national security and cyber issues. He was willing to hear Smith out, but he soon grew a bit suspicious of him and even more about his supposed Dark Web contact.

Smith was cagey in talking about whoever this Dark Web source was. He never identified the person or explained how they connected. After a few conversations, Tait warned Smith that his mysterious source might be part of a Russian clandestine influence campaign—to entice Smith and end up supplying him with doctored emails. But Smith was undeterred.

Even more concerning for Tait, Smith gave the impression he was somehow involved with the Trump campaign—that he was in touch with Michael Flynn, Flynn's son, and other top campaign aides. He talked like a Trump insider, sharing tales from the campaign. He even was planning to set up an off-the-books oppo research operation for Trump. He sent a memo to Tait—presumably by mistake—that described a company Smith had set up as a Delaware LLC called KLS Research to conduct opposition research for the Trump campaign, but in a way "to avoid campaign reporting." The memo noted that several senior Trump campaign aides were involved in the project, including Steve Bannon, Kellyanne Conway, Michael Flynn, Sam Clovis, and Lisa Nelson. Tait's name was also listed, though he had not agreed to be part of this project—and would not have, if asked.

Whether Smith ever had any contact with Trump insiders was never clear to Tait, whose conversations with Smith petered out. Bannon and Conway would both later say they didn't know who he was. But Smith plowed ahead on his quest for the Clinton emails, enlisting other technology experts, including a Russian-speaking investigator in Europe. After the election, Smith would tell the *Wall Street Journal* that he had found five groups of hackers that claimed to have the Clinton emails, including two that were Russian. He said he had obtained batches of these emails, but he could not determine if they were genuine. He suggested to the hackers they should take them to WikiLeaks.

The whole episode was murky save for one piece of intriguing intelligence that the *Journal* came across in reporting its story: U.S. intelligence agencies had collected information indicating that Russian hackers were indeed discussing how to find Clinton's emails and how to get them to Flynn through a cutout. Whether Smith was the cutout was never determined.

In May 2017, about ten days after he discussed his campaign project with the *Journal*, the eighty-one-year-old Smith committed suicide by asphyxiating himself in a hotel room in Rochester, Minnesota. According to local authorities, he left a note that said, "no foul play whatsoever."

CHAPTER 17

"It also could be somebody sitting on their bed who weighs four hundred pounds, OK?"

By mid-September, Glenn Simpson was getting frustrated.

The memos from Christopher Steele were still coming in with more wild and fascinating—but unconfirmed—tidbits from his Russian émigré collector. The new reports, if anything, were more incriminating than the first ones. In his initial June report, Steele had written that the Kremlin had been "cultivating" Trump for "at least 5 years." A report Steele sent to Simpson on July 30 went further. It quoted a source claiming there had been a "regular exchange" of information between Trump and the Kremlin "for at least 8 years." Putin was supposedly relying on Trump and his associates for intelligence on the activities of Russian oligarchs inside the United States, a subject of great interest to the Russian president. In exchange for the "high levels of voluntary co-operation," the Russians had "promised" not to use their *kompromat* on Trump.

And *kompromat* there was—"plenty" of it, according to Steele.

It wasn't only the "golden showers" incident in the Moscow hotel room. A Steele report dated September 14 cited "two knowledge-able St Petersburg sources" claiming that Trump had paid bribes during visits to that city to try to get business deals and "partici-pated in sex parties." Aras Agalarov, Trump's business partner in the Miss Universe pageant, supposedly knew all about these esca-pades. But "all direct witnesses" had been silenced—"bribed or coerced to disappear."

Simpson would read these reports and throw up his hands. The main purpose of opposition research was to develop informa-tion about the rival candidate that could be of some utility to the client—as material for television attack ads or talking points dur-ing a debate. What was he supposed to do with this stuff? What could the Clinton campaign possibly do with it? There was no way to verify most of it. "Chris' stuff was almost unusable," Simpson would later tell colleagues.

Even Steele's partner, Chris Burrows, had his doubts about the veracity of some of this material. But one factor mitigated any con-cerns: Everyone assumed Clinton was going to beat Trump. "We were fairly relaxed about producing stuff about a candidate that is not going to win," Burrows later said privately.

And yet, for all the sensational and uncorroborated claims, Steele had clearly stumbled upon a larger truth: There was indeed an ambitious campaign by the Kremlin to influence the American electorate. The DNC hack and the dumping of emails by WikiLeaks had proven that. And it was a campaign that, according to Steele's reporting, had produced turmoil within the Kremlin. Peskov, Putin's trusted spokesman who was allegedly overseeing the campaign, was supposedly "scared shitless" that he would be scapegoated if there were a backlash against Russia's interference in the election. A Rus-sian diplomat in Washington who was said to have been involved in the operation had been withdrawn for fear his role might be exposed. (It would later turn out that a Kremlin diplomat with a similar name was in fact sent back to Moscow around this time.) Yet Putin himself appeared to be not worried. He was, Steele wrote, "generally satis-fied with the progress of the anti-CLINTON operation to date."

There was a warning in Steele's latest reports to Simpson: More was coming. The Russians had additional *kompromat* on Clinton, and consideration was being given to releasing it through "plausibly deniable" channels. More Clinton email dumps? That tracked with what Julian Assange—and Roger Stone—had been telegraphing.

At this point, Simpson knew something that almost nobody else did: Steele had given his initial reports to the FBI and the Bureau was reviewing them. So he figured out a way to put Steele's material to use. He would bring Steele to Washington and have him brief a small number of reporters. Then, he hoped, the reporters would tap their sources and sniff out what the FBI was doing with all of this. It might even prod the Bureau to take Steele's reports more seriously.

Simpson focused on one of Steele's reports that had nothing to do with sex parties: the memo about the trip Carter Page, a member of the Trump foreign policy team, had made to Moscow in early July. Steele's report alleged that while there Page had met with senior Russian officials—including Rosneft chief Igor Sechin, a Putin crony sanctioned by the United States over the Russian intervention in Ukraine. Page and Sechin supposedly discussed a possible deal about the lifting of sanctions under a Trump presidency. It was provocative and possibly checkable information that could well be evidence of collusion between the GOP candidate's campaign and the Kremlin.

Simpson wasn't the only one thinking along these lines. In late August, Democratic Senate leader Harry Reid, while in his hometown of Las Vegas, had received an unexpected call from CIA director John Brennan. Could he find a location where they could have a secure phone call? Brennan asked him. This was unusual. Of course, Reid said. He arranged to go to the local FBI office where he got a fifteen-minute briefing on a secure line on the latest intelligence about the Russian interference in the U.S. election.

What Brennan told him that morning was the same briefing he was giving to the Gang of Eight—the majority and minority leaders of the House and Senate and the top Democrats and Republicans on the two congressional intelligence committees. But the fact that he had reached out during the congressional recess to speak, one on one, with Reid was a sign of urgency.

Brennan provided Reid the full picture. The intelligence community had concluded Moscow had pulled off the hacks of Democratic targets and the subsequent dumps of documents, and Putin was behind it. Worse, there were indications Moscow's covert tech operatives might try to mess with election systems and even tamper with the results. Brennan also shared the suspicions within the intelligence community that Trump associates had been in contact with Russians and possibly involved in the Russian clandestine campaign.

After the call, Reid seemed shaken, according to an aide traveling with him. Reid also had the impression that Brennan had an ulterior motive. He concluded the CIA chief believed the public needed to know about the Russian operation, including the information about the possible links to the Trump campaign. When Reid later was asked if Brennan directly or indirectly had enlisted him to push information held by the intelligence community into the public realm, he told an interviewer, "Why do you think he called me?"

So Reid went public. On August 27, two days after his briefing, Reid wrote FBI director Comey an extraordinary letter. He had recently become concerned "that the threat of the Russian government tampering in our presidential election is more extensive than widely known and may include the intent to falsify official election results." Then he added: "The evidence of a direct connection between the Russian government and Donald Trump's presidential campaign continues to mount. . . . The prospect of a hostile government actively seeking to undermine our free and fair elections represents one of the gravest threats to our democracy since the Cold War."

These were startling claims. But Reid, every bit as fierce a partisan as his GOP counterpart McConnell, had an agenda. He wanted the FBI to investigate the Trump campaign—and he wanted the public to know about it. The links between the Trump campaign and the Kremlin, he wrote, needed to be probed "thoroughly and in a timely fashion." And he set a deadline for the Bureau to release its findings to American voters: before the election.

Reid was a twenty-nine-year veteran of the Senate who had received many intelligence briefings. He knew Senate rules and the law as well as anybody: He couldn't use any details Brennan had told him in a classified briefing in a public letter. To back up his assertions of possible links between Trump operatives and the Russians, he mostly cited media reports. He mentioned an individual "with long ties to Donald Trump"—a reference to Roger Stone— who had claimed to be in communication with WikiLeaks. He talked about how the Trump campaign had employed people with "significant and disturbing ties" to the Kremlin—an apparent reference to Manafort and Flynn.

Then Reid cited something else that had not been the subject of any media coverage. He referred to a "series of disturbing reports" about a Trump adviser who gave a speech in Moscow in July and met with "high-ranking sanctioned individuals"—a clear reference to Page.

But there had been no news stories about such a meeting, and Reid didn't say what "disturbing reports" he was referring to or how he knew about them. Simpson had not briefed Reid. But Elias, the Clinton campaign lawyer who was the attorney for Reid's Super PAC, had informed Mook about the alleged Page meetings in Moscow, and Clinton campaign officials were in regular touch with Reid.

However Reid learned about the Page allegation, his reference to a meeting with "sanctioned individuals" was significant. Though no reporters picked up on that sentence, it was the first time Steele's unconfirmed reporting had seeped into the public discourse.

Two weeks after Reid's letter to Comey, Simpson and his Fusion GPS partner, Peter Fritsch, booked a private room at the Tabard Inn, a bohemian hotel and bar long a favorite of Washington journalists. It would serve as something of a private salon for Steele and reporters. Simpson invited investigative journalists who covered national security, not politics. He told them they would get to meet an impeccable source: a well-connected former intelligence operative who had some important information about Trump and the Russians. Among those Simpson invited for individual briefings at the Tabard that day were reporters for the *New York Times*, the *Washington Post*, and CNN, and Yahoo News' Michael Isikoff.

It was the first time Isikoff met Steele, and the journalist was impressed by his credentials. Steele explained who he was—a former MI6 spy who had served in Moscow. Wearing a starched white shirt, he was grave and all business. He was not there for small talk. Emphasizing that he believed what he had discovered was truly disturbing, Steele laid out his story about Carter Page and his trip to Moscow. He told Isikoff what had been reported to him from sources inside Russia: that Page had met with Rosneft chief Sechin, one of Putin's closest intimates, and they had discussed a possible deal for the lifting of sanctions. Steele also mentioned Page's supposed meeting with Igor Diveykin, a top Putin aide. Steele wouldn't say anything about his sources. That was strictly confidential. After all, this was Russia—where sources could be shot or poisoned for talking about such matters.

But Steele did mention that all this information had been reported to the FBI. That, more than anything, got Isikoff's attention. He pressed Steele: Had he personally briefed the FBI? You can assume that, Steele said, although he wouldn't say who he had briefed. What was the Bureau's reaction? Were they inclined to pursue it? Yes, Steele told Isikoff. There were people in the Bureau taking this very seriously. When Isikoff heard this, he realized he might have a potentially explosive lead: The FBI was investigating somebody in Trump's campaign.

There were strict ground rules for this meeting. It was on background. That meant Steele could not be quoted by name or referred to as an ex-MI6 officer. He was to be described as a Western "intelligence source"—which was true, since he had been a steady source of intelligence for the FBI. But when Isikoff left the Tabard, after a conversation that lasted about an hour, he figured he had more than enough to work with.

When he got back to the office, Isikoff called Jonathan Winer at the State Department; he had known Winer for years. Simpson had told him Winer could vouch for Steele. Yes, Steele was an absolutely reliable source, Winer said. Isikoff called another State Department official who had worked on Russian affairs. The source didn't know about Page's alleged meetings in Moscow but knew about Page. U.S. officials had taken notice of his previous trips to Russia, as well his provocative comments critical of U.S. policy and sympathetic to Putin. "He was pretty much a brazen apologist for anything Moscow did," the official said.

Isikoff also reached out to Page. He left him two voice mails and sent him two emails. In the last email, he said he wanted to talk to Page about his meetings in Moscow in July before writing any story. Page never responded. But Isikoff did get through to a senior U.S. law enforcement official. He asked about Reid's letter and its obvious reference to Page's alleged meeting with Sechin. "It's on our radar screen," the official said. "It's being looked at."

Isikoff's story ran on the Yahoo website on September 23. "U.S. Intel Officials Probe Ties Between Trump Adviser and Kremlin" was the headline. It reported that officials were "seeking to determine" if Page had private communications with senior Russian officials about the possible lifting of economic sanctions if Trump became president. The story quoted Reid's letter and sources who said concerns about Page were raised in intelligence briefings for senior members of Congress. It cited a "Western intelligence source" (Steele) confirming "intelligence reports" (Steele's own reports) provided to U.S. officials about the allegation that Page had met with Sechin. Such a meeting, "if confirmed," Isikoff wrote, would be viewed by U.S. officials as serious given that Sechin had been blacklisted by the Treasury Department.

It was the first story to reveal a U.S. intelligence investigation into the Russian ties of a Trump campaign figure.*

A month later, the FBI obtained a secret Foreign Intelligence

---

* In September 2017, Page sued Oath Inc., which owned Yahoo and HuffPost, filing a complaint claiming this article had defamed him and endangered his life. He was acting as his own lawyer.

Surveillance Court warrant to monitor Page's communications after persuading a federal judge that there was "probable cause" to believe he was "acting as an agent of a foreign power."*

A few days after the Yahoo story, the *Washington Post*'s Josh Rogin heard from Page and wrote a column. Page told him the allegations in the article were "just complete garbage" and that he had never met with Sechin or Diveykin. Still, Page told Rogin, he was taking a leave of absence from the Trump campaign.

Page gave Rogin a copy of a letter he had sent to Comey after the Yahoo story was posted. In the letter, Page said he would "eagerly await" the call from FBI agents so he could respond to these "outrageous" allegations. He didn't mention in the letter that while in Moscow he had met with one of Sechin's deputies and that after his trip he had emailed the Trump campaign to say that he had obtained "incredible insights" from Russian legislators and "senior members" of Putin's regime.

In Brooklyn, Clinton campaign officials jumped on Isikoff's story and promoted it to reporters. "It's chilling to learn that U.S. intelligence officials are conducting a probe into suspected meetings between Trump's foreign policy adviser . . . and members of Putin's inner circle while in Moscow," Glen Caplin, a Clinton aide working on the Russia issue, said in a statement released by the campaign. "This is serious business and voters deserve the facts before election day."

By this point, reporters were beginning to call and tell campaign officials they were pursuing leads and rumors about other possible Trump-Russia ties—and they asked what the Clintonites had picked up. One story making the rounds among Washington reporters was that there was an unusual link between an email

---

* In February 2018, Republicans on the House Intelligence Committee released a memo alleging Steele's reports were improperly used by the FBI in its application to obtain the FISA warrant. The memo claimed the application "extensively cited" Isikoff's story. The FBI said it had "grave concerns about material omissions" in the memo that "fundamentally impact" its accuracy.

server associated with Trump's company and Alfa Bank, the largest private commercial bank in Russia. Clinton officials pushed journalists hard to dig into this, hoping that this would be the story to break through and define Trump as a Putin stooge. Coincidentally or not, Steele had just filed a new memo flagging the "current closeness" of the "Alpha Group-PUTIN relationship" and that "significant favours continued to be done in both directions."

Elias, the Democratic lawyer, was circumspect about what he did with Steele's memos. He would at times brief Mook on their contents. But he didn't want hard copies floating around and didn't share the actual reports with the campaign. An episode from 2012 was guiding his thinking. That year, the DCCC put out a press release claiming GOP billionaire megadonor and casino owner Sheldon Adelson was tied to the Chinese mob and a prostitution ring. Adelson threatened to sue the DCCC for defamation and libel, and with his deep pockets he could have mounted a legal action that would crush the party organization. The DCCC issued a retraction and publicly apologized. Elias was not eager for a repeat of that experience—not with the famously litigious Trump. He knew what might result if any of Steele's memos, filled with unverified allegations, ever became public.

And the dumps kept coming. DCLeaks posted emails stolen from the Gmail account of Ian Mellul, a young Democratic operative who had moved from the White House staff to Clinton's campaign. Days later, several media outlets posted a hacked audio that had been part of Mellul's email files, and it captured Clinton at a February fundraiser describing Sanders supporters as "children of the Great Recession" who are "living in their parents' basement." Clinton's foes jumped on this remark, claiming she was being dismissive of young people supporting Sanders—though her campaign maintained she had been expressing sympathy for frustrated young adults.

Yet Trump once against exploited the Russian hacking operation, blasting Clinton for demeaning Sanders voters. In a tweet, he exclaimed, "Crooked H is nasty to Sanders supporters behind closed doors. Owned by Wall St and Politicians, HRC is not with you."

September had not been kind to Clinton. Early in the month she had given a speech decrying Trump for attracting racists, misogynists, homophones, xenophobes, and Islamophobes, and she remarked that half of Trump supporters were a "basket of deplorables"—a phrase that backfired against her politically. And a few days later, she had almost collapsed at a 9/11 memorial service in New York City. She had been battling pneumonia at the time but had kept that a secret. Donna Brazile, the interim DNC chair, would later write that she was so concerned about Clinton's health that she began thinking of ways to replace her on the Democratic ticket. Moreover, the polls tightened at the start of the month, though Clinton still maintained a close but respectable lead.

Both campaigns were now planning for their first big showdown—the first of three debates. This one would be held at Hofstra University on Long Island. There was no question the Russia issue would come up. About two-thirds of the way into the contentious debate, the moderator, NBC News anchor Lester Holt, asked Clinton: What could be done to thwart cyberattacks on the United States?

Clinton hit the Russia connection hard. "There is no doubt now that Russia has used cyberattacks against all kinds of organizations in our country," she said. "And I am deeply concerned about this. I know Donald's very praiseworthy of Vladimir Putin, but Putin is playing a really tough, long game here. And one of the things he's done is to let loose cyberattackers to hack into government files, to hack into personal files, hack into the Democratic National Committee. And we recently have learned that, you know, that this is one of their preferred methods of trying to wreak havoc." Then she brought up Trump's invitation to hack her deleted emails. "I was so shocked when Donald publicly invited Putin to hack into Americans. That is just unacceptable."

Trump, predictably, was dismissive of the whole issue, including the idea that Moscow had hacked the DNC. "She is saying Russia,

Russia, Russia. But I don't—maybe it was. I mean, it could be Russia, but it could also be China, it could also be lots of other people. It also could be somebody sitting on their bed who weighs four hundred pounds, OK?" He then wandered off to a strange place: "So we have to get very very tough on cyber and cyber warfare. It is a huge problem. I have a son—he's ten years old. He has computers. He is so good with these computers. It's unbelievable."

On September 28, Jim Comey sat down at a table in a committee room of the House Rayburn Office Building and prepared to be grilled by members of Congress. The occasion was a regular public oversight hearing conducted by the House Judiciary Committee. But the most pressing question for the Democrats was what the FBI was doing to investigate connections between the Trump campaign and Russia.

"Is the FBI investigating the activities of Mr. Trump or any adviser to the Trump campaign with respect to any line of communication between the campaign and the Russian government?" Representative John Conyers of Michigan, the senior Democrat on the panel, asked. Comey replied without hesitation: "I can't say, sir. . . . We don't confirm or deny investigations." Another Democratic member asked if the FBI had questioned Roger Stone about his communications with Julian Assange or his interactions with WikiLeaks. Comey answered, "I can't comment on that." What about Paul Manafort and his work in Ukraine? Again, no comment. Comey was asked about the statement recently issued by Feinstein and Schiff that said, "Russian intelligence agencies are making a serious and concerted effort to influence the U.S. election." Comey responded, "I can't comment on that in this forum."

Democrats on the panel became exasperated. There was no word coming out of the federal government about the Russian assault—which was targeting their party and its nominees—or the suspicions widely held within the intelligence community that there were some odd associations between Trump's world and Moscow.

Comey, the Democrats pointed out, had in a rather public manner discussed the Clinton email server investigation, in a major departure from FBI policy. So why not be evenhanded and disclose whether the Trump campaign was the subject of an investigation. "Is there a different standard for Secretary Clinton and Donald Trump?" asked Representative Jerry Nadler of New York.

"No," Comey replied. "Our standard is we do not confirm or deny the existence of investigations. There is an exception for that: when there is a need for the public to be reassured; when it is obvious it is apparent, given our activities, public activities, that the investigation is ongoing. But our overwhelming rule is we do not comment except in certain exceptional circumstances."

Comey was in a box. In the case of Clinton, the Bureau's probe had become public because the inspectors general of the intelligence community and the State Department had each made referrals to the Justice Department about the former secretary's handling of classified information—and that step had been reported to Congress. But the Trump campaign probe fell into a different category. It was a counterintelligence investigation—by its nature, classified. It involved ongoing activity involving suspected Russian intelligence agents. There was no way Comey could publicly confirm its existence without tipping off some of the suspects and sabotaging the work of his own agents.

In early October, Steele traveled from London to Rome to meet with FBI agent Mike Gaeta. It was a follow-up session to their earlier meeting in London in July. Headquarters considered this a highly serious matter; four senior FBI counterintelligence officials flew over from Washington to sit in. Gaeta had told Steele that the Bureau was prepared to cover his travel expenses.

The FBI pumped Steele for information about his memos: who were his sources and how was the material collected. Steele was careful; he couldn't reveal much without endangering the lives of his "sub-sources" who were talking to his main "collector."

FBI meetings with informants and sources are often one-way streets: The agents take in what the subjects say and reveal little, if anything, of what they already know. But Steele was a former officer in an allied intelligence service and had a solid track record. So the agents disclosed a striking piece of intelligence to him. The Bureau, he was told, had received information on contacts between suspected Kremlin cutouts and George Papadopoulos. This was a reference to the report the Australian government had passed to Washington two months earlier revealing that Papadopoulos had told an Aussie diplomat that Russia had dirt on Clinton.

The Bureau wanted to determine what Steele might have to add. It made Steele an offer: The Bureau would provide him a $50,000 contract if he worked with the FBI and supplied information about links between the Trump campaign and Moscow.

Later on, Steele would insist that the money was beside the point. (The contract would never be implemented, and Steele would not even be reimbursed the £1,200 he spent on the Rome trip.) "I wasn't asking them for money," he told colleagues. "I was coming forward because it was my duty. We were seeing stuff on the ground that affected national security. It was fucking obvious what was going on." That is, there was a Russian active-measures operation to penetrate the Trump campaign. "We were doing the right thing," he added. And he would defend his work: "You think if I was peddling false information about Russia, I'd still be in business?"

In the early days of October, Roger Stone once again began to stir the pot. At 12:52 A.M. on Sunday, October 2, Stone tweeted, "Wednesday@HillaryClinton is done. #Wikileaks." Later that same day, Stone appeared on the show of Infowars conspiracy theorist Alex Jones and declared, "I'm assured the motherlode is coming Wednesday." The release would be "devastating," he predicted. He also asserted that Assange was scared "the globalists and the Clintonites are trying to figure out how to kill him." And on October 3, Stone put out this tweet: "I have total confidence that @Wikileaks and my hero Julian Assange will educate the American people soon #LockHerUp."

Clinton aides were watching Stone's tweets the way seismologists look for tremors before the big quakes. And these tweets were seen as a code-red warning sign. But they weren't the only ones paying close attention.

Donald Trump Jr. had intermittently been in private contact with WikiLeaks, and now he wanted to know more about Stone's taunting prediction. A couple of weeks earlier, on September 20, the WikiLeaks Twitter account had sent Trump Jr. a private message asking him about a new election blog called PutinTrump.org that had been created by a political action committee funded by a liberal internet entrepreneur. "Off the record I don't know who that is, but I'll ask around," Trump Jr. replied. And he had emailed Bannon, Kushner, and Conway about his exchange with WikiLeaks.

Now, on October 3, WikiLeaks contacted him again with a private request. "Hiya, it'd be great if you guys could comment on/ push this story," WikiLeaks suggested, attaching an article alleging (probably falsely) that Clinton had once suggested she wanted to "just drone" Assange. "Already did that earlier today," Trump Jr. responded. "It's amazing what she can get away with."

Two minutes later, Trump Jr., now looking for some inside information, messaged WikiLeaks. Referring to the Stone tweet, he asked, "What's behind this Wednesday leak I keep reading about?" Trump Jr. asked. In this instance, WikiLeaks didn't respond.

In the weeks since Obama had warned Putin to "cut it out," White House officials had continued to grapple with what to do about Russia's actions. With the failure to win over McConnell, Obama and his top advisers had decided that the administration itself would have to issue a statement tagging Moscow as responsible for the hacks. Some Cabinet members disagreed, arguing that intelligence sources and methods could be compromised or that issuing an attribution might in and of itself undermine the election.

But the intelligence kept getting stronger. One report based on intelligence intercepts—labeled Top Secret/SCI (for Sensitive Compartmented Information)—revealed that after WikiLeaks had dumped the DNC emails in July, Kremlin officials were congratulating themselves on a job well done. "We all looked at it, and said 'fuck,'" one official who reviewed the report later said. "The

Russians were talking, telling one another, 'great job.' It was pretty specific. They were celebrating their success." One Russian official referred to the operation having been done "at the direction of our leadership."

"In the end, we concluded we had to tell the public what we knew, and that it would be unforgivable if we did not," Jeh Johnson, the homeland security secretary, recalled. Clapper, too, now argued forcefully for saying something. "If the election did go south for one reason or another, and then afterwards it was learned that we knew about what the Russians were doing and sat silent, there'd be hell to pay," he subsequently said.

The intelligence community was instructed to compose a statement that could be released. To do so meant crafting language that would not blow any secret sources or methods. After working on this for over a month—an amount of time that White House officials considered excessive—the agencies finally had a draft that represented the consensus of the various spy services agencies that Russia was the culprit.

In early October, the principals met twice to discuss the statement and assess the status of the Russian operation. Clapper and Brennan both reported that Russian cyberattacks related to the election seemed to have diminished since Obama's meeting with Putin. There was some activity, but it was hard to figure out how significant it was. There was no intelligence suggesting major new cyber pokes at the election system. "We thought we could ride out the influence campaign the Russians were running [against the Democrats] and that it was not a big deal," one participant in these meetings recalled. "We were still much more agitated the Russians could rig the election." The White House and the intelligence community were oblivious to the other major element of Putin's operation: a vast social media campaign targeting the American electorate.

The intelligence community had come up with a statement that attributed the hack-and-dump operation to the Russian government and that noted the probing of state election systems was related to Russian servers. It did not state that the Kremlin operation aimed to place Trump in the White House. The intelligence on this point was not yet definitive.

All the relevant agencies, including the FBI, CIA, NSA, and DHS, signed off on the conclusions. But over the course of the two meetings, the principals reviewed the wording carefully, even discussing the moving of commas. The intent was to make sure the statement came across as professional and even a bit banal. Just the facts, nothing unnecessarily dramatic. "We were being overly cautious," one participant later noted. "If we played this wrong, we could play into the Russians' hands."

One sentence in particular was debated during these meetings: the one that stated that Putin had authorized the operation.

A near-to-final draft asserted that Putin had personally okayed the information warfare campaign. Given that Putin was the leader of an authoritarian regime, it certainly made sense. But there was concern among some principals that explicitly naming Putin as the ringleader would be an overly provocative step—and could possibly endanger some of the intelligence community's sources. After much discussion, Putin's name was deleted. Instead, the principals opted for less specific wording, fingering senior Kremlin officials.

The final draft was produced, and it bore the logos of all the intelligence agencies involved to show that the entire intelligence community—the FBI, the NSA, the CIA, and others—agreed on the finding. Then in the final principals meeting, Comey raised an objection. He did not want to attach the FBI to the statement.

"It was a jaw-dropping moment," one participant recalled. This was especially so because during the summer Comey had drafted that newspaper op-ed blaming the Russians that the White House had scuttled. But now, with the election closer, Comey had second thoughts.

Is this because you don't agree with the conclusions? Comey was asked.

No, Comey said. He told the others he was worried that it would look as if the FBI was putting its thumb on the scale right before an election. There had long been a tradition of the Bureau not engaging in public actions close to an election that might influence a race.

He did not want to tarnish the FBI's reputation by signing on to a statement that could be viewed as political. Comey did not share what was still a closely held secret: that the Bureau had already launched its counterintelligence investigation of Kremlin contacts with the Trump campaign.

The absence from the statement of the FBI—which had principal responsibility for counterintelligence inside the United States—would look curious and undoubtedly raise questions. Comey's move could undermine the whole point of issuing an assessment, some officials feared.

The principals discussed other options. At one point in the Situation Room, Clapper slipped Johnson a note saying, "Why don't we just issue a joint statement?" And Johnson proposed that DHS and the Office of the Director of National Intelligence, which represented the entire intelligence community, release the statement in their agencies' names. That settled the matter. No one would know that Comey had been unwilling to have the FBI identified with it.

Obama and his advisers decided it would be best to release the statement with little fanfare, with no comment from the president. Obama would not use his bully pulpit to heighten the message being delivered by the intelligence community. The White House wanted to squeeze politics out of this as much as possible. "We were wearing self-imposed handcuffs," a senior White House aide later said. "We would not allow anyone to suggest the president had stepped out of bounds and was using this for political ends."

There was a last-minute hiccup. In the principals meetings, Kerry suggested delaying the statement until after his upcoming talks with Sergey Lavrov in Lausanne, where once again he would be trying to resolve the Syrian conflict. But Obama and other principals wanted the statement out right away. It was scheduled to be released on Friday, October 7.

CHAPTER 18

"Only Russia's senior-most officials could have authorized these activities."

October 7 began with a hurricane—a real one. A category 4 storm named Matthew had wreaked havoc in the Caribbean. And now it was heading toward the Florida coast. Homeland Security Secretary Jeh Johnson was at the White House updating Obama on disaster preparations, when he received a call saying that the Clinton campaign had requested a briefing for the candidate. Sure, Johnson thought, but to be fair he would also have to offer one to Trump.

Shortly after noon, he called Clinton from FEMA headquarters. She asked a few smart questions, including about an arcane matter related to disaster relief legislation that had passed when she was in the Senate.

Afterward, Johnson called Trump and had a conversation he would later describe to colleagues as surreal.

On the speakerphone in his Trump Tower office, the candidate was gregarious. "Hey Jeh, how ya doing?" Trump said. "You're doing a great job. Everybody says you're doing a great job." Johnson filled him in on the government preparations for the hurricane.

Then Trump asked, "What are you doing when you leave office?" Johnson replied he would be returning to his law firm in New York. "When this is over," Trump said, "why don't you come over to the Tower and we'll have lunch?"

Johnson was taken aback. Trump was running for president. If he won, he would be in the White House, not Trump Tower. "There are some scenarios," Johnson gently pointed out, "where we might have to have lunch in Washington, not New York."

"Oh, yeah," Trump replied, as though he had not considered the possibility. Johnson's top aides, who were listening in on the call, were incredulous. It seemed like Trump hadn't given any thought to the idea that he might actually win.

After Johnson got off the phone, his attention turned toward the joint statement he and Clapper had agreed to put out that day officially attributing the hack to Russia. The Office of the Director of National Intelligence was finishing its declassification. It would be released within hours on a Friday afternoon. Having spoken to both candidates, Johnson pondered the weirdness of the moment. "They had no idea of the bombshell we're about to drop on both of them," he thought. The U.S. government in modern times had never accused a foreign nation of intervening in the American political process. Johnson was convinced the release would drive the news cycle. He was wrong.

That morning, Clinton's debate team had set up at the Doral Arrowwood resort in Rye Brook, New York, for a prep session with the candidate. In two days, Clinton would face Trump for their second debate. The group included Jennifer Palmieri, Jake Sullivan, John Podesta, Joel Benenson, the campaign's chief strategist, longtime Democratic advisers Ron Klain, Jim Margolis, and Mandy Grunwald, and others (no Bill Clinton). Playing Trump was Philippe Reines, who had been Clinton's combative—and abrasive—spokesman at the State Department. Clinton arrived around midday, and they began work.

About 3:00 in the afternoon, the news broke: the Office of the Director of National Intelligence (ODNI) and the Department of Homeland Security (DHS) had released the statement declaring that the intelligence community was "confident that the Russian Government directed the recent compromises of e-mails from US persons and institutions, including from US political organizations." It noted the release of the stolen material by DCLeaks, WikiLeaks, and Guccifer 2.0 was "consistent with the methods and motivations of Russian-directed efforts. These thefts and disclosures are intended to interfere with the US election process." And it stated that "only Russia's senior-most officials could have authorized these activities." The statement added, "Some states have also recently seen scanning and probing of their election-related systems, which in most cases originated from servers operated by a Russian company. However, we are not now in a position to attribute this activity to the Russian Government." But it seemed clear—by its inclusion in the statement—that the intelligence community suspected Moscow had targeted America's electoral infrastructure.

The Clintonites were ecstatic. The White House had not tipped them off. But it was exactly what they wanted. Finally, the Obama administration was backing up what the campaign had been saying for months. "It seemed like this would have to reshape the conversation of the remainder of the campaign," Benenson said. Now the media finally would have to make this story a priority, Benenson and other campaign aides believed. Clinton was somewhat more skeptical. Although she was delighted with the statement, she told her aides she wasn't quite certain that reporters covering the campaign would pay sufficient attention to it.

In Brooklyn, the senior Clinton aides not doing debate prep huddled in Mook's office and got the debate group on the phone. They decided to put out a statement designed to apply pressure on Trump to acknowledge the Russians were meddling in the election. After that was done, Mook and other Clinton officials or surrogates would contact reporters to talk up the development. The Clinton aides believed they now had a solid basis for asking the media to reject future email dumps and concentrate on what they considered the real story: the Russian war on the 2016 election.

Across the East River, in Trump Tower, the Republican candidate was in the twenty-fifth-floor conference room with his top advisers doing his own debate prep. When news of the Russia statement reached them, they didn't pay it any mind. "It was so unimportant," David Bossie, the Trump campaign's deputy manager, recalled. The campaign's tactic had been to ignore the Russian story, give it no oxygen—that is, when Trump and his advisers were not dismissing it in public. Besides, Trump and his team had something much bigger to worry about.

In the middle of the prep session, Bossie's phone rang. On the line was campaign spokeswoman Hope Hicks. She had been contacted by *Washington Post* reporter David Fahrenthold. He was asking for a comment from the campaign about a story he was about to publish.

Fahrenthold had been sent a video of Trump making lewd comments about women. The footage was shot in 2005 when Trump was a guest on the *Access Hollywood* entertainment news show. Trump was riding on the *Access Hollywood* bus with host Billy Bush. Not realizing his mic was live, Trump crudely boasted about sexually pursuing a married woman and sexually assaulting women. "You know I'm automatically attracted to beautiful—I just start kissing them," he told Bush. "It's like a magnet. Just kiss. I don't even wait. And when you're a star, they let you do it. You can do anything. . . . Grab them by the pussy. You can do anything."

Fahrenthold had sent Hicks a transcript of Trump's comments on the video. Bossie's initial thought was "pure and simple" this was a last-minute Clinton oppo-research hit to influence the Sunday debate. He and campaign chairman Steve Bannon left the room to discuss how to respond. Soon they were joined by Kushner, Hicks, and Jason Miller, the campaign communications director. Those inside the conference room could see through a glass wall that something was happening. The group outside went back in, joining Trump, Christie (who was playing Hillary Clinton), and Reince Priebus, the Republican Party chair. They showed Trump the transcript. He dismissed it. "It doesn't sound like me," he said. Then Hicks got an update from Fahrenthold. The *Post* had decided to send the campaign the video. Together, they all watched on Bossie's iPad. Still, the candidate was unfazed. He didn't dwell on the contents. "What are we gonna do about it?" he asked his aides.

By now, Ivanka Trump was in the room. Her eyes welled with tears, her face reddened. She urged her father to make a full-throated apology. Christie did the same. Trump didn't want to do it. Instead, he, Bannon, Bossie, and Miller quickly drafted a statement for the *Post*. It was short and considerably less than what Ivanka was pleading for. Naturally, it took a shot at the Clintons: "This was locker room banter, a private conversation that took place many years ago. Bill Clinton has said far worse to me on the golf course—not even close. I apologize if anyone was offended." Hicks sent it to the *Post*.

With the statement from Trump, Fahrenthold and the *Post* wrapped up their story. At 4:02 P.M., Fahrenthold tweeted: "stand by for some news about @realDonaldTrump." One minute later, his story went live.

At the White House, officials were bracing for what they assumed was going to be a huge news day driven by the Russia statement. And at first it was. The release of the statement capped months of speculation about what the administration knew about Russia's interference in the election—and pinning it on the highest levels of the Russian government was a surprise. "My phone was ringing constantly" recalled Ned Price, the NSC spokesman. He was inundated with emails from reporters asking about the statement. And then, suddenly, Price said, "the phone stopped ringing." At first, he didn't realize why. Then he understood.

Todd Breasseale, the senior spokesman at the Department of

Homeland Security, filled Price in on what was happening. Breasseale had just been on the phone with a top network correspondent who was planning a piece that evening about the ODNI/DHS statement. This was huge, it was unprecedented, the correspondent was saying. The United States was calling out Russia for screwing with our democracy. Then Breasseale heard the correspondent barking to a colleague: "Oh fuck! Unmute the TV!" The cable news channels were playing the *Access Hollywood* tape nonstop, showing Trump time and again making his outrageous comments about women. "You're not going to fucking believe this! There goes my story!" the correspondent shouted over the phone. "I got to go." The correspondent hung up.

At the Doral Arrowwood, Clinton and her aides were taking a break from debate prep when the news reports of the *Access Hollywood* video hit. At first, no one said anything. Clinton stared at the screen in absolute disbelief. After a short discussion with her senior staff about what, if anything, she should say, Clinton put out a brief statement on Twitter: "This is horrific. We cannot allow this man to become president."

Many top Republicans at that moment were having the same thought. At Trump Tower, the candidate and his advisers were watching their support from the party establishment crumble. Jeb Bush tweeted, "As the grandfather of two precious girls, I find that no apology can excuse away Donald Trump's reprehensible comments degrading women." Mitt Romney declared, "Hitting on married women? Condoning assault? Such vile degradations demean our wives and daughters and corrupt America's face to the world." Reince Priebus commented, "No woman should ever be described in these terms or talked about in this manner. Ever." Paul Ryan disinvited Trump from a campaign event, saying he was "sickened" by Trump's remarks. Senator John McCain announced, "the disclosure of his demeaning comments about women and his boasts about sexual assaults make it impossible to continue to offer even conditional support for his candidacy." Utah Representative

Jason Chaffetz called Trump's words "some of the most abhorrent and offensive comments that you can possibly imagine" and withdrew his support.

It looked like a death blow to Trump's campaign.

As devastating as the video was to Trump, some Clinton campaign staffers still wanted to keep the focus on Russia. Ignoring the nonstop cable coverage of the video, Brian Fallon, the press secretary, and Glen Caplin, the oppo man, had crafted a statement: "The world now knows, beyond a shadow of a doubt, that the hack of the Democratic National Committee was carried out by the Russian government in a clear attempt to interfere with the integrity of our elections," it declared. "The only remaining question is why Donald Trump continues to make apologies for the Russians."

The Clinton staffers hit the phones, calling reporters they had worked with, urging them to give more attention to the Russia story. They weren't having much luck. And the surprises that day weren't over.

At 4:32 P.M., came the WikiLeaks tweet: "RELEASE: The Podesta Emails." At that moment, the group was posting about two thousand of Podesta's emails from his personal Gmail account—and reporting that it had more than fifty thousand of his emails in its possession. It was the October Surprise the Clinton people had anticipated and feared. Palmieri pulled Podesta out of debate prep to let him know his emails were out. Podesta and other Clinton aides were convinced: This was strategically timed to fuck them—and distract from both the Russia statement and the grab-them-by-the-pussy video. They even suspected—given Stone's public tweets—that it was coordinated with the Trump campaign. "The timing was not coincidental," Podesta later said. "They needed Fox News to have something to talk about."

This day had become almost too intense for some Clinton officials. The swings were overwhelming. Palmieri could barely stand the increased stress. At one point, she had to call a time-out for herself. She left her colleagues and walked the perimeter of the resort, listening to a Bruce Springsteen song: "Take 'Em as They Come."

Perkins Coie, the campaign's law firm, began to download the Podesta material and make sure the documents were not laced with malware or other cyber bombs. In the Brooklyn headquarters, handling email dumps had become routine. The campaign already had a war room set up for reviewing hacked material. The previous day, DCLeaks had released emails from Capricia Marshall, a longtime Clinton confidante, and now a dozen or so researchers turned from those messages to scouring the Podesta emails.

Though campaign officials had feared that Podesta's emails would be leaked, the campaign had not preemptively reviewed them. Podesta had not wanted campaign researchers sifting through all his messages. He knew there was sensitive material within this trove—emails that could bruise feelings and cause unease within the conflict-ridden Clinton world. But now Podesta had no choice. The campaign needed to know what was in these emails—especially since WikiLeaks had released only a small slice of the collection of tens of thousands. Presumably more were coming. He gave the campaign access to his account.

The researchers in the war room soon began combing through the full Podesta cache, starting with the ones WikiLeaks had dumped. Looking for material that might cause problems, they conducted key word searches. The list was obvious: email server, the Clinton Foundation, Benghazi, Goldman Sachs, Obama, Sanders.

Campaign officials—Mook, Caplin, Fallon, and others—tried their own effort at damage control. They jumped on the phone with reporters and urged them not to write about the WikiLeaks dump. The message they pushed out was simple: This is a Russia-orchestrated October Surprise, and our campaign is being attacked by Putin. As Mook saw it, it was as if a criminal Russian super PAC working on behalf of Trump had stolen information from Podesta and was releasing it to save a candidate who was now facing annihilation. They asked the journalists to think twice before reporting on the material.

But it was a futile exercise. The Clinton folks could not challenge the authenticity of the emails or point to any that had been doctored. And, it was soon clear, there was plenty of juicy material to be mined.

Some of it was merely amusing, like a June 2015 email thread about a request from CNN's Tapper to interview Clinton. "Why is Jake Tapper such a dick," Podesta had written. Tapper posted Podesta's comment with his own commentary: "It's a question that has confounded millions of people for hundreds of years."

Within hours, more serious emails were discovered. A January 25, 2016, email to Podesta and other top campaign officials contained excerpts of Clinton's paid speeches to various groups including Goldman Sachs and other financial institutions.

Through the course of the campaign, Clinton had refused to release the transcripts of these speeches. They were a reminder of her unseemly buck-raking from Wall Street banks and other special interest groups during the run-up to her presidential campaign—an issue that was an easy target for Sanders and his supporters. It reminded many in the media of her well-documented penchant for secrecy. Campaign officials knew what was in the speeches. They had dissected them at the start of the primary season and urged Clinton to make them public, arguing there was nothing embarrassing or troubling enough that was worth the flack she was taking for her failure to do so. But Clinton refused to budge. "I'm being asked to put out more information than other candidates," she complained to her aides. Once Trump emerged as the GOP nominee, she had a new argument: Why should I release my speeches, if he won't release his tax returns?

Now that decision came back to haunt her. The first significant stories on the Podesta emails focused on the Clinton campaign's own internal assessment of the speech transcripts and the passages that could be exploited by her opponents. In one speech to a 2013 Brazilian bank, Clinton had said, "My dream is a hemispheric common market with open trade and open borders." Reporters and Trump supporters latched on to "open borders." Was Clinton suggesting the elimination of border controls? (Clinton insisted she was referring to cross-border energy supplies.) In a 2013 speech hosted by Goldman Sachs, she had suggested that Wall Street insiders could be tapped to better regulate the financial industry. "And the people that know the industry better than anybody are the people who work in the industry," she said. In a 2014 speech to Goldman and BlackRock, another big Wall Street firm, she described herself as "kind of far removed" from the middle-class upbringing she grew up in.

Perhaps more worrisome for the campaign was an excerpt from a 2013 speech to an apartment industry group in which she discussed the need for a politician to balance the "public and the private efforts" needed to pass legislation and implement policy. "Politics is like sausage being made," she had said. "It is unsavory. . . . So you need both a public and a private position." The initial news reports zeroed in on this remark as evidence of Clinton's political hypocrisy. The Republican National Committee jumped on the emails. "It's not hard to see why she fought so hard to keep her transcripts of speeches to Wall Street banks paying her millions of dollars a secret," RNC chair Priebus said in a statement. "The truth that has been exposed here is that the persona Hillary Clinton has adopted for her campaign is a complete and utter fraud."

The Clintonites realized that no matter how hard they tried they could not sell the Russian attack as the main story. "There were no stories saying, 'Holy shit, this Russian stuff is incredible,'" said Mook. As for Clinton, she was frustrated. But she was used to this. She told her advisers that she had taken incoming attacks through her entire political life and cautioned them not to become distracted.

Trump and his advisers had bigger problems. They were confronting mounting calls for him to drop out of the race. They realized his initial statement to the *Post*—with its reference to "locker room banter"—was not enough. They rushed out a video statement late that evening in which a stern-looking Trump, speaking awkwardly into the camera, made more of an effort to apologize: "I've said and done things I regret, and the words released today on this more-than-a-decade-old video are one of them," Trump said. "Anyone who knows me knows these words don't reflect who I am. I said it, I was wrong, and I apologize." Moments later, he pivoted: "I've said some foolish things, but there's a big difference between the words and actions of other people. Bill Clinton has actually abused women, and Hillary has bullied, attacked, shamed, and intimidated his victims. We will discuss this more in the coming days. See you at the debate on Sunday."

One of Trump's rules over his decades in public life was simple: Never apologize. And this was as grudging an apology as he could muster. Immediately, it was dubbed "a hostage video" by reporters and even some of his supporters.

At the day's end, Hurricane Matthew had skirted Florida but caused flooding along the coast. It would make landfall the coming day in South Carolina as a fierce but diminished storm. And each campaign was now facing its own crisis. Each was being hammered by an October Surprise. One of them had originated in Moscow. The U.S. presidential race was essentially in chaos.

And October 7 was Vladimir Putin's sixty-fourth birthday.

CHAPTER 19

"We've been ratfucked."

The next morning, October 8, Jeh Johnson picked up the copy of the *New York Times* delivered to his home. He had expected to see a story on the Russia statement at the top of the front page with a large headline. Instead, the big story was the *Access Hollywood* tape. An article on the U.S. accusations against Russia was there on the front page, but toward the bottom. And it wasn't getting much attention on cable news. "The press had gone off to the other end of the pasture," Johnson said later, "because of greed and sex and groping."

In Trump's private apartment in the tower that bore his name, the Russia statement was the last thing on anybody's mind. The candidate and his senior advisers were trying to figure out how to survive. The inner circle was there—Bannon, Conway, Bossie, Hicks, Christie, and Rudy Giuliani. Priebus arrived late, having taken the train back from Washington. What are you hearing? Trump asked him. "With all due respect, sir," he answered, "you have two choices: One, you lose by the biggest electoral landslide in American history... or you can drop out of the race." The room fell silent. "This is something that I will get through and it will not be a problem," Trump said. "But more importantly, Reince, I'm going to win." Bannon bucked him up. "One hundred percent victory, not even a question about it," he said, when Trump went around the room and asked his advisers to assess his chances.

Bannon had concocted a plan for Trump, and he put it in motion the next day. Ninety minutes before the second debate was to start at Washington University in St. Louis, the press pool covering Trump was ushered into a conference room. The under-sieged Republican nominee sat at a table with two women on each side of him. A reporter asked, "Mr. Trump, does your star power allow you to touch women without their consent?" Trump, with a grim expression, ignored it. He introduced the four women: Kathleen Willey, Juanita Broaddrick, and Paula Jones—who each years ago had accused Bill Clinton of sexual misconduct or assault—and Kathy Shelton, a rape victim whose assailant had been defended by Hillary Clinton when she was a court-appointed defense lawyer in Arkansas forty-one years earlier.

The goal was to change the subject and rattle Hillary Clinton— as Bossie later put it, "to get people to talk about Bill Clinton, not Donald Trump." For months, Bannon had been talking to Roger Stone about how to deploy these women. They had considered having them appear at a rally on Trump's behalf. That never happened. But at Trump's most desperate moment, Bannon was using them to turn the tables on Clinton.

Each one made a short statement, and in about three minutes, the meeting was done. This might have been an act of desperation, but Clintonites would later concede it worked to a degree. "Everyone was disoriented by that and by Trump's aggressive raising of these past controversies," Fallon recalled. "It was a strange and unprecedented move, but it did succeed in muddying the waters." Bannon was exultant. He later saw this as the turning point of the campaign.

To no one's surprise, the debate started out with a question about the *Access Hollywood* tape. Trump denied he had bragged about sexually assailing women. Clinton asserted the video "represents exactly who he is."

About halfway through, Clinton was asked about the Podesta

email that referred to her having public and private positions on issues. Clinton campaign officials cringed. The question was entirely legitimate. But this was a watershed moment. Clinton's comments had only come to light courtesy of Russian intelligence. The Kremlin's hack-and-dump influence campaign had just scored one of its biggest payoffs: It was driving the discussion at an American presidential debate.

And that, Clinton insisted, was the real issue. "We have never in the history of our country been in a situation where an adversary, a foreign power, is working so hard to influence the outcome of the election," she said. "And believe me, they're not doing it to get me elected. They're doing it to try to influence the election for Donald Trump." She pressed Trump to explain why he had praised Putin.

"Anytime anything wrong happens, they like to say the Russians are—she doesn't know if it's the Russians doing the hacking," Trump responded. "Maybe there is no hacking. But they always blame Russia. And the reason they blame Russia because they think they're trying to tarnish me with Russia." He insisted, "I don't deal there. I have no businesses there," failing to mention his two attempted deals in recent years—including one while he was running for president—to build a Trump Tower in Moscow.

Watching the debate at home, Jeh Johnson shook his head. The statement his DHS and the ODNI had issued two days earlier apparently had not settled anything.

After the St. Louis debate, Trump's advisers thought the pre-debate surprise and his performance on the stage added up to a big victory. And now with the Podesta emails, they would have almost an unlimited supply of fresh ammo to hurl at Clinton. The next day, at a rally in Pennsylvania, Trump would read excerpts from Clinton's speeches and shout, "I love WikiLeaks." The audience would respond with a chant of "Lock her up." Two days later, WikiLeaks sent Trump Jr. a private Twitter message: "Hey Donald, great to see you and your dad talking about our publications." WikiLeaks passed along a link to the Podesta emails and asked Trump Jr. to share it publicly. Days later, he did.

Clinton aides, too, had also been satisfied with the outcome of the debate, but less so. They realized the debate had not been a slam dunk. For all the predictions that Trump's candidacy was about to collapse, he was still very much in the race—as Joel Benenson, the Clinton campaign pollster, discovered to his chagrin. Five days after the *Access Hollywood* video emerged—with several women now accusing Trump of sexual misconduct—the contest was still tight. Clinton was maintaining a narrow two- to four-point lead. "We would hear in focus groups, 'Yeah, Donald Trump throws bombs. He says outrageous things, but he doesn't mean all those things. He won't be like that as president. He'll change,'" Benenson later said.

After a few days of quiet, WikiLeaks began releasing more Podesta emails, putting out batches of a couple thousand or so emails daily that would eventually tally about sixty-four thousand.

Assange had altered his tactics. In July, WikiLeaks had posted all twenty-two thousand of the Russian-stolen DNC emails at once. That was in keeping with the group's previous practices and with its claim of being a champion of whistle-blowing and accountability. If WikiLeaks had no agenda other than transparency, there was no need to dribble out the disclosures. It could just throw the documents into the world for all to see.

This time was different. WikiLeaks made a strategic adjustment: It would release the Podesta emails in installments, each tranche with enticing nuggets, to keep the story going. Whether this was done with the complicity of the Russians was unknown.

Either way, it worked. The WikiLeaks emails were constantly in the news. When Clinton supporters went on television, they were confronted with the latest Podesta emails release. Whatever rhetoric, spin, or message they hoped to promote was often smothered by questions about the latest revelation. Clinton herself later compared the releases to "Chinese water torture."

There were emails about Bill Clinton's speaking fees, the Clinton Foundation, and the never-ending rivalries within the often-fractious Clinton circle. Some highlighted Clinton's vulnerabilities, such as her penchant for secrecy. In one email about the email server story, Neera Tanden, one of Clinton's closest (and most candid) advisers, vented to Podesta, "Why didn't they get this stuff out like 18 months ago? So crazy." She blamed Clinton staffers Cheryl Mills and Philippe Reines: "i guess I know the answer. they wanted to get away with it."

The most damning emails documented the ceaseless fund-raising and money-chasing that the media had long ago dubbed "Clinton Inc." A thirteen-page memo by Doug Band, for years a top Bill Clinton aide, spelled out how he had arranged for corporate clients of his consulting firm, Teneo, to kick in big contributions to the Clinton Foundation, pay Clinton huge speaking fees, and provide "in-kind services for the President and his family—for personal travel, hospitality, vacation and the like." He boasted of having helped secure "more than $50 million" in support of Bill Clinton's "for-profit activity," with $66 million in future contracts "to be paid out over the next nine years."

Hillary Clinton's role in Clinton Inc. also was covered in the emails. One set of emails revealed that Clinton advisers worried about Hillary Clinton's decision to fly to Morocco for the May 2015 meeting of the Clinton Global Initiative. The event was scheduled for a few weeks after her presidential campaign announcement, and it was being partially underwritten by a $1 million contribution from a Moroccan phosphate mining firm that profited from operations in disputed international territory in Western Sahara. The king of Morocco, these emails revealed, had offered to contribute $12 million for the event and the Clinton Foundation—so long as Hillary Clinton showed up. Her aides were beside themselves. "This was HRC's idea," Huma Abedin, a top Clinton aide, explained to others. She added, "She created this mess and she knows it." Mook fretted about the unseemly optics—his soon-to-be-announced candidate flying overseas to gather foreign cash for her foundation. "We really need to shut Morocco and these paid speeches down," he wrote Podesta. (He succeeded. Clinton did not go to Morocco.) Trump would point to these emails and claim this was evidence of the Clinton's pay-to-play ways.

Whether Russian intelligence had planned this or not, it had managed to sock Clinton where it could hurt the most. Putin's operatives were exploiting a weakness that Clinton herself had created years ago when she set up her private email server.

The emails were producing one cut at a time. But the damage was deeper than whatever embarrassing material was in them. When the Clinton campaign convened focus groups in key battleground states, they learned that voters made no distinction between the emails on Clinton's private server and the Podesta emails hacked by Russian intelligence. It was all a blur. When the voters saw headlines about the emails hacked from Podesta's Gmail account, "people thought this was all about her own server, that the emails were the stuff she had been hiding," Mook recalled. So why, these voters wondered, was Clinton talking about the Russians? Was she trying to blame Moscow for her own email troubles?

Some aides believed the problem might be beyond remedy. The more the campaign responded to the Podesta emails—even if only to denounce Russia's role—the more it could bolster the sense that the email scandal had returned. "Any day that Hillary Clinton and the word 'emails' are in a story was going to be a bad day for us," Benenson later observed.

To the dismay of the Clinton camp, the intelligence community's Russia statement had not made any difference. When the campaign raised the issue of Russian intervention, political reporters covering the race mostly ignored them. Clinton was frustrated. "Why can't you get people to take this seriously?" she asked her aides. Just about every morning she called Sullivan to press him about the Russia matter: "What are you doing today?"

The campaign explored ways to promote the Russia issue. After the statement was released, its social media team produced a slew of Russia-related content: explainer videos, websites, graphics with Russian dolls popping up, an interactive map—all to highlight Trump's real and suspected connections to Russia and to emphasize that the release of the Podesta emails was part of a Russian plot. The scripts were written in Signal—an encrypted messaging app—out of concern campaign emails might be intercepted by the Russians. But much of this product ended up being shelved.

"There was a concern that people would see us as crazy," Rob Flaherty, the campaign's deputy digital communications director, later remarked. "It seemed too conspiratorial, too tinfoil." Instead, the campaign issued statements and posted a six-minute-long video making the case that Trump was in cahoots with—or at least countenancing—Russia's attempt to undermine the election.

The campaign was also pissed off with the White House. The ODNI/DHS statement had come out and then there was no follow-up. No announcement of new sanctions, no response. Clinton and her aides were mystified by the White House's low-key reaction. "We could not understand why there was not more visibility from the president," a top Clinton adviser recalled. "Why was there not an immediate policy response?"

The NSC staffers who had worked on the rejected cyber responses were also disappointed. Celeste Wallander, the top Russian expert on the NSC staff, believed the October 7 statement was largely irrelevant. "I was not focused on what we said," she later explained. "The Russians don't care what we say. They care what we do."

Inside Trump Tower, the candidate's top advisers could not have cared less about Russia. It was, they thought, irrelevant—an issue made up by the Clintonites that was not registering with the public. They believed the idea that they were colluding with the Russians was ludicrous. "We couldn't coordinate with the RNC over what to do in Pennsylvania," Bannon would later tell colleagues. "We were the Keystone Kops." Of all the issues Bannon worried about, Russia didn't make the list.

By mid-October, after it was clear the *Access Hollywood* tape had not been the knockout punch that many had anticipated, Bannon saw reason for optimism: Clinton's persistent weakness in the polls. As Bannon viewed it, Clinton was a flawed candidate with serious baggage—she was old, tired, and the epitome of a Washington establishment that many voters viewed as corrupt and out of touch. He took more than a little credit for that. A book he helped orchestrate—with research funded by conservative hedge-fund financier Robert Mercer—that came out the year before, *Clinton*

Cash, had spawned front-page stories in the *New York Times* and other publications—and the issue was now being given new life by the Podesta emails.

Though Bannon considered Clinton vulnerable, he realized voters still needed "permission" to vote for Trump—and he knew his candidate had more than his own share of problems. There were allegations of mob ties and dodgy business practices, as well as his lewd talk and comments about women. And most of all, there were questions about his mental stability—whether Trump was going to trigger a nuclear war and blow up the world. Against all that, Bannon thought, Russia was a "fucking zero." When asked, all Trump ever said about the issue was, "I don't know any Russians."

During the third and final debate between Clinton and Trump, in Las Vegas on October 19, both candidates were in the shadow of the recent controversies. Trump again was on the defensive about the allegations of sexual harassment and assault.

When faced with a question based on the stolen Podesta emails, Clinton once more tried to make Putin and the Russian operation the topic. In response, Trump pointed out that Putin had said "nice things about him." And that triggered a rowdy exchange in which Clinton shot back, "Well, that's because he'd rather have a puppet as president of the United States." Trump replied in schoolyard fashion: "No puppet. No puppet. You're the puppet." As Clinton tried to reference the administration's official statement, Trump kept on denying Moscow meddling: "Our country has no idea. Yeah, I doubt it." Russian intelligence had yet again succeeded in shaping a presidential debate—and this time causing an unruly scene that cast the Russia issue as mainly political fodder.

After the debate, top Clinton advisers fretted that their candidate, though still in the lead, was vulnerable. The campaign was not building momentum. "We were dead in the water, just sitting there," Palmieri recalled. Whatever message Clinton was putting out was not sparking media attention or winning over swing state voters. To gin up a little excitement, on October 28, while Clinton was flying to Iowa for a rally, Mook was planning to tell reporters on the plane that she would be campaigning in a few days in Arizona, a reliably red state. It was a typical end-of-campaign head fake—make the other guys think you know something they don't by invading their territory. (The campaign wasn't heeding organizers on the ground reporting that Clinton needed to shore up her position in key Midwestern states, including Wisconsin.)

While Clinton was in the air that Friday, a single tweet set off a political earthquake. It was from Representative Jason Chaffetz, the Republican chair of the House Oversight Committee, and he wrote: "FBI Dir just informed me, 'The FBI has learned of the existence of emails that appear to be pertinent to the investigation.' Case reopened." He was referring to the Clinton emails. It was the biggest October Surprise of all.

That day, Comey had sent a letter to eight Republican congressional committee chairmen explaining that he needed to supplement his previous testimony to their committees in which he said that the FBI's Clinton email server investigation was completed. He wrote that the FBI had discovered emails that could be related to that inquiry. The Bureau would "review those emails to determine whether they contain classified information, as well as to assess their importance to our investigation." Comey noted the FBI had no idea whether the material might be significant or how long this review would take.

It was eleven days before the election, and Clinton's email server controversy—one of her most critical vulnerabilities—was back in the news. For weeks, the Russia-WikiLeaks operation had steadily reminded voters of Clinton's email server problem, providing a competing plot line to the accusations regarding Trump and women. The Russians had inadvertently set the stage for this final stunner.

Comey had learned only the day before of the existence of these new emails. He didn't say so in his letter to Congress, but they had been found as part of a separate FBI investigation of former

Representative Anthony Weiner, Huma Abedin's husband, for sexting with a 15-year-old girl. When they seized Weiner's laptop, agents discovered a large number of Clinton's emails. Apparently, they had been forwarded to Abedin and somehow wound up on a laptop she shared with her husband, from whom she had recently separated.

As soon as Comey had been briefed on this development in the Weiner probe, he realized he faced a dilemma. He had told Congress the Clinton investigation was done. But now it seemed to be back—at least temporarily for a review of this material. The emails could turn out to be duplicates of what the FBI had already reviewed—or not. If he said nothing and allowed his testimony to stand, Comey worried it could look like he had concealed pertinent information from Congress. But if he said anything, he also realized, he could be accused of a game-changing intervention in the presidential race.

There was yet another complication. Earlier in the year, agents in the FBI's New York office had argued internally that the Clinton Foundation should be investigated for influence peddling and financial crimes. The Justice Department decided there was not enough evidence to warrant a probe. Discussions between the department and agents over this matter were at times tense. Some agents were steamed. The word got around that the New York office was home to agents who had a beef with Clinton. It was within this charged environment that New York field agents had discovered the emails on Weiner's laptop.

The FBI hadn't yet obtained a search warrant to begin examining all the emails. Still, Comey and his advisers worried that if they didn't act quickly, FBI agents nursing a grudge against the Clintons could leak word about the discovery. "We were facing one big pile of shit," a Comey adviser said at the time. "The question was, from which side are you going to eat?"

Palmieri was on the campaign plane with Clinton when a reporter approached her and asked if she had heard about the Comey letter. She didn't know what the reporter was talking about. The internet connection on the plane was not working. She could only load the headlines of stories about the letter. "This has to be a mistake," she kept telling herself. She knew the rules of the road. As an election approached, the FBI and Justice Department were supposed to avoid moves that could affect the outcome.

She and Mook went to tell Clinton. The candidate was stoic. She focused on the immediate challenge: how to handle the matter. "It was as if she knew she would not get through the last two weeks without something horrible happening," Palmieri recalled.

With the lousy Wi-Fi connection on the plane, it took twenty minutes or so for Clinton and the aides traveling with her to reach Brooklyn. As they consulted over the phone, Clinton and her aides vented their outrage over Comey's action. The director of the FBI had just revived an issue that could destroy her candidacy—without being able to point to any new evidence that she had done anything wrong. Podesta—whose emails had caused so much damage that month—was among the most upset. He thought, "We've been ratfucked."

CHAPTER 20

"This is the real reset of the Western world."

At a raucous Trump rally in New Hampshire that Friday, October 28, the chants were more boisterous than ever: "Lock her up! Lock her up!" Trump himself was ebullient. "Perhaps, finally, justice will be done," he told his supporters. "Hillary Clinton's corruption is on a scale we have never seen before."

Comey's letter had scrambled the election. Trump's candidacy had been given a powerful boost. Clinton had been blindsided. Her team decided not to challenge Comey directly but pressed him for more information and a speedy resolution.

Senator Harry Reid, the Democratic minority leader, was determined to do something. This was, he thought, a monstrous injustice. The FBI was reopening a closed investigation into his party's nominee while staying silent about an investigation into the campaign of her rival. He fired off an angry letter to Comey, accusing him of violating the Hatch Act, a federal law that bars U.S. government officials from using their office to influence an election. The letter, which Reid made public, accused Comey of a double standard. "As soon as you came into possession of the slightest innuendo related to Secretary Clinton, you rushed to publicize it in the most negative light possible," Reid complained. Yet Comey had not done the same with Trump. "In my communications with you and other top officials in the national security community, it has become clear that you possess explosive information about close ties and coordination between Donald Trump, his top advisors, and the Russian government.... The public has a right to know this information."

Reid didn't say what the "explosive information" was. But this was one last chance to put the issue of the Trump campaign's Russia ties into play. If voters knew the Bureau was digging into links between Trump's world and the Kremlin, Reid thought, maybe, just maybe, it would make a difference and prevent Comey's letter from derailing Clinton's campaign.

For the past two months, David Corn, a reporter for *Mother Jones* magazine in Washington, had been poking into the Trump-Russia connection. The letter that Reid had sent Comey the previous August—referring to "evidence of a direct connection between the Russian government and Donald Trump's presidential campaign"—had been a tantalizing lead. Weeks later, Michael Isikoff had reported U.S. intelligence agencies were probing Carter Page and his July trip to Moscow. And in Washington rumors swirled of FBI investigations, FISA warrants, and a supposed link between a computer server associated with Trump's business and Russia's Alfa Bank. There was talk of intelligence intercepts capturing incriminating conversations. Yet there was no hard information and few leaks. Reid's new letter denouncing Comey was a clue there was a story here. What, Corn wanted to know, was this "explosive information"?

That weekend, Corn checked in with Glenn Simpson of Fusion GPS. He had known Simpson for years—as a colleague, a social acquaintance, and an occasional source—and he was aware that Simpson was doing opposition research on Trump, including his links to Russia. He asked if Simpson had any last-minute leads that warranted independent investigation.

Let's meet today, Simpson told him.

* * *

Ever since his trip to Washington in mid-September, Chris Steele had continued to file reports to Simpson. One suggested that the Kremlin had "buyer's remorse" over its U.S. election meddling. Yet Russian officials were said to be upset that the dump of hacked anti-Clinton emails had not made more of a splash. A foreign ministry official also told one of Steele's contacts that the Kremlin believed that even if Trump lost, he would continue to be a divisive force within American politics. The Russians would win, even if Trump did not.

Another report alleged new details of the supposed meeting between Igor Sechin of Rosneft and Carter Page. Citing a source close to Sechin, Steele reported that the Rosneft chief had offered Page and other Trump associates an interest in the gigantic broker-age fee that would come from the upcoming privatization sale of 19 percent of Rosneft. The memo also claimed that Michael Cohen, Trump's lawyer, was playing a "key role in the secret TRUMP campaign/KREMLIN relationship." An additional memo alleged Cohen had secretly met in Prague with Kremlin representatives in August to "clean up the mess" after news stories appeared about Manafort's relationship with the corrupt Yanukovych regime in Ukraine and about Page's July trip to Moscow. (Cohen would later say he had never been to Prague and never been in any such meeting.)

Simpson had flown Steele to Washington in October to once again brief reporters on his research. But other than Isikoff's article on Page in late September, nothing else had been reported. Simpson still had not handed out copies of the memos. Yet after the Comey letter—a violation of Washington norms that could have a devastating impact on the race—Simpson decided it was time to be more aggressive.

Corn and Simpson met at a Le Pain Quotidien in Dupont Circle. "I got some crazy shit," Simpson told the reporter. He then recounted the story of Steele and his memos. This stuff is almost unbelievable, Simpson said. He noted he had briefed a few reporters on some of the material, but the biggest elements of the Steele story—his claim Moscow had secretly co-opted Trump and the fact the FBI had been digging into ties between the Trump camp and Russia—had not broken through.

"Let me see the memos," Corn said.

Later that day, Corn was at Simpson's office, reading through all the Steele reports. The allegations were stunning: Moscow running a secret project to cultivate Trump for years (and dangling business opportunities in front of him), the Trump campaign and Moscow covertly exchanging information, and the Russians possessing blackmail material on Trump, including a "golden showers" video. It certainly fit the "explosive" description in Reid's letter. Corn arranged to speak via Skype with Steele, who was in London.

During that conversation, Steele came across, as he had to Isikoff, as somber and professional. He described his information as "hair-raising" and said he had been "shocked" by the allegations. He acknowledged that his memos were works in progress, containing unconfirmed information. But he was confident that the big picture—secret connections existing between Trump and Moscow—was accurate. He added, "My track record as a professional is second to no one." And he disclosed that he had been sharing his information with an FBI investigation that was under way.

Steele explained that he was reluctant to be cited in any article. "Someone like me stays in the shadows," he remarked. But he said he was genuinely concerned about the implications of his reports. He had been cooperating with the FBI for months, and he hadn't seen any public signs of the FBI inquiry. He believed voters needed to know that a presidential campaign was under investigation. "I think [Trump's] own party should be aware of this stuff as well," he remarked, adding, "The story has to come out." Steele said that Corn could quote him but not name him in any article he might write. He could only be identified as a former senior counterintelligence official for a Western country.

Could he be identified as British? Corn asked. No, Steele said. That would be going too far. He needed to be protected.

After speaking with Steele, Corn confirmed Steele's identity and expertise. He contacted Jonathan Winer to ask him about Steele. (Isikoff, too, had called Winer about Steele.) Speaking on background, Winer told Corn that he had worked with Steele and that he had a solid track record of collaborating with U.S. government agencies and providing them accurate and valuable information about sensitive national security matters.

Later that day, *Mother Jones* published a story by Corn reporting Steele's allegations that Moscow had been deeply involved in the campaign. Headlined "A Veteran Spy Has Given the FBI Information Alleging a Russian Operation to Cultivate Donald Trump," the article was pegged to Harry Reid's recent letter, and it reported that a former senior intelligence official for a Western country who specialized in Russian counterintelligence had provided the FBI with reports contending the Russian government had been trying to covertly co-opt and assist Trump. The story said this former intelligence officer was working with an American firm—a reference to Fusion GPS—on a project financed by a client "allied with Democrats." It quoted from the memos but did not report the salacious (and unconfirmed) details. It did note that the reports claimed Russian intelligence had "compromised" Trump during his visits to Moscow and could "blackmail him." The story cited Steele calling his findings "an extraordinary situation."

The most important element in the article was that the FBI apparently was investigating Trump-Russia ties and material within the Steele reports. The story quoted the unidentified intelligence officer remarking, "It's quite clear there was or is a pretty substantial inquiry going on." An FBI spokeswoman refused to acknowledge receiving Steele's memos. "Normally, we don't talk about whether we are investigating anything," she told Corn.

This was the first media account to reveal the existence of Steele's memos—and their allegations that Trump was colluding with Moscow and vulnerable to Russian blackmail.

That same day, Halloween, Obama sent a message to Putin using the so-called Red Phone, the link established during the Cold War for communication between Washington and Moscow in times of crisis. It actually was not a phone. It was an email connection from a special computer housed within the State Department. The message, crafted by Michael Daniel, the White House cyber chief, was an iteration of Obama's earlier warning. It asserted that the United States had in recent months observed activity that was a "direct threat" to the U.S. election system. "International law, including the law for armed conflict, applies to actions in cyberspace," the message read. "We will hold Russia to those standards."

This was the first time the Obama administration had resorted to this communications channel. The Kremlin soon responded. "Thank you for the note. Please furnish us the evidence of this," its reply read, according to a White House official who reviewed the exchange. Then in the same message the Russians engaged in another round of "Whataboutism"—Putin's practice of hurling any and all U.S. accusations back in Washington's face by making similar charges against the American government. "We are observing the same activity against our infrastructure," read the Kremlin email message. The response, the official said, "was laughable."

About the time Corn's *Mother Jones* piece went up, *Slate* posted an article on the murky relationship between the Trump business server and Alfa Bank. The piece cited the research of several cybersecurity experts who had analyzed internet traffic and discovered what they thought were unexplained communications between the Trump Organization and the bank. The article reached no hard and fast conclusion. But it said there was a "suggestive body of evidence" pointing to a computer link between the two organizations.

In Brooklyn, Clinton officials, looking at these stories, wondered if the dam was about to break. Clinton tweeted out the *Slate* piece, noting, "It's time for Trump to answer serious questions about his ties to Russia." Perhaps, Clinton aides thought, the final October Surprise of this crazy race would be news of an FBI investigation into Trump and Russia.

Then came another story.

Since mid-September, two *New York Times* reporters, Eric Lichtblau and Steven Lee Myers, had been chasing the allegations of a Trump-Russia connection. Initially, they were focused on the purported Trump–Alfa Bank story, which was being privately promoted to journalists by Clinton campaign aides. The *Times* reporters had learned that the FBI had been investigating this matter and had held senior-level briefings on the subject in Comey's office. The Bureau at one point even asked the *Times* reporters not to publish a story on this server link, fearing that would undermine the FBI probe.

But the FBI soon cooled on the server inquiry, finding insufficient evidence to pursue it any further. The Bureau concluded the communications most likely were some form of routine commercial traffic—spam or marketing emails. But in the course of their reporting, Lichtblau and Myers had learned the Bureau was conducting a wider investigation focused on interactions between Trump associates and Russia. They had talked with Steele, at meetings arranged by Simpson, and they learned the FBI probe possibly involved supersecret FISA warrants that would allow the Bureau to snoop on Trump associates.

But *Times* editors were reluctant to go with the story. It was close to the election. To publish an incendiary article about an FBI investigation involving one of the two presidential candidates—when the reporters weren't precisely sure what or who the Bureau was investigating—made the editors nervous. And a mistake could backfire and cause a storm in the final days of the campaign. "Conversations over what to publish were prolonged and lively, involving Washington and New York, and often including the executive editor, Dean Baquet," the paper's ombudsman later wrote. And Baquet had the deciding vote. The story didn't run.

Once Reid released his letter to Comey, hinting at an FBI investigation, the *Times* had a reason to revive it. And the newspaper posted an article shortly after the *Mother Jones* and *Slate* articles were up. But the *Times* piece, carrying Lichtblau and Myers's co-byline, did not bolster the burgeoning Trump-Russia narrative. Instead, the article smothered it.

Headlined "Investigating Donald Trump, F.B.I. Sees No Clear Link to Russia," the story concentrated on the fact that the Bureau had not yet found a "conclusive or direct link between Mr. Trump and the Russian government." The main point, though, was in the tenth paragraph: U.S. intelligence agencies had been compelled by "apparent connections between some of Mr. Trump's aides and Moscow" to "open a broad investigation into possible links between the Russian government and the Republican presidential candidate."

The FBI's investigation was still under way. It was not surprising that the Bureau had not yet uncovered hard and fast evidence of direct connections. But the editors at the *Times* had cast the absence of a conclusion as the article's central theme rather than the fact of the investigation itself. The headline and the thrust of the piece downplayed what Lichtblau and Myers wanted to highlight. (Baquet later defended the paper's handling of the story. What was published then was "all we could report at that moment," he said.)

The *Times* article changed Steele's plans. At Simpson's request, he was considering flying to Washington that week to speak with members of Congress. Simpson was even thinking of holding a press conference with Steele on the steps of the Capitol. (Simpson later told friends, "You wouldn't want to live with yourself for the rest of your life without having tried everything.") This would be his final attempt to get the Trump-Russia story into the headlines before Election Day—and possibly detonate one last October Surprise.

But the *Times* piece spooked Steele. The ex-spy was already reluctant to become further involved and do anything that might push him into the spotlight. And he didn't see why the FBI was being so coy about this investigation. It looked to him as if the Bureau had misled the newspaper and downplayed its own probe. "Glenn," he told Simpson, "something is going on we don't understand."

And once Steele was effectively outed in Corn's piece—his existence if not his name—the Bureau quickly concluded he was too hot to handle and cut its ties to him. As FBI officials saw it, Steele seemed more interested in getting the story out rather than quietly working with them on the investigation. "There was clearly an agenda on his part," one senior FBI official later said.

Steele turned down Simpson's request to come back to the United States. As he figured it, he had done what he could do to warn the Americans. Now he would watch the end of the election from the quiet of his London home.

The Clintonites were sorely disappointed by the *Times* article. "We had been waiting for the Alfa Bank story to come out," Podesta recalled. "Then—boom!—it gets smacked down." The campaign—although it had no real proof to substantiate it—had prepared a video promoting the Trump–Alfa Bank server connection and was poised to make an all-out push through social media. That plan was canned.

That same day, CNBC reported that Comey had agreed with the October 7 ODNI/DHS assessment but had decided not to attach the FBI's name to the statement. Comey, the report noted, argued it was too close to the U.S. election to issue such a judgment. In Brooklyn, Clinton aides, ignoring the differences between a criminal probe and a counterintelligence investigation, saw this as stark hypocrisy. At a congressional hearing the previous month, Comey had declined to tell Democratic legislators whether he was investigating Trump-Russia ties. Now Comey had publicly injected the Clinton email case into the political news cycle during the final stretch of the election.

By the end of this day, it appeared to Clinton and her aides that the nation was going to reach Election Day without any public accounting of the mysterious links between Trump and Russia. Putin had essentially gotten away with mounting an operation to subvert an American election, and Trump had escaped significant scrutiny of the strange assortment of associations between his world and Moscow. At least, the Clinton team could take comfort in the fact they were still leading in the polls.

It was two days before the election, and Clint Watts was still trying to warn America. The former FBI analyst and two colleagues—Andrew Weisburd and J. M. Berger—published a report in the *War on the Rocks* online magazine, noting that they had monitored more than seven thousand social media accounts in the previous thirty months and had discerned a "small army of social media operatives" with the goal of "moving misinformation and disinformation from primarily Russian-influenced circles into the general social media population." They saw an integrated and coordinated Russian attack that included the hacks and information dumps. Guccifer 2.0, they pointed out, had recently claimed that the Democrats might "rig the elections"—reinforcing a message that Trump had been pushing.

In August 2016, Watts had been stunned to see Paul Manafort, then Trump's campaign manager, citing Russian propaganda—the fake story about angry protesters almost taking over a U.S. airbase in Turkey. Since then, he and Weisburd, a fellow at the Center for Cyber and Homeland Security, had analyzed Twitter traffic and discovered that many of the tweeters pushing this made-in-Russia story were also Trump fans.

Now, Watts and his two coauthors were convinced that America was being trolled by Russia. "Posting hundreds of times a day on social media," they pointed out in *War on the Rocks*, "thousands of Russian bots and human influence operators pump massive amounts of disinformation and harassment into public discourse." And, they added, the "most overwhelming element of Russia's online active measures over the last year relate to the presidential campaign of Donald Trump."

Watts and his colleagues didn't see the full picture, but they were close. Putin's information war against the United States included a wide-ranging and creative clandestine social media operation aimed at exploiting the United States' iconic high-tech companies— including Facebook and Twitter—to influence American voters. But by this late date there was no time to do anything to counter the digital Russian invasion. Watts and his coauthors did offer a warning: "Trump isn't the end of Russia's social media and hacking campaign against America," they wrote, "but merely the beginning."

There had been signs of this Russian social media campaign, but only a few observers were paying attention. Two years earlier, the secret source in the Kremlin had warned the U.S. embassy about Russia's information warfare buildup. That same year, whistle-blower Lyudmila Savchuk had exposed the Internet Research Agency in St. Petersburg. The *New York Times* investigated this troll farm in mid-2015. For that article, Adrian Chen, the author, had created a list of Russian trolls. And in December of that year, as the presidential campaign was intensifying, Chen discovered an intriguing development. As he said at that time, "I check on [the list] once in a while, still. And a lot of them have turned into conservative accounts, like fake conservatives. I don't know what's going on, but they're all tweeting about Donald Trump and stuff." Russian trolls for Trump—it seemed obvious.

In early 2016, Andrey Krutskikh, a senior Kremlin adviser, gave a hair-raising talk at a Russian information security forum and hinted at what his country was unleashing. "You think we are living in 2016?" he said. "No, we are living in 1948. And do you know why? Because in 1949, the Soviet Union had its first atomic bomb test. And if until that moment...the Americans were not taking us seriously, in 1949 everything changed and they started talking to us on an equal footing." Krutskikh added, "I'm warning you: We are at the verge of having 'something' in the information arena, which will allow us to talk to the Americans as equals." This new information weapon, he predicted, would allow Moscow to "dictate to the Western partners [the United States and its allies] from the position of power."

Months later, in June 2016, the Russian Institute for Strategic Studies, which was managed by retired Russian intelligence officials appointed by Putin's office, had circulated within the Kremlin a confidential report calling for Moscow to initiate a propaganda campaign on social media and Russian media outlets to persuade U.S. voters to elect a president who would adopt a softer approach toward Russia. Not until after the election would U.S. intelligence learn of this report—and a later report proposing Russian propaganda efforts push the idea of voter fraud to undercut the legitimacy of the U.S. election and undermine the presidency of Clinton, should she win.

And throughout the campaign, some of Clinton's digital media aides, looking at fake news attacks on Clinton on Facebook and Twitter assaults against their candidate, did wonder if Moscow had a hand in some of this. "We had a sense that Russia was playing a role but no idea the depth of it," Rob Flaherty, a member of the Clinton digital media team, recalled. But the Clinton campaign's overall digital strategy was not amenable to seeking out and confronting online malefactors. The plan was to use social media to reach Clinton's supporters, fire them up, and get them to contribute money to Clinton—not to engage or persuade voters who were not already with her and who might be met with an online barrage of fake news stories, conspiracy theories, and bot-driven anti-Clinton messages. After the campaign, top Clinton aides would acknowledge they had screwed up by ceding this territory. "This left us naked," Podesta later observed. "A lot of puke was sloshing around in social media, particularly Facebook. And for swing voters, there was more of that than direct communications from us."

The Trump campaign, though, had fixated on Facebook. Jared Kushner was in charge of overseeing this effort. Using both a social media firm run out of San Antonio by Brad Parscale and Cambridge Analytica, the secretive data firm owned by right-wing hedge-fund billionaire Robert Mercer, the campaign—working with the Republican National Committee—was employing micro-targeting and other data-driven techniques. It zeroed in on Facebook not just as the place to engage existing supporters but to win over potential Trump voters.* And its work, whether the Trump campaign realized it or not, was aided by the anti-Clinton messages generated by Russian trolls and others.

Putin's covert social media campaign was employing a host of tactics. The Internet Research Agency's worker bees deployed thousands of phony Twitter accounts. Posing as Americans, they posted

* In June, as Cambridge Analytica was beginning to work for the Trump campaign, its chief executive, Alexander Nix, had contacted WikiLeaks and asked if it would share with his firm Clinton-related emails Assange at that point had hinted he possessed. WikiLeaks declined.

comments at major U.S. media outlets. Using fake accounts and VPNs—virtual private networks, which hide the origins of internet communications—they attacked Clinton on Twitter and Facebook and depicted her as corrupt. When Trump begrudgingly rejected birtherism, Russian trolls echoed his claim that it had been Clinton who had kick-started the birther conspiracy theory. And when the *Access Hollywood* video was posted, Russian Twitter accounts rushed to Trump's defense, attacking Clinton, and then promoted WikiLeaks' Podesta dump.

"We had a goal to set up the Americans against their own government," an IRA troll who went by the pseudonym Maksim explained in a Russian television interview after the election. "To cause unrest [and] cause discontent." To better understand American politics and how to craft messages, Maksim said, he and his colleagues were given an important homework assignment: Watch the Netflix series *House of Cards*.

Long after the election, Twitter would identify more than thirty-six thousand accounts that had generated automated, election-related material and were possibly associated with Russia. These accounts posted 1.4 million election-related tweets that received about 288 million impressions in the fall election period. (Some social media analysts believed Twitter's numbers were low.)

On Facebook and Instagram, hundreds of IRA operatives bought thousands of ads—about $100,000 worth, not a large amount but an audacious move on the part of the Kremlin's secret online propagandists. Many of the messages were issue ads—inflammatory and divisive, but not necessarily tied to the election itself. They focused on hot-button issues, including LBGT rights, race, police brutality, immigration, and gun rights. An ad placed by South United, a Facebook group set up by the Russians, depicted a Confederate flag with the text: "Heritage, not hate. The South will rise again!" Another Russian-created group, Secured Borders, ran an ad showing a border fence and declaring, "No Invaders Allowed."

But Clinton was often a target. A Russian-backed ad posted by a group called Army of Jesus showed Satan arm-wrestling Jesus and proclaiming, "If I win Clinton wins." The text of the ad warned,

"Hillary is Satan, and her crimes and lies had proved just how evil she is." Yet another Russian ad—designed to look as if it came from a U.S. veterans organization—showed a flag-draped coffin of a dead solider accompanied by the text, "Hillary Asks, 'What Difference Does It Make?'" A fake Born Liberal group circulated an ad with Bernie Sanders saying, "Clinton Foundation is a 'problem.'"

About 5 million people in the United States saw the Russian ads before the election.

The Russian effort went beyond ads. The Internet Research Agency set up 120 or so Facebook pages and circulated inflammatory posts. A Russian-backed Facebook page called Being Patriotic organized pro-Trump rallies across Florida, succeeding in at least two cities to bring together Trump supporters. The page also promoted a "Down With Hillary!" protest outside her Brooklyn headquarters. And the Russians backed YouTube videos in which two African-American men talked trash about Clinton, calling her a "racist bitch" who was "going to stand for the Muslims."

Facebook would estimate that the fake Russian accounts produced about eighty thousand posts over two years that were seen by about 126 million Americans.

How much of a difference did all this activity make? Many of the Facebook ads were not placed in the final weeks of the campaign. Swing states were not always targeted the most. The total number of Russian-linked tweets were a tiny fraction of the overall amount of election tweets. Yet Moscow had mounted a clandestine propaganda endeavor, stretching across social media platforms and in sync with the cyberattacks and the output of RT and Sputnik, which was largely missed by the U.S. government.

Whatever information the intelligence community had about these Russian actions, it did not get the whole picture. In briefings with members of Congress, U.S. intelligence officials discussed Russian propaganda efforts in the most general terms. They gave no indication they were aware of this substantial undertaking. And in the highly secretive principals meetings in the White House Sit Room, Obama and his top national security advisers had pondered the details and implications of the Kremlin's hack-and-dump operations and Russia's attempts to probe and penetrate state election systems. But there was no talk of Moscow's infiltration of American social media and its propaganda campaign. "It was not part of the conversation," a participant in those meetings later conceded. This was an intelligence failure.

By the end of the campaign, top Trump advisers and supporters were amplifying the Russians' secret handiwork. Two days before Election Day, Kellyanne Conway tweeted a post from @Ten_ GOP—a Twitter account that billed itself as the "Unofficial Twitter account of Tennessee Republicans." That tweet read, "Mother of jailed sailor: 'Hold Hillary to same standards as my son on Classified info' #hillarysemail #WeinerGate." Weeks earlier, Parscale, the Trump campaign's digital director, also had retweeted an @ Ten_GOP tweet, this one saying, "Thousands of deplorables chanting to the media: 'Tell The Truth!' RT if you are also done w/ biased Media!" Donald Trump Jr. retweeted a post from this account warning about Clinton voters committing voter fraud in Florida. And Flynn and his son Michael Flynn Jr. retweeted posts from @Ten_GOP.

The @Ten_GOP account was operated by the Internet Research Agency. Trump's top advisers were advancing covert Russian propaganda. (Parscale later said he had no idea this account was a Russian fake: "I got fooled.")

On November 6, Comey sent a letter to Congress noting that the FBI had completed its review of the emails found on Anthony Weiner's laptop. After the uproar caused by his letter a week earlier, Comey saw that the Bureau could not leave this question hanging. He had the FBI's techies and analysts work around the clock to examine these messages. And now he declared, "We have not changed our conclusions that we expressed in July." The emails on this computer were mainly duplicates of what the Bureau had previously examined.

Clinton officials were relieved. But the damage had already been done. The headline on the *Washington Post* story on this announcement reported, "FBI Director Comey says agency won't recommend charges over Clinton's email." It was another reminder that Clinton had been under FBI investigation. Trump denounced Comey and the FBI. "Hillary Clinton is guilty," he proclaimed at a Michigan rally. "She knows it, the FBI knows it, the people know it."

Clinton's post-Comey slide in the polls had stopped by the middle of the final week of the race. But she had dropped from a 4.7 percent lead on October 28 to a 2.9 percent lead now. Before the Comey announcement, Clinton had an 81 percent chance of winning the election, according to the model of analyst Nate Silver. Two days out, it was at 65 percent. The campaign's own polling numbers showed Clinton remained ahead in the states her advisers believed she needed to win.

On Election Night, Clinton collected 65,844,610 votes to Trump's 62,979,636 votes. But Trump won a decisive majority in the Electoral College by eking out narrow victories in Wisconsin, Michigan, and Pennsylvania—triumphing in each Rust Belt swing state by less than 1 percentage point. A swing of 77,000 votes in these three states would have yielded the opposite outcome.

In the White House, Obama and his aides, like political observers throughout the nation and the world, were shocked by the results. They believed they had accomplished their mission: Election Day was free of disruption and chaos. But that was little comfort. It had taken the White House months to inform the public of the Russian attack. Obama had threatened Putin but had not imposed sanctions on Moscow. And a large question would linger: Had they truly protected American democracy from Putin's information warfare?

With the margin of victory so slender, any element of the race could have been the decisive factor: Clinton's own messaging problems, her ad buys, the decisions where to campaign and deploy resources in the final weeks, her inability to hold on to a greater number of Sanders voters, her self-created email server problem, Comey's last-minute revival of that controversy, and much more—including the Russian hacks, the WikiLeaks dumps, and Putin's covert social media blitz. Clinton and her aides, jolted and devastated, believed one factor in their loss was Putin's under-handed intervention. Late on Election Night, when it seemed Trump was going to win, Senator Claire McCaskill, a Missouri Democrat close to Clinton, walked past a reporter and muttered, "Can you believe this? The fucking Russians."

But as Trump saw it, any talk of the Russians tainted his cam-paign. He had repeatedly refused to acknowledge the Russian operation, even after the U.S. intelligence community had declared that Putin's attack on America was real. And it worked. In his vic-tory speech, he declared, "Now it is time for America to bind the wounds of division, have to get together."

"Trump! Trump! Trump!" The crowd at the bar roared, as the election results came in. There was a large, life-sized photo of Trump in one corner, where Trump fans could take selfies. And a photo of Putin. The bar was in downtown Moscow. At a late-night/early-morning Marathon for Trump, ultra-nationalists, pro-Kremlin academics, government-friendly journalists, and other Russian Trump fans had gathered to cheer on the Republican candidate. Alexei Zhuravlyov, a legislator who chaired the ultra-patriotic Rodina party, praised Trump's pro-Russia stance. "This is the real reset, not the Clinton reset," Dmitry Drobnitsky, a writer for pro-Kremlin outlets, exclaimed. "This is the real reset of the Western world."

Hours later, the Russian Duma burst into applause when informed Trump was the victor. Putin's operation—which had fueled divisions within the United States and influenced an Ameri-can presidential election—had succeeded.

CHAPTER 21

"We got a sinking feeling. . . . It looked like a season of *Homeland*."

T he morning after Election Day, Barack Obama walked into the Oval Office for his daily intelligence briefing, and he shouted to his administrative staffers, "Chin up, people, we have shit to do." He then called in his communications and political teams, about thirty people, who were utterly dejected.

"History zigs and zags," he told them. "It is not a straight line. A lot of what we achieved can be sustained. Don't be discouraged. There's two months left and a lot to do." One of his aides got the sense Obama was talking to himself, as well.

The president was trying to be as upbeat as possible. On Election Night, as it appeared Trump would win, he had told senior staff that his soon-to-be successor was more a blowhard showman than an ideologue. Maybe Trump would be responsible. Maybe he would only tweak Obamacare, not trash it, and remain within the Paris climate accord. Obama was hoping for an easy and efficient transition period in which Trump could be smoothly guided into his new role as head of the U.S. government and custodian of the nation. But the Russian issue would not go away—and it would shape and undercut one of the United States' oldest and most important political traditions: the handover of power.

New questions began to mount almost immediately. Two days after the election, Russian deputy foreign minister Sergei Ryabkov told a Russian news agency "there were contacts" between the Kremlin and the Trump team during the campaign. "Obviously, we know most of the people from his entourage," Ryabkov said. "Those people have always been in the limelight in the United States and have occupied high-ranking positions. I cannot say that all of them, but quite a few have been staying in touch with Russian representatives."

Ryabkov's comments were striking. What contacts was he talking about? Ryabkov provided no further details, and Hope Hicks, the Trump campaign spokeswoman, quickly issued a comprehensive denial: "It never happened. There was no communication between the campaign and any foreign entity during the campaign." It was a statement that would not hold up well.

At the same time, the intelligence on the Russian role in the election continued to harden. The National Security Agency chief, Adm. Michael Rogers, speaking at a conference in the days after the election, was asked about the WikiLeaks release of hacked information during the campaign. "This was a conscious effort by a nation-state to attempt to achieve a specific effect," he said. "This was not something that was done casually. This was not something that was done by chance. This was not a target that was selected purely arbitrarily." These were strong words. The intelligence community had identified Moscow as the culprit in the hacks of Democrats in October. But it had only said then the release of the material was "consistent" with the methods and motivations of Russian-directed efforts. Rogers was now going further—and setting the stage for what would soon become a bruising confrontation between the U.S. intelligence community and the newly elected president.

*   *   *

The U.S. intelligence community's conclusions about Russia hadn't made a dent in the thinking of the incoming administration. Trump told reporters that he had received a "beautiful" letter of congratulations from Putin. The two men spoke by phone on November 13 and, according to a Kremlin statement, discussed ways "to normalize relations and pursue constructive cooperation on the broadest possible range of issues."

Trump tapped Michael Flynn to be his national security adviser. Within a few days of his appointment, Flynn called a U.S.-based advocate for the Syrian opposition to President Bashar al-Assad—the brutal dictator whom the Russians had propped up. "We're going to have to work with the Russians," Flynn told him. The Trump team's strategy, as he explained it, was to put aside the Obama administration's prior demand that Assad step down and focus for now on destroying ISIS and its base in the Syrian city of Raqqa—a goal that Flynn believed could best be accomplished in coordination with the Russian military. Flynn mentioned he had already discussed the subject with Sergey Kislyak. In follow-up conversations with the advocate, Flynn spoke freely about the conversations he was having with the Russian ambassador. "He was talking to Kislyak a lot," the activist recalled. The talks became so routine that Flynn—a professional military intelligence officer—never considered that they were all being monitored by U.S. intelligence.

About the time that Flynn, on behalf of Trump, was reaching out to the Russians to resolve the Syrian crisis, Secretary of State John Kerry had given up trying to work with Moscow. During the summer and into the fall, Kerry had raised objections to taking actions against the Russians that would interfere with his efforts to work out a deal with Foreign Minister Lavrov to end the bloody Syrian civil war. But by the fall, Kerry realized he was getting nowhere with Lavrov. And, amid rising anger among his former Democratic colleagues in the Congress over Russia's meddling in the election, he pushed a novel proposal to get to the bottom of what happened.

In early December, at a National Security Council meeting,

Kerry—who was in Brussels for a NATO gathering and participating via video—recommended creating an independent and bipartisan investigation to investigate the Russian hack-and-release attack. He had asked the policy shop at the State Department to draw up a proposal for such a body, and officials there had drafted a memo noting that this inquiry could be modeled on the highly acclaimed 9/11 Commission. "We thought this was the only chance to get the truth out," a State Department official later said. "If we don't do it, it won't happen in the Trump administration."

But Kerry had the sense that Obama was not keen to fully confront the Russia question during the transition. At the meeting, Obama and other Cabinet officials reviewed Kerry's proposal. And the president nixed it. During the heat of the campaign, Obama had worried that if he made a public comment about the Russian cyberattacks, it would come across as too partisan. Now, after the election, he had the same fear: Establishing a commission to investigate what happened would look political.

That's it, Kerry thought. There will be no response. The Russians will get away with this. "After the election, we were all thrown for a loop, and any consideration of the Russia operation just languished," one senior administration official recalled. "I didn't think the president would do anything."

The first order of business for Trump was to form a Cabinet. And, on November 19, while hunting for a suitable secretary of state, the president-elect had a surprising visitor at his mansion in Bedminister, New Jersey: Mitt Romney.

The idea that the former Massachusetts governor might be offered the most prized position in Trump's Cabinet seemed improbable. Trump had famously called Romney a "choke artist" after his 2012 defeat to Obama. And Romney during the GOP primary campaign had ripped into Trump, deriding him as a "phony" and a "fraud" who had played the American public for "suckers." But there was another reason that Romney as Trump's secretary of state seemed to make no sense. When he was running for president four years earlier, Romney had called Russia the country's "number one geopolitical foe"—a statement that Obama had ridiculed (and misrepresented) at the time but which now seemed prescient.

Romney said little about his talk with Trump as he departed. "We had a far-reaching conversation with regard to the various theaters in the world," he told reporters. Speculation that he was to be named to the Cabinet was rampant.

It was soon after this that Christopher Steele in London picked up a new thread of intelligence from one of his sources in Moscow. He was no longer working for Simpson and Fusion GPS, but he still felt obliged to share what had come in.

He dashed off another report to Simpson—a brief memo that would never be made public. "Speaking on November 29 2016, a senior official working at the Russian MFA reported that a rumour is currently circulating there that US President-elect TRUMP's delay in appointing a new Secretary of State is the result of an intervention by President PUTIN/the Kremlin," Steele wrote. "The latter reportedly have asked that TRUMP appoint a Russia-friendly figure to this position, who was prepared to move quickly on lifting Ukraine-related sanctions and cooperation ('security') in Syria."

Steele added: "The source assumes the Kremlin's reported intervention was in response to the possibility that Mitt ROMNEY, viewed as hostile to Russia, might be appointed Secretary."* (A Trump White House official later said, "There is no indication the Russians were in communication or sought any influence in this decision, and had they done so, they would have been promptly rebuffed.")

On December 12, Trump announced that he would nominate Rex Tillerson, the CEO of ExxonMobil, as his secretary of state. It was an unusual pick. Tillerson had no diplomatic or even government experience. But he did have very close relations with senior leaders in the Moscow. As Exxon chief, he had flown repeatedly to Russia to cut huge energy deals with Igor Sechin, chief of Rosneft,

---

* In mid-December, Steele sent his final report to Simpson. The memo cited a source claiming a Russian tech executive and his companies deployed botnets and porn traffic to hack the Democratic Party leadership. The Russian and his companies would later deny this and sue Steele in London.

the Russian energy giant, and the two of them once toasted each other with champagne to celebrate. In 2013, Putin awarded Tillerson a medal—the Order of Friendship.

Obama was under increasing pressure from congressional Democrats and officials within his own administration to provide a full accounting of what happened during the election. The U.S. intelligence community had been reviewing its intelligence reporting and some officials were getting unnerved. A secret CIA assessment concluded that Russia's cyberattacks had been launched not merely to foment chaos, but specifically to elect Trump. Why was this only discovered belatedly? "We vacuum up a lot of intelligence that is not exploited in real time," a senior administration official later explained. "Things sat in databases until queried. Not until after the election did analysts go into these databases and find a lot of stuff that changed the assessments. Plus, intelligence picked up certain Russians high-fiving after the election."

In early December, Obama directed Lisa Monaco, his homeland security adviser, to announce the intelligence community would conduct a "full review" of Russian interference in the campaign and make a public report before he left office. There were other reasons for Obama to act beyond pressure from Capitol Hill. His aides and some members of Congress concluded that intelligence documents on the Russian operation needed to be preserved right away—before Trump's team could bury or even destroy them. "It was imperative to get as much down on paper and briefed to the Hill during the transition," a White House aide recalled. "Otherwise, Trump would sweep it under the rug."

Having decided it was time to get tougher with the Russians, the Obama White House had trouble figuring out how to do so. After a brief overseas trip, Obama had ordered a new review to determine if sanctions were warranted.

There was no appetite for the far-reaching economic sanctions that could wreak havoc on Russia. The intelligence community warned that this would be seen by Putin as a final Obama attempt to bring about regime change—and provoke a crisis that the new Trump team would not be equipped to deal with.

The State Department dusted off the punishments it had drafted earlier in the year, which included tossing Russian diplomats—including spies—out of the United States and shutting down Russian facilities in America used as centers for Russian intelligence operations. But Kerry was hesitant to boot too many Russians, for fear Moscow would retaliate and cripple the State Department's—and the intelligence agencies'—ability to operate within Russia.

Some administration officials—still uninformed about the depth of the Russian social media campaign—argued that maybe extreme measures weren't called for anyway. "We thought in terms of the Russian cyber activities, that it had stopped about the time of Obama's warning to Putin," a senior official involved in these deliberations recalled. "By the time we were responding, some officials were of the view we had successfully deterred them. So we did not have to impose the extreme measures that had been cooked up."

When Obama held his annual end-of-year press conference, the first question posed was a sharp query about the Russia matter. AP's Josh Lederman asked, "There is a perception that you are letting President Putin get away with interfering in the U.S. election and that a response that nobody knows about or a lookback review just don't cut it. Are you prepared to call out President Putin by name for ordering this hacking, and do you agree with what Hillary Clinton now says, that the hacking was actually partially responsible for her loss?" Obama responded with a long and defensive reply. "I think we handled it the way it should have been handled," he said.

Finally, on December 29, Obama did unveil a response to Moscow's interference. He sanctioned the GRU and the FSB, four senior officers of the GRU, and three companies that provided material support to the GRU's cyber operations. And the State Department would shut down the two Russian compounds, one in Maryland, the other in New York, which were used for intelligence operations, and declare thirty-five Russian diplomats who were suspected intelligence operatives persona non grata. They would have three days to leave the United States. "These actions are not the sum total of our response to Russia's aggressive activities," Obama said. "We will continue to take a variety of actions at a time and place of our choosing, some of which will not be publicized." No other punishments, if they existed, were ever revealed.

What impact these moves had was questionable. GRU officers did not have a habit of traveling to the United States or putting their money in American bank accounts that could be seized by the Treasury Department. Schiff, the top Democrat on the House Intelligence Committee, considered the expulsion of diplomats "minor." Over time, some senior Obama officials believed the president had blown it. Later, Susan Rice would think it was reasonable to conclude the administration should have gone further. "Maybe we should have whacked them more," said one senior official.

The incoming Trump team didn't want the Russians whacked at all. And the Russians weren't pleased, either—especially about the closure of their compounds. The day before the sanctions announcement, Kislyak had met at the State Department with officials who informed him of Obama's decision. The ambassador was irate. He threatened Moscow would retaliate. Trump, too, was not happy with the sanctions. "I think we ought to get on with our lives," he told reporters at Mar-a-Lago.

The next day, Flynn placed several calls to Kislyak. He urged the Russians not to respond, promising there would be better relations with Washington once Trump was in office. Afterward, he informed his deputy, K. T. McFarland, of the conversation, and she sent emails to other transition officials notifying them of Flynn's discussion with the Russian. Moscow got the message. Contrary to all expectations, Putin did not retaliate by expelling any U.S. diplomats from Russia. Trump praised the Russian president in a tweet: "Great move on delay (by V. Putin)—I always knew he was very smart!" Soon Kislyak called Flynn to tell him Putin had held back in response to Flynn's request, and Flynn let other senior Trump advisers know this. His backdoor communication with Kislyak had worked.

Putin's restraint surprised the White House. "We had intelligence that showed the Ministry of Foreign Affairs was preparing retaliation," a senior Obama official later noted. "Then Putin turned it off." Administration officials wondered what had happened. It would only be a few days before they found out. Flynn's calls to Kislyak had been intercepted by U.S. intelligence, and word of the incoming national security adviser's request to the Russians spread within the national security community.

Flynn and Trump were trying to reset relations with Moscow—as Obama had tried eight years earlier—but under very different circumstances. In the context of what had just taken place during the election, the Trump efforts looked suspicious to White House and intelligence officials. And the Trump transition officials weren't observing a basic tenet of American government: They were supposed to wait to take office before making foreign policy. In fact, they were actively undermining U.S. policy.

Two weeks earlier, the United Nations Security Council had been due to vote on a resolution condemning Israel for its settlement activity on the West Bank. Obama, fed up with Israeli Prime Minister Benjamin Netanyahu and his persistent refusal to make any accommodations to the Palestinians, had decided the United States would abstain rather than exercise its usual veto of anti-Israeli resolutions. The Trump transition officials, at the request of the Israelis, moved to secretly intervene and sabotage Obama. The entire Trump senior team—Steve Bannon, Jared Kushner, Reince Priebus, Michael Flynn, and Nikki Haley, Trump's designated UN ambassador—divided up the list of Security Council members and began calling the ambassadors to ask that they delay or abstain from the resolution. Flynn, after consulting with Kushner, called Kislyak. This time, Russia wouldn't go along. Like Flynn's other contacts with the Russian ambassador, the call was intercepted by the NSA.

Senior White House officials viewed these and other communications between the Trump team and the Russians with increasing alarm. It was hardly unusual or improper for transition officials to meet with foreign diplomats. But the Trump team's actions seemed to go well beyond the norm. Flynn and Kushner had also met with

Kislyak at Trump Tower on December 1. The ambassador told them that Russian generals had information they wanted to provide to the transition officials about Syria. But they preferred to do so privately—not through official U.S. government circles. Was there a secure line in the transition office they could use? Kislyak asked. There wasn't. But Kushner suggested Flynn could go to the Russian embassy in Washington to use a secure line there to talk to Russia's generals—a surprising proposal since the only reason to do this would be to make sure the NSA couldn't eavesdrop.

Twelve days later, Kushner—at Kislyak's request—had another meeting, this time with someone the Russian ambassador described as having a direct line to Putin. It was Sergey Gorkov, the head of Vnesheconombank, known as VEB, a Russian state-owned bank that the U.S. had sanctioned after the Crimea annexation. (Kushner, soon to become a senior White House adviser for his father-in-law, would fail to disclose his contacts with Kislyak, Gorkov, and dozens of other foreign officials when applying for a top secret security clearance.)

For Obama officials, the pattern of contacts—and the nature of discussions—was disturbing. They were reading reports of U.S. intelligence intercepts of Russian officials communicating with Americans whose identities, under the law, were not revealed to protect their privacy. Rice, UN Ambassador Samantha Power, and others asked intelligence officials to "unmask" the names of these Americans—a procedure that was rare but permitted so policy-makers could better understand intelligence reports. The unmasking revealed the names of Flynn and other Trump aides. And some Justice Department officials believed the Trump team was possibly violating the Logan Act, a 217-year-old law (never successfully prosecuted) that bars private citizens from interfering with diplomatic relations between the United States and foreign governments. "We got a sinking feeling, a feeling of dread," an Obama aide recalled. "Were the incoming national security adviser and Trump's son-in-law in the bag with the Russians? It looked like a season of *Homeland*."*

---

* In recent months, Flynn, even as he advised candidate and then President-elect Trump, had been busy as a consultant. He was advising a project that aimed to

* * *

Ten days after the election, Senator John McCain—one of Capitol Hill's most ardent anti-Russia hawks—was at the annual Halifax International Security Forum in Nova Scotia when he heard about the Steele dossier from Sir Andrew Wood, a former British ambassador to Russia and an associate of Steele at Orbis. McCain dispatched David Kramer, a former State Department official who was a fellow at the nonprofit McCain Institute, to see Steele in England and obtain a copy. They met in Surrey on November 28, and Steele showed Kramer the memos. Kramer was shocked. He told Steele that these reports potentially raised grave issues of national security and needed to be reviewed in Washington. But Steele wouldn't give Kramer a copy. Too risky, he told him. Steele worried that Kramer's bags would be searched by customs officials and the memos seized. "You don't want them crossing the border," Steele explained to Kramer. He advised the American to fly back to Washington and get the dossier from Simpson.

Once Kramer was in Washington, he went to Simpson's office in Dupont Circle and retrieved a copy—under the explicit understanding that it was only for McCain. Kramer brought the dossier to McCain. Alarmed by the idea that Putin might possess *kompromat* on Trump, the senator took the unusual step of hand-delivering it to Comey. The Bureau already had the memos. But now that one of the Senate's most influential members was worked up about the Steele dossier, it became a more urgent matter.

In early December, CIA director John Brennan called up Director of National Intelligence James Clapper to alert him to a report that

---

build nuclear power plants in Saudi Arabia and throughout the Middle East and that at one point involved Russian companies. He also was working as a consultant and lobbyist for Turkey—though he had not registered as one. In September 2016, he met with Turkish government officials in New York City to discuss how to deal with a Muslim cleric in the United States who was a critic of the Turkish government. One participant in the meeting, James Woolsey, a former CIA chief, later said there was a discussion of kidnapping the cleric and returning him to Turkey. A Flynn spokesman insisted there had been no talk of any illegal actions.

had just come into his possession: the Steele dossier. "You need to read this thing," Brennan told him. Clapper did and instructed his analysts to start reviewing it. He had no idea how consequential this would become.

By now, talk of the memos—and their explosive, if uncorroborated, allegations—was spreading like wildfire through official Washington. Members of Congress knew about them. Reporters were calling their sources in U.S. intelligence agencies asking if it was really true that the Kremlin had a sex tape of the incoming U.S. president.

As U.S. intelligence officials were preparing the report on Russian meddling in the election that Obama had ordered, they had to deal with a vexing question: Should the dossier's allegations be part of it?

According to Clapper, it was not an easy call. As the U.S. intelligence community's top Russia analysts dug into the document, they realized they had nothing to corroborate the sensational claims of sexual blackmail or active collusion between the Trump camp and the Kremlin. But there were passages in the dossier that, Clapper thought, matched later U.S. intelligence reports about the Russian influence campaign—and the underlying reasons behind it, especially Putin's hostility toward Hillary Clinton. In July, Steele had written about how Putin was motivated by his "fear and hatred of Hillary CLINTON." In August, he had described the Russian campaign as an effort "to aid TRUMP and damage CLINTON"—a conclusion Clapper's own intelligence analysts had not yet reached. "I probably didn't appreciate the depth of the animus that [Putin] had to the Clintons," Clapper subsequently said.

In the end, the FBI and Clapper's analysts couldn't reach a firm conclusion about the dossier. There were some obvious mistakes—Steele had gotten (slightly) wrong the name of the Russian diplomat who had been recalled from Washington during the height of the influence campaign. His sourcing was murky and mysterious. The lurid sex claims were wild and completely unsubstantiated. But based in part on Comey's word that Steele had been regarded as a "credible" source by the FBI, a reference to the dossier was included in an early draft of the report. "There was debate about that," recalled Clapper. Then the mention was taken out.

The leaders of the U.S. intelligence community came up with an alternative plan for how to handle the dossier. Before publicly releasing the IC's report, they would be briefing Obama at the White House and Trump at Trump Tower about the assessment. The meeting with Trump, they all realized, would be the dicey one. The intelligence chiefs—Comey, Clapper, Brennan, and Rogers—would each present different sections of the report. Then they would leave—except for Comey. He would privately give a two-page synopsis of the dossier to Trump. He would tell the president-elect he was doing so because the dossier was being "shopped around" and they wanted—as a courtesy—to give him a heads-up. The group huddled in Clapper's office days before the briefing, fully aware of the gravity of what they were about to do. "Are we all OK with how we're going to do this?" one of Clapper's briefers asked them. They voted one by one—Clapper, Brennan, Rogers, and Comey—giving their assent.

The report they had prepared wouldn't need the dossier to get headlines. Its findings were stark and dramatic enough. With "high confidence," the assessment stated, "Russian President Vladimir Putin ordered an influence campaign in 2016 aimed at the US presidential election. Russia's goals were to undermine public faith in the US democratic process, denigrate Secretary Clinton, and harm her electability and potential presidency. We further assess Putin and the Russian Government developed a clear preference for President-elect Trump." What prompted Putin to order the attack? It was "most likely" because the Russian president wanted to discredit Clinton because he blamed her for the 2011 protests in Russia and all these years later still held a grudge for the disparaging comments she had made about him.

What was most striking was the depth and scope of the Russian operation: the cyberattacks, the information dumps through WikiLeaks, the creation of phony online personas like Guccifer 2.0 and DCLeaks, the deployment of online trolls by the Internet Research Agency, the use of state propaganda outlets—RT and Sputnik—to advance the Kremlin's messaging. That was all in the public version.

* * *

On Thursday, January 5, 2017, the day before its public release, the intelligence chiefs briefed Obama and his senior staff. White House officials were taken aback. It was "the first time all the pieces came together for us," one senior official said. "It seemed a much grander conspiracy than it was during the election. This was an intelligence failure and a failure of the imagination." And when Biden was briefed about intelligence reports on the connections between various players in the Trump orbit and the Kremlin, he had a visceral reaction. "If this is true," he exclaimed, "it's treason."

A few days earlier, Rice had encouraged Clapper during the daily intelligence briefing to tell Obama about the "golden showers" allegation. Obama turned to Rice and said, "Why am I hearing this?" He was incredulous. "What's happening?" he asked. Rice said the intelligence community had no idea if this story was true but that Obama needed to be aware the allegation was circulating. "You don't really expect to hear the term 'golden showers' in the President Daily Brief," a participant in this meeting later said, "or that the guy who is going to become president may be a Manchurian candidate."

On January 6, Clapper, Brennan, Rogers, and Comey went to Capitol Hill to brief the Gang of Eight congressional leaders on the report. Then a motorcade, complete with flashing lights and sirens, whisked them to Andrews Air Force Base, where they hopped a plane for Newark. They were on their way to Trump Tower.

Clapper was nervous. He didn't know how Trump would respond. When they arrived at Trump's office, they were greeted by the president-elect, along with his senior leadership: Vice President-elect Mike Pence, Mike Flynn, Sean Spicer, K. T. McFarland, and Tom Bossert, who would soon be Trump's homeland security adviser in the White House. Trump was cordial when they arrived and at first listened closely to Clapper and the others. Clapper handed Trump a copy of the main report, as well as a classified annex that detailed the forensic analysis that supported the IC's conclusion that Russian intelligence had done the hacking.

Trump did question whether the intelligence was truly solid. It was clear to Clapper that Trump was obsessed with anything that might challenge the legitimacy of his election victory. The real problem, Trump suggested, was that the DNC had no security for its servers, leaving them vulnerable, unlike the RNC, which had better security. Clapper explained that the Russians had also infiltrated GOP computers but were likely saving that material for a later day. Then, as they had planned, Clapper, Brennan, and Rogers exited, and Comey stayed back to deal with the more sensitive matter— handing Trump the two-page synopsis of the Steele memos. He let Trump know this information was circulating. Trump looked at the material and took it in. None of it is true, he told Comey.

After Comey left, Trump reviewed what had just happened with his advisers, now joined by Bannon. The president-elect was furious. This claim about him watching women urinate at the hotel. "It's bullshit," Trump said. He explained, as he would later do publicly, that he was a germaphobe who would never be around anything like that. Then Bannon fed Trump's anger: "What the fuck is the head of the FBI giving that to you for? Is that an official FBI document? Has it been vetted?" Bannon turned to Flynn and Priebus. Why did you let this happen? By even touching the document, Bannon told them, Trump had turned it into an official presidential record. Why did you even take it? Bannon said to Trump.

Trump ruminated some more and—in his own mind—figured it out. This was a "shakedown," he said. Comey was trying to blackmail him—letting him know that he had something on him. It would later occur to Bannon that he had planted a seed in Trump's mind—doubts about the loyalty of the FBI director. Within a few months, it would result in one of the biggest disasters of Trump's presidency: the decision to fire Comey. "I put the idea in his head," Bannon later told colleagues regretfully.

After the briefing, Trump publicly focused on one slim portion of the IC's official assessment, tweeting, "Intelligence stated very strongly there was absolutely no evidence that hacking affected the election results." Actually, the report had noted the intelligence community had not evaluated this point, explaining it was not the

IC's job to analyze domestic political matters: "We did not make an assessment of the impact that Russian activities had on the outcome of the 2016 election."

Late on the afternoon of January 10, CNN reported that the FBI director had given Trump a two-page synopsis of a dossier containing allegations that Russia had "compromising personal and financial information" about the president-elect. The network reported that the memos had been compiled by a former British intelligence operative—who it did not name—and that their contents were being investigated by the FBI. CNN did not disclose the details of the potentially compromising material "as it has not independently corroborated the specific allegations."

The dam had now burst. Almost immediately, Buzzfeed posted a full set of the Steele memos—with all the details about golden showers, prostitutes, and sex parties. There had been some debate within the online news organization about the advisability of doing so, with some reporters arguing it would be irresponsible to throw out inflammatory allegations that had not been corroborated. But Buzzfeed editor Ben Smith contended that with CNN reporting that the dossier was being taken seriously by the intelligence community, the public deserved to read and decide for itself what the controversy was all about.

Trump was now livid. He took to Twitter and called it "Fake News." The next morning, he tweeted, "COMPLETE AND TOTAL FABRICATION, UTTER NONSENSE." In another tweet, he exclaimed, "I HAVE NOTHING TO DO WITH RUSSIA—NO DEALS, NO LOANS, NO NOTHING." And then came this: "Intelligence agencies should never have allowed this fake news to 'leak' into the public. One last shot at me. Are we living in Nazi Germany?"

At a press conference that day, Trump lashed out left and right—at the intelligence community which he blamed for leaking the memos, at CNN for first reporting them, and at Buzzfeed ("a failing pile of garbage") for publishing the material. When asked about his tweet comparing the U.S. intelligence community to the Nazis, he didn't back down: "I think it was disgraceful—disgraceful that the intelligence agencies allowed any information [out] that turned out to be so false and fake out....That's something that Nazi Germany would have done and did do."

In his office, Clapper was watching Trump on the console with four televisions and fuming. He could scarcely believe that the president-elect had just compared the men and women he worked with to the Gestapo. "I just went nuts," Clapper recalled. "It was an affront to the entire U.S. intelligence community. I couldn't let that go."

Clapper decided he would call Trump out. It was an audacious move for a lifelong military man, confronting the soon-to-be commander in chief. But, he figured, what the hell? He only had nine more days in office. "I felt I had to stand up for the intelligence community," he later explained. He checked with the White House, obtained approval, and asked his secretary to set up a call with Trump for the next morning.

When the time came, Trump got on the phone, and Clapper was as direct as he could be. Mr. President-elect, you have disrespected the entire U.S. intelligence community, which has done so much to keep this nation safe, he told Trump. "Yeah, they're great people," Trump replied, going on about the fine work the intelligence community had done and steering the conversation away from the Nazi analogy.

Then Trump had a request for Clapper. Could he issue a statement refuting the allegations in the dossier?

Clapper was uncomfortable. "I don't know that I could do that," he told Trump. "That wasn't an IC document. Our only purpose in giving that to you was to warn you that it was out there." And with that, the conversation ended. Clapper felt a sense of catharsis, but he didn't think he made any inroads with Trump.

Clapper was right. In the days that followed, Trump kept tweeting about the dossier—and attacking the intelligence community for leaking it. In one tweet, he claimed, "Clapper called me yesterday to denounce the false and fictitious report that was illegally circulated." That was untrue. Clapper had never said that. The following day Trump claimed this "FAKE NEWS" was "probably released by 'intelligence.'" And he tweeted, "Those intelligence chiefs made a mistake here."

The same day as Trump's press conference, Chris Steele's world changed. A *Wall Street Journal* report identified him as the author of the now-famous memos. The article also named his firm, Orbis Business Intelligence, and his partner Christopher Burrows. To avoid further unwanted publicity, the former spy left town and went into hiding.

Any hope Trump might have had that he could contain the damage from both the intelligence assessment and the dossier disappeared on January 13 when the leaders of the Senate Intelligence Committee, Republican chairman Richard Burr of North Carolina and Democratic vice chairman Mark Warner of Virginia, announced the panel would conduct a broad investigation of the Russian attack on the American election including "any intelligence regarding links between Russia and individuals associated with political campaigns." The House Intelligence Committee soon followed suit.

On January 20, Trump appeared on the steps of the U.S. Capitol and was sworn in as the forty-fifth president of the United States of America. "From this moment on, it's going to be America First," he declared in his inauguration speech.

But it was Russia that would consume the first year of his presidency.

AFTERWORD

"Please, my God, can't you stop this?"

In the early days of Trump's administration, Steve Bannon was in the White House talking to the president about the mushrooming controversy over his campaign's ties to the Kremlin. Trump was enraged by the scandal that had tarnished his victory and was now tainting his presidency. Suddenly, Trump had an epiphany. He looked straight at Bannon, jabbed at him with his finger, and summed it up in one phrase: "Witch hunt!"

Brilliant, Bannon thought, just brilliant. Trump—the master marketer—had come up with the right way to craft the White House political narrative for an investigation that posed a mounting threat to his presidency.

In the weeks and months that followed, it was a phrase Trump returned to time and again—on Twitter, in press conferences, during meetings with members of Congress, and whenever the subject came up or merely crossed his mind, which it did all the time. As the investigations by Congress and the FBI proceeded, garnering ever more media coverage, the framing got repackaged with typical Trumpian hyperbole. "This is the single greatest witch hunt of a politician in American history!" the president tweeted at 7:52 A.M.

on May 18, the morning after Robert Mueller was appointed special counsel in charge of the Russian investigation.

Throughout his first year in the White House, Trump railed constantly about the investigations. He tweeted about Russia more than a hundred times, often declaring the entire issue a "hoax." He decried the media's coverage of the scandal as "fake news." Trump dismissed reporting on the covert Russian social media assault as phony. He called for investigations of Hillary Clinton. As he had done throughout the campaign, Trump, a longtime fan of chaos, was throwing up dust to cloud the public debate about the Russian attack on American democracy and its role in helping to elect him president.

Trump's Russia scandal posed a fundamental challenge for the American political system. Never before had a president's election been so closely linked to the intervention of a foreign power. Never before had a president so openly disputed the findings of his own intelligence community. And not since Richard Nixon during Watergate had a president so brazenly sought to interfere with a duly authorized criminal investigation that targeted his campaign and his associates.

Trump also had no interest in punishing Putin. In the first days of Trump's presidency, officials in the State Department's Bureau of European Affairs and Eurasian Affairs got an unusual "tasking" order from the new team on the seventh floor: Draw up options for improving relations with Russia to secure Moscow's cooperation in the war against ISIS. The options were to include an easing of sanctions Obama had imposed for Moscow's meddling in the election. Officials in the European bureau were stunned and upset. Weeks earlier, they had worked on the order to shut down the compounds in Maryland and New York that Russia used for spying in the United States. Now they were being instructed to undo what they had done and essentially give the Russians a free pass.

Daniel Fried, the State Department sanctions coordinator, received what he later described as "panicky" calls from colleagues about this new plan. They implored him: "Please, my God, can't you stop this?" Fried, who had served in the department for more than thirty years, contacted lawmakers and aides on Capitol Hill, urging them to pass legislation to codify the Russia sanctions already in place and force the White House to submit any changes for congressional review. So too did Tom Malinowski, an Obama appointee who had just stepped down as assistant secretary of state for human rights and who had received similar calls. The gambit—a blatant move to block the Trump White House's plans from inside the bureaucracy—worked. In a rare bipartisan move, Congress would overwhelmingly pass a tough bill intensifying sanctions on Russia—over a veto threat from Trump. He reluctantly signed the measure. But in early 2018, the Trump administration would announce it was not implementing the new sanctions—even though that same day, Trump's CIA chief, Mike Pompeo, said he expected Moscow to "target" the mid-term elections later that year.

The expanding Trump-Russia scandal hung over Trump's presidency and prompted concerns about his integrity, his autocratic impulses, and his disregard for one of the core principles of modern American government: U.S. law enforcement should be free of political interference. Nothing showed this more than his dealings with James Comey.

On January 27, three weeks after Comey had infuriated Trump (and sparked his paranoia) by handing him the two-page synopsis of the Steele memos, Trump invited him to the White House for dinner. "I need loyalty," Trump told him, as they sat at a small table, served by White House waiters. There was an awkward silence. The two men stared at each other. When Trump renewed the request later in the dinner, Comey dodged. "You will always get honesty from me," he replied.

Two and a half weeks later, at the end of an intelligence briefing in the Oval Office, Trump asked Comey to stay behind. Michael Flynn, Trump's national security adviser, had been forced to resign the day before over disclosures he had lied about his conversations with Kislyak during the transition.* He was now the subject of an

---

* In February, Kislyak told the *Washington Post* that he also had been talking to Flynn before the election, but he declined to say what they had discussed.

FBI investigation. "He is a good guy. I hope you can let this go," Trump said, according to Comey's account. Stunned that the president would seek to influence an ongoing criminal investigation, the FBI director left the meeting and immediately started typing a memo documenting Trump's extraordinary request—a practice he had begun with the new president.

Then on March 20, Comey appeared before the House Intelligence Committee and gave testimony that was devastating for Trump. He confirmed for the first time there was an ongoing counterintelligence investigation into the Trump campaign's ties to the Russians—and that it had been under way since the previous July.

Comey was asked about Trump's recent tweet claiming that Obama had "had my 'wires tapped' in Trump Tower just before the victory. Nothing found. This is McCarthyism!" The claim seemed preposterous on its face—and was yet another Trump attempt to deflect attention. Still, if Trump Tower had been tapped, it would have been the FBI's job to do it. Comey said the FBI and the Justice Department "has no information that supports those tweets." The FBI director had, for all intents and purposes, just called the president a fabulist.

Trump was now obsessed with one goal: getting Comey to publicly say he was not under investigation. The Russia scandal was complicating his job as president. During a phone call, Egyptian President Abdel Fattah el-Sisi had asked Trump about the investigation, according to a White House official. The fact that a foreign leader would raise the issue incensed Trump.

On March 30, Trump called Comey and told him he "had nothing to do with Russia" and "had not been involved with hookers" there. What could Comey do, he asked, to "lift the cloud"? Comey had already privately briefed congressional leaders on the Bureau's probe, identifying the players who were under investigation—and this did not include Trump. But to state that publicly would create a problem. What happens if something changed? Would Comey need to publicly announce that as well? The FBI once again sidestepped the request and told Trump the bureau would do its work "as quickly as we could." On April 11, Trump called Comey and made the same request, asking if he would "get out" the fact Trump was not a direct target. Comey politely told Trump he should have the White House counsel take the matter up with the Justice Department.

On May 9, while he was visiting the FBI's Los Angeles field office, Comey looked up at a TV set and learned that he had been fired. The White House initially said it was because Deputy Attorney General Rod Rosenstein had written a memo criticizing Comey for his handling of the Clinton email investigation. But Trump quickly contradicted that—in a meeting with Russian officials. The morning after the firing, he had a jovial get-together at the White House with Foreign Minister Sergey Lavrov and Ambassador Sergey Kislyak. There were smiles all around. "I just fired the head of the FBI. He was crazy, a real nut job," Mr. Trump told them, according to notes of the meeting. "I faced great pressure because of Russia. That's taken off." The next day, Trump told NBC News anchor Lester Holt that he had in mind "this Russia thing" when he dismissed Comey.

Jared Kushner reportedly had told his father-in-law that if he dumped Comey, Democrats would cheer the move. But Trump's firing of Comey backfired. Immediately, there were questions as to whether the president was seeking to obstruct justice. As Bannon had warned Trump, "You can fire the FBI director, you can't fire the FBI."

By this point, the Russia scandal had already upended his administration. Attorney General Jeff Sessions, facing a storm of criticism over his failure to disclose his own contacts with Kislyak during the campaign, had recused himself from the investigation. Trump was angered by Sessions's move. He wanted his own guy— a loyal guy—in charge. "Where's my Roy Cohn?" Trump vented to his aides at one point.

Instead, Rosenstein was now overseeing the probe, and he soon tapped the seventy-two-year-old Mueller to get to the bottom of the Russian affair. Mueller was the worst possible pick for Trump. He was a ramrod straight, Marine veteran who had served as FBI director for twelve years. According to friends and colleagues,

Mueller had one supreme passion in life: making criminal cases and putting malefactors behind bars.

Trump's "witch hunt" approach made it much tougher for the Republican-led Congress to do its job and investigate the Russia scandal.

Excessive partisanship had already poisoned Capitol Hill. Now with Trump insisting there was nothing to investigate, many of his Republican comrades demonstrated little desire for digging deep into the Russian attack and any Trump-Moscow connections. No special committees were formed. The relevant panels did not greatly expand staff resources, were reluctant to use their subpoena power, and, in many instances, only conducted a cursory review of documents. Most important, throughout 2017, they held all their interviews of key witnesses in private. A major purpose of congressional investigations for decades—from Teapot Dome to Watergate to Iran-Contra to the campaign finance abuses of the 1990s—was to educate the country through public hearings. Yet the Russian probes were being run almost entirely behind closed doors. Several key Republicans were focused not on pursuing Trump's ties to the Russians but on Glenn Simpson and Christopher Steele's ties to the Democrats. For the Republican leaders, the goal appeared to be to protect Trump and get through it as fast as possible—before the mid–term congressional elections of 2018.

A prime example of this GOP effort came in February 2018, when Representative Devin Nunes, the chair of the House Intelligence Committee, released a memo that some of his fellow Republicans said revealed shocking FBI abuses worse than Watergate. The memo claimed that Steele's dossier had been "an essential part" of the FBI's October 2016 application for the FISA surveillance warrant for Carter Page; that the Bureau had failed to disclose to the FISA court Steele's payments from the DNC and the Clinton campaign; and that Steele had "lied" to the FBI about his contacts with journalists—a claim Steele denied. (Weeks before the memo was made public, two GOP senators had asked the Justice Department to investigate Steele for allegedly making false statements to the FBI.) The memo prominently cited the reporting of the authors of this book.* Trump proclaimed the memo "vindicates" him and proved the Russia probe was an "American disgrace" and, of course, a "Witch Hunt."

But the FBI, Justice Department officials, and congressional Democrats challenged the memo's accuracy. The document also undercut the GOP argument that the Page warrant was illegitimate. It revealed that the surveillance of Page was renewed three times by federal judges—which could only have happened if the FBI had demonstrated the wiretap was yielding useful information. Moreover, the Nunes memo shot down the conspiracy theory pushed by some Republicans and conservative advocates led by Fox News' Sean Hannity that it was the unverified, Democratic-funded Steele dossier that had kicked off the Russia probe. The memo actually confirmed that months before the Page warrant the FBI investigation was triggered by the report that the Bureau had received about Papadopoulos. The release of the Nunes memo was widely criticized as a dud and a deflection.

Mueller's appointment had guaranteed that a fierce and thorough investigation on the part of the FBI would continue—unless Trump tried to stop it. Mueller signed up prosecutors experienced in bringing organized crime, money laundering, cybercrime, and white-collar crime cases. And they went to work.

As all the investigations proceeded, news broke of the Trump Tower meeting in June 2016, when Donald Trump Jr., Paul Manafort, and Jared Kushner talked with Natalia Veselnitskaya, the Kremlin emissary, in the expectation she was bringing them derogatory information on Clinton. (Trump Jr. and the White House, with the president's participation, put out misleading

---

* The memo suggested the FBI's application had relied heavily on Isikoff's story, without noting all the other information used by the Bureau to make its case that Page might be a Russian agent. It also pointed to Corn's October 31, 2016, *Mother Jones* article to suggest Steele was leaking information and, consequently, an unreliable source for the FBI. But the FBI had filed its FISA application for Page ten days before Steele spoke to Corn.

explanations of the meeting—an episode that caused Trump critics to suggest the Trump team had committed another obstruction of justice.) Manafort's home was raided by federal agents. Evidence of Moscow's wide-ranging covert social media campaign surfaced.

In October, Mueller indicted Manafort and Rick Gates on twelve counts, including money laundering and failure to file as registered foreign agents for their work on behalf of Yanukovych's pro-Russia party. As soon as the indictments were announced, the White House began distancing itself from Manafort, claiming the charges had nothing to do with the campaign or any interactions with Russia. Yet on the same day, before this spin could take hold, Mueller announced that Papadopoulos had pleaded guilty to lying to the FBI about his contacts during the campaign with Russians. Here was another example of the Trump campaign at least trying to interact with the Kremlin.

Information about Manafort's contacts with Deripaska, Page's trip to Moscow, Kushner's meeting with a Russian banker, the 2016 Trump Tower meeting, and Trump's attempt to develop a Moscow tower with Felix Sater during the campaign had already come out. But the Papadopoulos plea agreement was the first official confirmation that there had been ongoing private—or secret—communications between a Trump campaign adviser and the Russians.

And a month later, Mueller announced a plea deal with Flynn. Trump's former national security adviser—who had led the chant of "lock her up" at the Republican convention—admitted he had lied to FBI agents about his conversations with Kislyak. Flynn had been indicted on only two counts. He was cooperating with Mueller. But the question was, what information was he sharing with Mueller and who might it implicate?

Throughout it all, Trump fumed about the investigation and the FBI. In fits of rage, he vowed to fire Mueller. And GOP lawmakers were attacking the probe and the Bureau. At one point, Trump ordered White House counsel Don McGahn to dismiss Mueller. But McGahn refused and threatened to quit. Trump's lawyers—including John Dowd and Ty Cobb, two Washington criminal defense veterans—kept having to talk Trump down, assuring the president that Mueller's probe would finish quickly. It would be over soon, they told him. A few weeks later, they would say that again. And then again. The deadlines came and went. No one in the White House knew if the lawyers could keep Trump from trying to kill the investigation.

For all the public controversy, there was still much about Putin's cyberattacks that was cloaked in mystery—especially what had happened in Russia. Five days after Trump's inauguration, the Russian business newspaper, *Kommersant,* published an eye-popping story: Sergei Mikhailov, the deputy director of the FSB's Center 18, its main unit assigned to investigate cybercrimes, had been secretly arrested after the U.S. election. He had been grabbed during a meeting at his FSB office and dragged out with a bag over his head. He was charged with treason. So, too, was one of his deputies, a stocky criminal hacker turned government agent named Dmitry Dokuchaev. Other Russian media reported the men had been accused of having been informants for U.S. intelligence, tipping off the CIA to Russia's hacks of state election systems during the election.*

Meanwhile, a former FSB general, Oleg Erovinkin, a top deputy to Rosneft CEO Igor Sechin (who figured prominently in Steele's dossier), was found dead in his car in the center of Moscow, purportedly of a heart attack. This fueled speculation of foul play that might be related to Steele's memos.

And then came a clearer reminder of Putin's bent for revenge. In one of its last acts, the Obama administration had expanded the list of Russians sanctioned under the Magnitsky Act to include the two former intelligence officers who had poisoned Alexander Litvinenko in London in 2006. A few weeks later—in an event Russian dissidents suspected was connected—Vladimir Kara-Murza,

---

* In March 2017, Dokuchaev was one of two FSB officers charged in the United States for being part of one of the largest cyberattacks in history: the Russian penetration of Yahoo's email network, which resulted in the theft of data from 500 million email users around the globe.

the Russian human rights activist who had lobbied for this law, was rushed to a Moscow hospital gagging for air and fell into a coma. He survived, but the diagnosis was chilling: toxic action by an undefined substance. It was the second time he had been poisoned.

Trump, who never got to meet Putin when he was in Moscow for the Miss Universe pageant in 2013, finally had the chance now that he was the president. The first time came in July at a G20 summit in Hamburg. The two men displayed warm smiles, as they shook hands in front of a phalanx of reporters. Trump said it was an "honor" to meet the Russian president. Putin said he was "delighted" to see Trump. "There was a clear positive chemistry," said Tillerson, who sat in on their meeting.

The session lasted more than two hours and covered a wide range of issues, including Syria. Trump, according to Tillerson, pressed Putin about "the concerns of the American people regarding Russian interference in the 2016 election." Putin denied any meddling. And Trump moved on, Tillerson said, putting aside "an intractable disagreement at this point."

That night, during a grand dinner for all twenty world leaders, Trump got up from his table and walked over to Putin's and sat down. They talked again for about an hour. Nobody else was present, other than Putin's English translator.

Following his talks with the Russian leader, Trump said that it was "time to move forward" with Russia and that he and Putin had agreed to set up "an impenetrable cybersecurity unit so that election hacking and many other negative things will be guarded and safe." After all that had happened in 2016, the idea of Russian-American cooperation on cybersecurity was immediately derided by members of Congress as absurd. "It's not the dumbest idea I have ever heard but it's pretty close," Senator Lindsey Graham remarked. Trump quickly dropped the proposal.

In November, Trump and Putin met again at an Asia-Pacific Economic Cooperation summit in Vietnam. They talked during the event, and Trump asked Putin once more about Russia's meddling in the election. As Trump subsequently told reporters on Air

Force One, "He said he didn't meddle. He said he didn't meddle.
I asked him again. You can only ask so many times." Trump continued: "Every time he sees me, he says, 'I didn't do that.' And I
believe, I really believe, that when he tells me that, he means it." He
added, "I think he is very insulted by it."

Trump had gotten the answer he wanted. This had been a
crime *and* an act of covert warfare. Yet Trump seemed more worried about Putin's reaction than Putin's attack.

During the campaign, Trump had encouraged Russia's hacking and dumping—of which he was the chief beneficiary. He had
praised the WikiLeaks releases, promoting them, and calling for
more—even after he had received a secret U.S. government briefing stating that the cyber break-ins and the dissemination of Democratic files were part of a Russian covert operation to undermine
the election. He had spoken positively about Putin and suggested
he was eager to undo sanctions and cut deals with the Kremlin—
even as the Russia information warfare campaign was under way.
Whether or not the investigations would ever turn up hard evidence of direct collusion, Trump's actions—his adamant and consistent denial of any Russian role—had provided Putin cover. In
that sense, he had aided and abetted Moscow's attack on American
democracy.

Now, after his second meeting with Putin, Trump was done
raising the subject with the Russian leader. There would be no
penalties for Putin—and nothing to stop him from doing it again.
But Trump's own unsettling conduct guaranteed the Russia scandal was far from over—for Mueller, Congress, and the American
people.

ACKNOWLEDGMENTS

It is customary, almost a cliché, for authors to declare that their books could have not been completed without the assistance of their agents and editors. We know of no case for which that is truer than this book. Our agent, Gail Ross, was indispensable from start to finish. She helped conceive this book and provided invaluable support along the way. Moreover, she has been a dear friend to each of us for years. We cannot thank her enough. Sean Desmond, the editorial director at Twelve and our editor, was our captain—and taskmaster and cheerleader. Throughout it all, he was indefatigable, doing whatever it took to keep this project moving forward, displaying grace, good humor, and a generous spirit. His encouragement, judgment, and editorial guidance were essential. We owe him much.

We greatly appreciate the support and hard work of the entire team at Hachette Book Group and Twelve. Everyone embraced this book from the beginning and motivated us with their high expectations. The list includes Michael Pietsch, Ben Sevier, Brian McLendon, Paul Samuelson, Rachel Molland, Rachel Kambury, Elisa Rivlin, Bob Castillo, Yasmin Mathew, Melissa Mathlin, Laura Eisenhard, and Jarrod Taylor.

Patrick Reevell, an intrepid reporter based in Moscow, did important legwork for us in Russia. Dan Michalski dug up details about Trump's June 2013 trip to Las Vegas and his visit to The Act nightclub. Noah Lanard and Kara Voght were tireless fact-checkers who worked late into the night to help us reach the finish line. We are grateful to them all.

MICHAEL ISIKOFF

I thank my editors and colleagues at Yahoo News. Top billing, of course, goes to Editor in Chief Daniel Klaidman—whose news smarts and wise counsel have informed my reporting ever since we chased scoops together back in our *Newsweek* days many years ago. (And quite the scoops they were!) I am eternally grateful for Danny's support and his friendship. Megan Liberman, after some initial, totally understandable reservations, finally gave the book her green light—and for that, a really hearty thanks. Lauren Johnston, Colin Campbell, Hunter Walker, Charity Elder, Bob Morrissey, Olivier Knox, Hunter Walker, Garance Franke-Ruta, and Jon Ward are valued colleagues and great sounding boards. Jerry Adler deserves special recognition: For the past two years, he has managed to corral my copy on Donald Trump and Russia and turn it into serviceable prose for Yahoo—no small feat.

Full disclosure: Glenn Simpson, a key player in these pages, is a longtime friend. Over many years, I have benefited enormously from Glenn's insights into Putin's Russia and American politics. In recounting this story, we have tried to do what he would have done: play it straight.

None of this could have been written without the aid, comfort, and unwavering love of my family. My wife and fellow journalist, Mary Ann Akers, lived through the first Isikoff-Corn collaboration more than a decade ago. How she managed to this time is beyond me. But somehow she did and (among her many talents) even managed to inject humor into the process. I owe her immeasurably for that, and much, much more. Mary Ann, whom I adore and love, is the anchor of our small family; her compassion, wit and love of life makes everything worthwhile and every day worth living. My son Zach's persistent question—"Are you done with your book yet?"—gave me just the right kick in the butt to actually finish. Now he and I can get back to more important business. Go Nats!

Acknowledgments

DAVID CORN

I thank all my colleagues at *Mother Jones* for their support and camaraderie. Chief Executive Officer Monika Bauerlein and Editor in Chief Clara Jeffery allowed me to pursue this project and duck certain daily responsibilities. More important, they have been valuable sources of encouragement and advice. I'm grateful and proud to be a member of the powerhouse team they have built. A special mention goes to the marvelous crew in the Washington, D.C., bureau: Daniel Schulman, Jeremy Schulman, Marianne Szegedy-Maszak, Aaron Wiener, Patrick Caldwell, Russ Choma, Andy Kroll, Dan Friedman, Hannah Levintova, Pema Levy, A. J. Vicens, Tim Murphy, Nathalie Baptiste, Rebecca Leber, Stephanie Mencimer, Clint Hendler, Ashley Dejean, Megan Jula, and Courtney Perna. It is an honor and pleasure to work each day with this group of driven reporters and editors to produce journalism that matters.

For years, I've been privileged to be a part of the MSNBC community. I thank my colleagues at the network—Chris Matthews, Joy Reid, Lawrence O'Donnell, Ari Melber, Phil Griffin, and all the hosts, producers, and bookers—for their encouragement and support and for sharing so many history-making moments with me. A very deep nod of gratitude goes to Rachel Maddow.

I am grateful for the essential life-support services provided during this project by friends and relatives who were there even when I was not: Ruth Corn, Gordon Roth, Barry Corn, Steven Corn, Amy Corn, Samantha Corn, Sarah Corn, Reid Cramer, Sally Kern, Stephen Kern, Bobbi Kittner, Sam Kittner, Ricki Seidman, Bobby Shaprio, Liz Nessen, Tony Alfieri, Ellen Grant, Lynn Sweet, Lara Bergthold, Steven Prince, Nick Baumann, Jill Sobule, Steve Earle, Margaret Nagle, and Chuck Lorre. And I greatly appreciate all my Twitter and Facebook friends—you know who you are—for the RTs, likes, and snark.

I owe Peter Kornbluh yet another special shout-out—and send one to Jon Corn, the bravest person I know.

Above all, I once again thank Maaike, Amarins, and Welmoed for the delight and sustenance they have supplied over the years. Having watched their father write books in the past, Maaike and Amarins this time knew what the family was in for, and they made the necessary allowances without complaint—and without realizing that their presence in my life, including the most mundane interactions ("can you drive me to..."), offered a most crucial and soul-nourishing distraction. Nothing has been more satisfying for me than watching them become strong, independent-minded, confident, engaged young women with missions of their own. Finally, this book was made possible by Welmoed, not only because she put with up with it (and me!), but because she is, when not attending to her own accomplished career, the visionary and creative genius that guides our family. I'm enriched by her insight, bolstered by her fortitude, and grateful for her support and love. With this book done, I eagerly await our next chapter.

As we have done before, we thank our sources, especially those who trusted us with their confidences. Any mistakes in this book belong only to the authors—and we can argue over who is to blame.

NOTES

It is challenging to write a book on a scandal that is not over—as the story and investigations continue to develop, with new revelations and possible subpoenas and indictments. Many of our sources remain involved in the controversy and, consequently, were reluctant to speak openly. They and others, though, were willing to provide important and essential information on background, meaning we could use the material but not cite them by name. Quotes attributed to characters in this book are based on either interviews with these persons or those with direct knowledge of the statements.

For this book, we conducted more than 100 interviews with Obama administration officials, Trump administration officials, past and present members of the U.S. intelligence community, key players in the Trump and Clinton campaigns, Trump business associates, cybersecurity experts, and many others. We submitted a long list of questions to the White House regarding Donald Trump's actions as a businessman, candidate, and president. The White House did not respond to most of them. In the few instances when the White House did reply, we note that in the text.

During the 2016 election, many elements of the Trump-Russia scandal were not covered by the media. Since then, several news outlets have done impressive work unearthing important pieces of this sprawling tale. Portions of our account rely on these stories, and below we note some of the more significant contributions.

INTRODUCTION: "IT'S A SHAKEDOWN."

For Comey's account of the Trump Tower meeting, see James Comey statement to the Senate Intelligence Committee, June 8, 2017. It can be found at https://www.intelligence.senate.gov/sites/default/files/documents/os-jcomey-060817.pdf.

CHAPTER 1: "MR. PUTIN WOULD LIKE TO MEET MR. TRUMP."

For other accounts of Trump's time in Moscow, see "The Day Trump Came to Moscow: Oligarchs, Miss Universe, and Nobu," *Bloomberg*, December 21, 2016, and "When Donald Trump Brought Miss Universe to Moscow," *Politico*, May 15, 2016. The GAO report on money laundering can be found at https://www.documentcloud.org/documents/3896773-CBO-REPORT-RUSSIAN-LAUNDERING-2000.html. For the description of The Act's performances, see *VV Level 178 Club, LLC v. The Shoppes at the Palazzo, LLC*, Case No. A-13-680945-B, "Amended Findings of Fact, Conclusions of Law and Order Granting Defendants' Joint Motion For Preliminary Injunction," October 30, 2013. For Trump's deal in Baku, see "Donald Trump's Worst Deal," *The New Yorker*, March 13, 2017. Schiller gave his account of the offer of women during private testimony to the House Intelligence Committee in November 2017. See "Trump Bodyguard Keith Schiller Testifies Russian Offered Trump Women, Was Turned Down," NBCNews.com, November 9, 2017. For Tokhtakhounov's presence at the Miss Universe contest, see "How Did an Alleged Russian Mobster End Up on Trump's Red Carpet," *Mother Jones*, September 14, 2016.

CHAPTER 2: "WE DID NOT RECOGNIZE THE DEGREE IT WOULD TICK PUTIN OFF."

The account of the Litvinenko case is based on *The Litvinenko Inquiry*, by Sir Robert Owen, January 21, 2016. It can be found at http://webarchive.nationalarchives.gov.uk/20160613090324/https://www.litvinenkoinquiry.org/report. For McFaul's background, see "Watching the Eclipse," *The New Yorker*, August 11, 2014. The Obama administration's reset memo was obtained by the authors. For more on Clinton's interactions with Putin, see *Hard Choices*, by Hillary Clinton, Simon & Schuster, 2014. The "illegals" spying case was widely reported. For Putin singing with the returned spies, see "Vladimir Putin sang patriotic songs with spies expelled from US," *Telegraph*, July 25, 2010. The *New York Times* reported on Bill Clinton's speech and the Uranium One deal in "Cash Flowed to Clinton Foundation Amid Russian Uranium Deal," April 23, 2015. A list of Bill Clinton's paid speeches can be found at http://i2.cdn.turner.com/cnn/2013/images/05/23/clinton.speeches.2001-2012.pdf. For Putin lecturing Bill Clinton, see "Putin Criticizes U.S. for Arrests of Espionage Suspects," *New York Times*, June 29, 2010. Clinton wrote about her memo calling for rethinking the U.S. approach to Putin in *Hard Choices*.

CHAPTER 3: "ARE WE HERE BECAUSE CLINTON TEXTED US?"

For Clinton's memos related to Russia, see *Hard Choices*. Clinton described her APEC meetings with Lavrov and Putin in *Hard Choices*. For details on the death on Sergei Magnitsky, see *Red Notice: A True Story of High Finance, Murder, and One Man's Fight for Justice*, by Bill Browder, Simon & Schuster, 2015. For Donilon's response to Clinton's exit memo, see *Alter Egos: Hillary Clinton, Barack Obama, and the Twilight Struggle Over American Power*, by Mark Landler, Random House, 2016. McFaul's experience with harassment was described in "Watching the Eclipse," *The New Yorker*. Readers can find the Gerasimov article at http://usacac.army.mil/CAC2/MilitaryReview/Archives/English/MilitaryReview_20160228_art008.pdf. The Nuland phone-call episode was described by Victoria Nuland in her interview with PBS's *Frontline* and can be found here https://www.pbs.org/wgbh/frontline/interview/victoria-nuland/.

CHAPTER 4: "YOU DON'T KNOW ME, BUT I'M WORKING ON A TROLL FARM."

Putin's remark to Cameron can be found in *Cameron at 10: The Inside Story*, by Anthony Seldon and Peter Snowdon, William Collins, 2016. Putin's speech defending his aggression was reported in *The New Tsar: The Rise and Reign of Vladimir Putin*, by Steven Lee Myers, Knopf, 2015. Adrian Chen's investigation of the Internet Research Agency appeared in "The Agency," *New York Times*, June 2, 2015. Oleg Kalugnin wrote about KGB active measures in his book, *Spymaster: My Thirty-Two Years in Intelligence and Espionage Against the West*, Basic Books, 2009. The story of the fake Henry "Scoop" Jackson memo can be found in *The Sword and the Shield*, by Christopher Andrew, Basic Books, 1999.

CHAPTER 5: "THIS IS THE NEW VERSION OF WATERGATE."

The account of the FBI's contacts with the DNC is based on internal DNC documents—including emails and a memo written by Yared Tamene—obtained by the authors. See also "The Perfect Weapon: How Russian Cyberpower Invaded the U.S.," *New York Times*, December 13, 2016. Various news outlets have reported the details of the phishing attack on Podesta. For more on the wider Russian cyberattack that included Podesta, see "Russian hackers pursued Putin foes, not just US Democrats," Associated Press, November 1, 2017.

CHAPTER 6: "FELIX SATER, BOY, I HAVE TO EVEN THINK ABOUT IT."

For Trump's quote to the Associated Press about Sater, see "Donald Trump picked Felix Sater, convicted stock fraud felon, as senior business adviser," *Newsday*, December 4, 2015. Details of the Trump-Sater Moscow deal were first reported by the *New York Times* and the *Washington Post*. See "Trump Associate Boasted That Moscow Business Deal 'Will Get Donald Elected,'" *New York Times*,

August 28, 2017; "Trump business sought deal on a Trump Tower in Moscow while he ran for president," *Washington Post,* August 27, 2017; and " 'Help world peace and make a lot of money': Here's the letter of intent to build a Trump Tower Moscow," *Business Insider,* September 8, 2017. Michael Cohen provided the authors with a statement regarding his involvement in this deal. The Russian tax registry filing for I.C. Expert was reviewed in Moscow by Patrick Reevell, a researcher for this book. For background on Trump's search for deals in Russia, see "For Trump, Three Decades of Chasing Deals in Russia," *New York Times,* January 16, 2017. For Trump's 1987 interview in Moscow, see "Trump Considered Business with the Russian Government in 1987, and Newsweek Met Him in Moscow," *Newsweek,* August 28, 2017. For Trump and Bernard Lown, see "Donald Trump Angled for Soviet Posting in 1980s, Says Nobel Prize Winner," *The Hollywood Reporter,* May 26, 2017. For Trump's attempt at a Moscow deal in 1996, see "Trump Lays Bet on New Moscow Skyline," *Moscow Times,* November 12, 1996. The Benza quote can be found in "Donald Trump's Craziest Interview Ever: 'Any Girl You Have, I Can Take From You,' " *The Daily Beast,* August 2, 2015. For Trump's interactions with organized crime figures, see "The Many Times Donald Trump Has Lied About His Mob Connections," *Mother Jones,* September 23, 2016.

Sater's past has been covered by many media outlets. See "Donald Trump and the Felon: Inside His Business Dealings with a Mob-Connected Hustler," *Forbes,* October 25, 2016; "Former Mafia-linked figure describes association with Trump," *Washington Post,* May 17, 2016; and "This Top Mueller Aide Once Worked on an Investigation of a Trump Associate Tied to the Russian Mob," *Mother Jones,* June 23, 2017. The *New York Times* story that revealed the Trump-Sater connection was published on December 17, 2007, under the headline, "Real Estate Executive With Hand in Trump Projects Rose From Tangled Past." The report Sater wrote for his lawyer describing himself as a "national hero" was obtained by the authors from a confidential source. Readers can find Trump Jr.'s 2008 remarks at the Manhattan conference about investing in Russia at http://www.eturbonews.com/5008/executive-talk-donald

-trump-jr-bullish-russia-and-few-emerging-ma. For Sergei Millian's background and purported interactions with Trump, see "The shadowy Russian émigré touting Trump," *Financial Times*, November 1, 2016, and "Investigators on the Trump-Russia Beat Should Talk to This Man," *Mother Jones*, January 19, 2017.

CHAPTER 7: "HE'S BEEN A RUSSIAN STOOGE FOR FIFTEEN YEARS."

The Manafort memo sent to Trump was reported by the *New York Times* in "To Charm Trump, Paul Manafort Sold Himself as an Affordable Outsider," April 18, 2017. Manafort's history of work in Ukraine is detailed in "Paul Manafort's Lucrative Ukraine Years Are Central to the Russia Probe," *Bloomberg*, May 22, 2017. For the history of Black, Manafort, and Stone, see "The Quiet American," *Slate*, April 28, 2016, and "The Slickest Shop in Town," *Time*, March 3, 1986. For Levinson's conversation with Manafort regarding Somalia, see "Trump chair Paul Manafort: Mercenary Lobbyist and Valuable Asset," *Guardian*, May 31, 2016. The U.S. cable about Deripaska was revealed by WikiLeaks. Associated Press disclosed Manafort's $10 million plan for Deripaska in a March 22, 2017, article headlined, "Before Trump job, Manafort worked to aid Putin." For Deripaska letter sent to McCain's office, see "Aide Helped Controversial Russian Meet McCain," *Washington Post*, January 25, 2008. For background on Konstantin Kilimnik, see "Manafort's man in Kiev," *Politico*, August 18, 2016. The U.S. embassy cable about Yanukovych's party hiring K Street veterans was released by WikiLeaks. The "blood money" text was described in "Manafort's Ukrainian 'blood money' caused qualms, hack suggests," *Politico*, February 28, 2017. Firtash's conversation with the U.S. ambassador was described in a U.S. embassy cable released by WikiLeaks. For an account of Deripaska's legal action against Manafort and Gates in the Cayman Islands over the Ukrainian cable investment, see "Trump's campaign chief is questioned about ties to Russian billionaire," Yahoo News, April 26, 2016. Manafort's emails to Kilimnik were revealed by the *Washington Post* in a September 20, 2017, article headlined, "Manafort offered to give Russian billionaire 'private briefings' on 2016 campaign." The *New York Times* reported that Kilimnik was the unidentified Manafort associate on December 4, 2017, in an article headlined, "Manafort Associate Has Russian Intelligence Ties, Court Document Says."

CHAPTER 8: "HOW THE FUCK DID HE GET ON THE LIST?"

For background on Carter Page, see "Trump's New Russia Adviser Has Deep Ties to Kremlin's Gazprom," *Bloomberg*, March 30, 2016. The account of Papadopoulos' interactions with intermediaries for Russia is based on the Statement of Offense filed on October 5, 2017, in U.S. District Court by Robert Mueller. See also "Who's who in the George Papadopoulos court documents," *Washington Post*, November 2, 2017, and "Mystery Professor in Mueller Case Had Contacts With Russian Officials," *Mother Jones*, October 30, 2017. For more on Trump meeting with his foreign policy team, see "Ex-Trump aide: Russian collusion story is 'hoax of the century,'" Sky News, November 3, 2017. The *New York Times* revealed Papadopoulos' barroom conversation with Downer in a December 30, 2017, article headlined, "How the Russia Inquiry Began: A Campaign Aide, Drinks and Talk of Political Dirt." For more on Torshin and Butina's efforts to make connections with the conservative movement and the Trump campaign, see "Operative Offered Trump Campaign 'Kremlin Connection' Using N.R.A. Ties," *New York Times*, December 3, 2017, and "Kushner failed to disclose outreach from Putin ally to Trump campaign," NBCNews.com, November 18, 2017. Flynn's rocky tenure at the DIA is detailed in "Head of Pentagon intelligence agency forced out, officials say," *Washington Post*, April 30, 2014. For Flynn's speaking fee for the RT event, see "Moscow paid $45,000 for Flynn's 2015 talk, documents show," Yahoo News, March 16, 2017. (This story reported Flynn also received $23,500 from Russia-connected firms for speeches delivered in Washington, D.C.) The account of the GRU officer bragging about an operation to pay back Clinton can be found in "Inside Russia's Social Media War on America," *Time*, May 18, 2017.

CHAPTER 9: "IF IT'S WHAT YOU SAY I LOVE IT."

The full thread of the emails between Trump Jr. and Goldstone can be found at http://www.cnn.com/interactive/2017/07/politics/donald-trump-jr-full-emails. For more on the Trump Tower meeting, see Statement of Jared Kushner to Congressional Committees, July 24, 2017, and Trump Jr.'s interview with Sean Hannity at http://www.foxnews.com/transcript/2017/07/11/donald-trump-jr-on-hannity-in-retrospect-wouldve-done-things-differently.html. *Foreign Policy* obtained and published the memo Veselnitskaya brought to the meeting. For the similarity between the Veselnitskaya memo and the Chaika memo, see "Memo Undermines Russian Lawyer's Account of Trump Tower Meeting," *Mother Jones*, October 17, 2017. Trump Jr.'s quote—"not illegal to listen"—was cited by Representative Jim Himes on *Meet the Press*, December 10, 2017. A security camera recorded the attack, and readers can watch the video at https://www.youtube.com/watch?v=DC10fyQgNqo.

CHAPTER 10: "WIKILEAKS HAS A VERY BIG YEAR AHEAD."

For more on the DNC response to the hack and the Guccifer 2.0 releases, see "The Perfect Weapon: How Russian Cyberpower Invaded the U.S.," *New York Times*, and "Inside Story: How Russians Hacked the Democrats' Emails," Associated Press, November 4, 2017.

CHAPTER 11: "I HAVE TO REPORT THIS TO HEADQUARTERS."

For background on Fusion GPS, see "'Journalism for rent': Inside the secretive firm behind the Trump dossier," *Washington Post*, December 11, 2017, and "Fusion GPS Founder Hauled From the Shadows for the Russia Election Investigation," *New York Times*, January 8, 2018. For more on Simpson's involvement and his interactions with Steele, see his August 22, 2017 testimony before the Senate Judiciary Committee. It can be found at https://www.nytimes.com/interactive/2018/01/09/us/politics/document-

Fusion-GPS-Simpson-Transcript.html. See also his November 8, 2017 testimony before the House Intelligence Committee. It can be found at https://intelligence.house.gov/news/documentsingle. aspx?DocumentID=850. The story of the Skuratov case can be found in *The New Tsar: The Rise and Reign of Vladimir Putin*. For an account of the Hudson episode, see "Was British diplomat set up by the Russian secret service?" *Independent*, July 9, 2009.

CHAPTER 12: "AS FOR THE UKRAINE AMENDMENT, EXCELLENT WORK."

Comey's July 5, 2016, statement can be found at https://www.fbi. gov/news/pressrel/press-releases/statement-by-fbi-director-james-b-comey-on-the-investigation-of-secretary-hillary-clinton2019s-use-of-a-personal-e-mail-system. For other accounts of Comey's handling of the Clinton email server case, see "Comey Tried to Shield the F.B.I. From Politics. Then He Shaped an Election," *New York Times*, April 22, 2017, and "How a dubious Russian document influenced the FBI's handling of the Clinton probe," *Washington Post*, May 24, 2017. Page's lecture in Moscow can be viewed at https://www.youtube.com/watch?v=1CYF29saA9w. For Page's 2014 blog post and his comments at the meeting with the Indian prime minister, see "Trump adviser's public comments, ties to Moscow stir unease in both parties," *Washington Post*, August 5, 2016. The *Telegraph* reported Dugin's reaction to Page's lecture in a July 8, 2016 story headlined, "Donald Trump aide slams America's policy on Russia during speech in Moscow." For Page's meetings with Dvorkovich and Baranov and his email to Gordon, see Testimony of Carter Page, House Intelligence Committee, November 2, 2017. It can be found at https://intelligence.house.gov/uploaded-files/carter_page_hpsci_hearing_transcript_nov_2_2017.pdf. The account of Page's interaction with the Russian spies is based on the indictment filed in *United States of America v. Evgeny Buryakov, Igor Sporyshev, and Victor Podobnyy*, January 23, 2015. For Isikoff's interview with Flynn at the Republican convention, see "Top Trump adviser defends payment for Russian speaking engagement," Yahoo News,

July 18, 2016. For Sessions' meeting with Kislyak, see "All the known times the Trump campaign met with Russians," *Washington Post*, November 13, 2017. For Denman's account, see "How Diana Denman's singular stand for Ukraine revealed the Trump campaign's soft spot for Russia," *Austin American-Statesman,* March 6, 2017. And see "Trump campaign guts GOP's anti-Russia stance on Ukraine," *Washington Post*, July 18, 2016. For Page's email to Gordon after the platform fight, see Page's testimony to the House Intelligence Committee.

CHAPTER 13: "NEXT THEY'RE GOING TO PUT POLONIUM IN MY TEA."

Manafort's offer to provide private briefings to Deripaska was reported by the *Washington Post* on September 20, 2017, in an article headlined, "Manafort offered to give Russian billionaire 'private briefings' on 2016 campaign." The role of the message from the Australian government in launching this probe was reported in "How the Russia Inquiry Began: A Campaign Aide, Drinks and Talk of Political Dirt," *New York Times.* Clapper's remarks at the Aspen Security Forum can be found at http://aspensecurityforum.org/wp-content/uploads/2016/07/directing-national-intelligence.pdf.

CHAPTER 14: "WE'VE BEEN TOLD TO STAND DOWN."

For more on Bortnikov's presence at the White House summit, see "U.S. invites a Russian fox in the chicken coop," *Washington Post*, February 19, 2015. John Brennan mentioned his invitation to Bortnikov in an interview with NPR that aired on February 24, 2016. The transcript can be found at https://www.npr.org/2016/02/24/467711098/transcript-nprs-interview-with-cia-director-john-brennan. Brennan described his August 2016 phone call with Bortnikov and his initial steps regarding Russia's cyberattack in public testimony to the House Intelligence Committee on May 23, 2017. For more on the White House deliberations regarding the Russian attack, see "Obama's secret struggle to punish Russia for Putin's election assault," *Washington Post,* June 23,

2017, and "Did Obama Blow It on the Russian Hacking?" *Politico*, April 3, 2017.

CHAPTER 15: "HE'S GOT ME AS THE FALL GUY."

Watts' article for the foreign policy think tank can be found at https://www.fpri.org/2015/10/russia-returns-as-al-qaeda-and-the-islamic-states-far-enemy/. The CIA proposal for a covert action program to counter Kremlin propaganda was reported by the *Washington Post* on December 25, 2017, under the headline, "Kremlin trolls burned across the Internet as Washington debated options." For more on the firing of Manafort, see *Let Trump Be Trump: The Inside Story of His Rise to the Presidency*, by Corey Lewandowski and David Bossie, Center Street, 2017. For more on the August 15 FBI meeting, see "In FBI Agent's Account, 'Insurance Policy' Text Referred to Russia Probe," *Wall Street Journal*, December 18, 2017. For more on the DCCC hack, see "Democratic House Candidates Were Also Targets of Russian Hacking," *New York Times*, December 13, 2016. For background on Stone, see "The Dirty Trickster," *The New Yorker*, June 2, 2008. Stone's speech to the Florida Republican group can be found at https://www.youtube.com/watch?v=K7oHyGyq1UM. For Stone's interactions with Guccifer 2.0, see "Roger Stone's Russian Hacking 'Hero,'" *The Smoking Gun*, March 8, 2017.

CHAPTER 16: "DOES IT EVEN MATTER WHO HACKED THIS DATA?"

For more on Comey and the draft op-ed, see "Comey Tried to Shield the F.B.I. From Politics. Then He Shaped an Election," *New York Times*. For more on Tait's involvement with the Smith operation, see "GOP Operative Sought Clinton Emails From Hackers, Implied a Connection to Flynn," *Wall Street Journal*, June 29, 2017; "GOP Activist Who Sought Clinton Emails Cited Trump Campaign Officials," *Wall Street Journal*, July 1, 2017; and "The Time I Got Recruited to Collude with the Russians," *Lawfare*, June 30, 2017.

CHAPTER 17: "IT ALSO COULD BE SOMEBODY SITTING ON THEIR BED WHO WEIGHS FOUR HUNDRED POUNDS, OK?"

The *Washington Post* reported on the FISA warrant for Page on April 11, 2017, in an article headlined, "FBI obtained FISA warrant to monitor Trump adviser Carter Page." For Rogin's article on Page, see "Trump's Russia adviser speaks out, calls accusations 'complete garbage,'" *Washington Post*, September 26, 2016. Comey's testimony before the House Judiciary Committee can be found at https://judiciary.house.gov/wp-content/uploads/2016/09/114-91_22125.pdf. For Trump Jr.'s contacts with WikiLeaks, see "The Secret Correspondence Between Donald Trump Jr. and WikiLeaks," *The Atlantic*, November 13, 2017.

CHAPTER 18: "ONLY RUSSIA'S SENIOR-MOST OFFICIALS COULD HAVE AUTHORIZED THESE ACTIVITIES."

For more on Johnson briefing Clinton and Trump and on the Trump and Clinton campaigns responding to the events of October 7, 2016, see *64 Hours: How One Weekend Blew Up the Rules of American Politics*, a Yahoo News documentary, October 6, 2017.

CHAPTER 19: "WE'VE BEEN RATFUCKED."

For more on Johnson's reaction to news coverage and on the Trump campaign's plan for the debate, see *64 Hours* and "Steve Bannon interview: Trump's 'Access Hollywood' tape was a 'litmus test,'" CBSNews.com, September 8, 2017. For Benenson on the polls after the *Access Hollywood* video, see *64 Hours*. For the FBI-Justice Department dispute over a Clinton Foundation inquiry, see "FBI in Internal Feud Over Hillary Clinton Probe," *Wall Street Journal*, October 30, 2016.

CHAPTER 20: "THIS IS THE REAL RESET OF THE WESTERN WORLD."

For more on Simpson's and Steele's actions in October, see Simpson testimony to the Senate Judiciary Committee and his testimony to the House Intelligence Committee. For the *Slate* article, see "Was a Trump Server Communicating with Russia?" *Slate*, October 31, 2016, and "Trump's Server, Revisited," *Slate*, November 2, 2016. For more on the *New York Times* article on the FBI investigation, see "Trump, Russia, and the News Story That Wasn't," *New York Times*, January 20, 2017. Baquet's quote—"all we could report"— was reported in "New NYT scoop on Russia raises questions about old NYT story on Russia," *Washington Post*, January 1, 2018. For the Watts, Weisburd, and Berger article, see "Trolling for Trump: How Russia Is Trying to Destroy our Democracy," *War on the Rocks*, November 6, 2016. Chen described Russian trolls tweeting for Trump in a *Longform Podcast* that can be found at https://longform.org/posts/longform-podcast-171-adrian-chen. Krutskikh's 2016 lecture was reported by the *Washington Post* on January 18, 2017, in a column headlined, "Russia's radical new strategy for information warfare." For the Russian Institute for Strategic Studies reports, see "Putin-linked think tank drew up plan to sway 2016 US election—documents," Reuters, April 19, 2017. Kushner's handling of the Trump campaign's social media effort is detailed in "Exclusive Interview: How Jared Kushner Won Trump the White House," *Forbes*, November 22, 2016. For Cambridge Analytica contacting WikiLeaks, see "Data Firm's WikiLeaks Outreach Came as It Joined Trump Campaign," *Wall Street Journal*, November 10, 2017.

For Russian trolls defending Trump on birtherism and the *Access Hollywood* video, see "Russia Twitter trolls deflected Trump bad news," Associated Press, November 10, 2017. For Maksim's remarks about the Internet Research Agency, see "Russian trolls were schooled on 'House of Cards,'" Yahoo News, October 15, 2017. For Twitter statistics related to Russian bot activity, see Testimony of Sean Edgett, acting general counsel of Twitter, to the U.S. Senate subcommittee on crime and terrorism, October 31, 2017. For statistics related to Russian activity on Facebook, see Testimony of Colin Stretch, general counsel of Facebook, to the U.S. Senate subcommittee on crime and terrorism, October 31, 2017.

For the Russian-backed ads and groups on Facebook and videos on YouTube, see "House Intelligence Committee Releases Incendiary Russian Social Media Ads," *New York Times*, November 1, 2017; "These Are the Ads Russia Bought on Facebook in 2016," *New York Times*, November 1, 2017; "Here Are 14 Russian Ads That Ran on Facebook During the 2016 Election," *Gizmodo*, November 1, 2017; "A color-in Bernie, hits on the Clinton foundation, and calls for Texas to secede: The Facebook ads Russia bought during the presidential campaign seen by 150 million," *Daily Mail*, November 1, 2017; "Russian-backed Facebook ads featured 'Buff Bernie,'" *New York Daily News*, November 1, 2017; "Exclusive: Russians Appear to Use Facebook to Push Trump Rallies in 17 U.S. Cities," *The Daily Beast*, September 20, 2017; and "Exclusive: Russia Recruited YouTubers to Bash 'Racist B*tch' Hillary Clinton Over Rap Beats," *The Daily Beast*, October 8, 2017. For the Trump campaign promoting @Ten_GOP tweets, see "Trump Campaign Staffers Pushed Russian Propaganda Days Before the Election," *The Daily Beast*, October 18, 2017. For Parscale quote—"I got fooled"—see "Top Trump campaign adviser admits he was 'fooled' by a Russian Twitter bot," Yahoo News, November 8, 2017. For accounts of the Moscow bar, see "Delight at Donald Trump Watch Party in Moscow," ABCNews.Go.Com, November 9, 2016, and "Inside Moscow's pro-Trump Election Night Bash," *Moscow Times*, November 9, 2016.

CHAPTER 21: "WE GOT A SINKING FEELING. . . . IT LOOKED LIKE A SEASON OF *HOMELAND*."

For more on the Obama White House post-election response to the election hack, see "Trump, Putin, and the New Cold War," *The New Yorker*, March 6, 2017. The brief Steele memo that never became public was obtained by the authors from a confidential source. For Flynn's transition conversations with Kislyak, see Statement of the Offense, *United States of America v. Michael T. Flynn*, November 30, 2017. See also "Inside the Trump Team's Push on Israel Vote That Mike Flynn Lied About," *Wall Street Journal*, January 5, 2018. For Kushner and Flynn meeting with Kislyak at Trump Tower, see Statement of Jared Kushner to Congressional Committees; "Kushner and Flynn Met With Russian Envoy in December, White House Says," March 2, 2017; and "Russian ambassador told Moscow that Kushner wanted secret communications channel with Kremlin," *Washington Post*, May 26, 2017. For Kushner's meeting with Gorkov, see "Explanations for Kushner's meeting with head of Kremlin-linked bank don't match up," *Washington Post*, June 1, 2017. For Flynn's involvement with the Middle East nuclear power proposal and with the Turkish officials, see "Exclusive: Mideast nuclear plan backers bragged of support of top Trump aide Flynn," Reuters, December 1, 2017, and "Ex-CIA Director: Mike Flynn and Turkish Officials Discussed Removal of Erdogan Foe From U.S.," *Wall Street Journal*, March 24, 2017. For more on McCain's involvement with the Steele memos, see "UK was given details of alleged contacts between Trump and Moscow," *Guardian*, April 28, 2017. For more on the intelligence agency heads briefing Trump, see Comey statement to the Senate Intelligence Committee.

AFTERWORD: "PLEASE, MY GOD, CAN'T YOU STOP THIS?"

For more on the effort to block the lifting of sanctions, see "How the Trump Administration's secret efforts to ease Russia sanctions fell short," Yahoo News, June 1, 2017. Comey detailed his interactions with Trump in the Comey statement to the Senate Intelligence Committee. A transcript of Comey's March 20, 2017, testimony to the House Intelligence Committee can be found at https://www. washingtonpost.com/news/post-politics/wp/2017/03/20/full-transcript-fbi-director-james-comey-testifies-on-russian-interfer-ence-in-2016-election/?utm_term=.3b56add4fee1. For the death of Erovinkin, see "Mystery death of ex-KGB chief linked to MI6 spy's dossier on Donald Trump," *Telegraph*, January 27, 2017. For the poisoning of Kara-Murza, see "World's most dangerous job: Putin critic Vladimir Kara-Murza on surviving poisoning, twice," Yahoo News, April 20, 2017.

INDEX

Index

Index

Index

Index

Herbalife, 140
Hermitage Capital Management, 40
Hicks, Hope, 103, 241, 278
Hillary for America, 144
Hofstra University debate, 230–231
Hohlt, Rick, 109
Holt, Lester, 230, 299
Horwitz, Jeff, 78
House Intelligence Committee, 294, 298
House Judiciary Committee, 231–232
Hudson, James, 149
Human Rights Accountability Global
    Initiatives Foundation, 121
Hurricane Matthew, 238
hybrid warfare doctrine, 44

I.C. Expert Investment Company, 80
information warfare, 44–47, 54, 183. *See
    also* Internet Research Agency
Instagram. *See* social media
intelligence community (IC). *See also* CIA
    (Central Intelligence Agency); FBI
    (Federal Bureau of Investigation)
    composing statement on Russian
      cyberattack, 235–237
    conclusions about Russia, 224, 278–279
    crafting memo on cyberattack response,
      195–196
    handling Steele dossier, 287–289
    investigating DNC hack, 176
    Russia statement, 240, 254
    Trump lashing out at, 292–294
    turf-crossing operation of, 184–185
interagency process, 184–185
Internet Research Agency, 56–59, 270, 274.
    See also information warfare; Russian
    social media campaign; troll farm
Isikoff, Michael, 162–163, 226–228, 261

Johnson, Jeh, 185–189, 216, 218, 235,
    237–239, 249
Jones, Alex, 208
Jones, Paula, 250

Kadyrov, Ramzan, 21n1
Kahl, Colin, 185
Kalugin, Oleg, 58–59
Kara-Murza, Vladimir, 34, 41, 303
Kasparov, Garry, 22, 24–25
Kaspersky, Eugene, 125

Kaspersky Lab, 125
Katsyv, Pyotr, 120
Kaveladze, Ike, 7, 121
Keene, David, 109
Kellogg, Keith, 104–105
Kelly, John, 104
Kemp, Brian, 189
Kerry, John, 43, 124, 185, 237, 279
Khodorkovsky, Mikhail, 8
Kilimnik, Konstantin, 97–98, 102–103, 173
Kislyak, Sergei, 115, 115n2, 164, 284,
    297n1, 299
Klain, Ron, 239
kompromat
    on Clinton, 223
    on Trump, 146–150, 221–222
Konst, Nomiki, 176
Kovalchuk, Yury, 51
Kozhin, Vladimir, 15, 16
Kramer, David, 287
Krutskikh, Andrey, 270
Kubic, Charles, 107
Kushner, Jared
    on Comey's firing, 299
    Dearborn and, 111
    firing Manafort, 201
    Gorkov meeting, 286
    on hiring Manafort, 94
    Kislyak meeting, 115n2, 285–286
    overseeing social media efforts, 271
    as owner of the *Observer*, 206
    reaction to *Access Hollywood* video, 241
    Veselnitskaya meeting, 119–123, 173, 300

LaBella, Chuck, 16
Lady Gaga, 4
Latham, Sara, 67
Lavrov, Sergey, 25–26, 37–38, 124, 237,
    299
Le Pen, Jean-Marie, 53
Ledeen, Simone, 113
Lederman, Josh, 283
Ledgett, Richard, 59–60
Levinson, Riva, 95
Lew, Jack, 185
Lewandowski, Corey, 158–159
Libya, 32
Lichtblau, Eric, 265–267
Liggett-Ducat Ltd., 83
Litvinenko, Alexander, 19–20, 170

Index

Index

Index

Index

Index

Index

ABOUT THE AUTHORS

Michael Isikoff is an investigative journalist who has worked for the *Washington Post, Newsweek*, and NBC News. He is the author of two *New York Times* bestsellers, *Uncovering Clinton: A Reporter's Story* and *Hubris: The Inside Story of Spin, Scandal, and the Selling of the Iraq War* (co-written with David Corn). He is a frequent guest on MSNBC, CNN, and other TV talk shows. Isikoff is currently the chief investigative correspondent for *Yahoo News*.

David Corn is a veteran Washington journalist and political commentator. He is the Washington bureau chief for *Mother Jones* magazine and an analyst for MSNBC. He is the author of three *New York Times* bestsellers, including *Showdown: The Inside Story of How Obama Battled the GOP to Set Up the 2012 Election* and *Hubris: The Inside Story of Spin, Scandal, and the Selling of the Iraq War* (co-written with Michael Isikoff). He is also the author of the biography *Blond Ghost: Ted Shackley and the CIA's Crusades* and the novel *Deep Background*.